'As a study and a celebration of some of [Australian] literature's finest blooms, *Australian Classics* is excellent.'

Richard King, *Sydney Morning Herald*

'*Australian Classics* is generously inclusive, written with flair, not bent on settling scores, but on reopening and reintroducing the rich and often eccentric body of our literature. It is an enterprise for which Gleeson-White ought to be commended.'

Peter Pierce, *The Canberra Times*

'It is in books like *Australian Classics* that our best hope lies for a healthy, productive Australian literature for many years into the future.'

Per Henningsgaard, *Journal of the Association for the Study of Australian Literature*, Vol. 8

'I wouldn't hesitate to recommend this book to someone who wanted a crash course in Australian literature, but there's also more to it than that . . . *Australian Classics* clearly has its uses not only for beginners but also for those who already know the field.'

Kerryn Goldsworthy, *Weekend Australian*

'I hope I'm not alone in saying that a book of this ilk is long overdue . . . This is a very readable reference book and would make a great gift.'

Julia Jackson, *Bookseller and Publisher*

Jane Gleeson-White has worked as an editor, writer and reviewer in Sydney and London since completing her degrees in English and Australian literature, and economics at the University of Sydney in 1987. She also worked as a student at the Peggy Guggenheim Museum in Venice, where she studied Byzantine, early Renaissance and modern art. Her first book, *Classics*, was published in 2005.

Australian Classics

Australian Classics

50 GREAT WRITERS
AND THEIR CELEBRATED WORKS

JANE GLEESON-WHITE

ALLEN&UNWIN

This project has been assisted by the Australian
Government through the Australia Council
for the Arts, its arts funding and advisory body.

This edition published in 2010
First published in 2007

Allen & Unwin
83 Alexander Street
Crows Nest NSW 2065
Australia
Phone: (61 2) 8425 0100
Fax: (61 2) 9906 2218
Email: info@allenandunwin.com
Web: www.allenandunwin.com

Cataloguing-in-Publication details are available
from the National Library of Australia
www.librariesaustralia.nla.gov.au

Internal design by Greendot Design
Typeset by Midland Typesetters, Australia
Printed in Australia by McPherson's Printing Group

10 9 8 7 6 5 4 3 2 1

Mixed Sources
Product group from well-managed
forests, and other controlled sources
www.fsc.org Cert no. SGS-COC-004121
© 1996 Forest Stewardship Council

The paper in this book is FSC certified.
FSC promotes environmentally responsible,
socially beneficial and economically viable
management of the world's forests.

For Michael Hill, who showed me Australia

CONTENTS

Introduction 1

1. *Robbery Under Arms* by Rolf Boldrewood 8

2. 'The Sick Stockrider' by Adam Lindsay Gordon 18

3. *Such is Life* by Tom Collins 24

4. *His Natural Life* by Marcus Clarke 32

5. 'The Chosen Vessel' by Barbara Baynton 40

6. 'The Man From Snowy River' by AB 'Banjo' Paterson 47

7. 'Nationality' by Mary Gilmore 54

8. 'The Drover's Wife' by Henry Lawson 60

9. 'Lilith' by Christopher Brennan 67

10. *Seven Little Australians* by Ethel Turner 75

11. *The Getting of Wisdom* by Henry Handel Richardson 81

12. 'The Gentle Water Bird' by John Shaw Neilson 87

13. *My Brilliant Career* by Miles Franklin 93

14. *The Magic Pudding* by Norman Lindsay 99

15. *Coonardoo* by Katharine Susannah Prichard 106

16. *10 for 66 and all that* by Arthur Mailey 112

17. *Lucinda Brayford* by Martin Boyd 118

18. *A Fortunate Life* by AB Facey 124

19. *Picnic at Hanging Rock* by Joan Lindsay 131

20. 'Five Bells' by Kenneth Slessor   137

21. *Capricornia* by Xavier Herbert   143

22. *The Man Who Loved Children* by Christina Stead   149

23. *The Pea-pickers* by Eve Langley   154

24. 'A Letter from Rome' by AD Hope   160

25. *Voss* by Patrick White   166

26. *My Brother Jack* by George Johnston   172

27. 'Woman to Child' by Judith Wright   178

28. *Tirra Lirra by the River* by Jessica Anderson   183

29. *Power Without Glory* by Frank Hardy   188

30. 'No More Boomerang' by Oodgeroo Noonuccal   195

31. *Storm Boy* by Colin Thiele   201

32. *The Lucky Country* by Donald Horne   208

33. *Milk and Honey* by Elizabeth Jolley   216

34. *The Acolyte* by Thea Astley   222

35. *The Glass Canoe* by David Ireland   228

36. *The Tyranny of Distance* by Geoffrey Blainey   234

37. *The Transit of Venus* by Shirley Hazzard   241

38. *An Imaginary Life* by David Malouf   248

39. *The Chant of Jimmie Blacksmith* by Thomas Keneally   254

40. *Visitants* by Randolph Stow   260

41. *Grand Days* by Frank Moorhouse   266

42. 'The Buladelah-Taree Holiday Song Cycle' by Les Murray   274

43. *The Fatal Shore* by Robert Hughes   280

44. *The Plains* by Gerald Murnane   288

45. *Monkey Grip* by Helen Garner   294

Contents

46. *Our Sunshine* by Robert Drewe   300

47. *True History of the Kelly Gang* by Peter Carey   306

48. *Lilian's Story* by Kate Grenville   312

49. *My Place* by Sally Morgan   317

50. *Cloudstreet* by Tim Winton   323

Index to boxes and Favourite Australian books   331

Bibliography   333

Permissions   337

Acknowledgements   338

To the literary mind there is a special interest attaching
to fiction or other matter written in and of Australia.
There are not many English-speaking lands left from which
we may look for new developments in English literature.
Australia is one of the few, and very interesting it is to watch
her progress in letters.

ATHENAEUM, LONDON, 1904

Few things are more potent than song or story in relating
peoples to their soil . . .

MILES FRANKLIN

Australian literature matters to Australia. It is part of our gift
to the world.

MARY GILMORE

Culture builds itself like a coral reef and like a reef it
entails much sacrifice.

CLIVE JAMES

Introduction

I set out to write *Australian Classics* with a simple intention: to make a book on 'Australian literature' as there are books on 'Australian art'. I wanted to create a book that would give a broad overview of Australia's writing and bring some of its key authors to a wide audience. As I thought about the idea, I also realised that by writing about Australian books over the last one hundred years or so—the earliest work in *Australian Classics* is 'The Sick Stockrider', Adam Lindsay Gordon's poem from 1869—I would be creating a sort of literary portrait of Australia, fragmented and partial though it might be, and I found this an intriguing prospect.

My earliest acquaintance with Australian writers came through my parents' bookshelves, where these authors lived alongside the writers of the world and were not singled out in any way as 'Australian'. They were Martin Boyd, Patrick White, Kenneth Slessor, Judith Wright, Donald Horne, Geoffrey Blainey, Robert Hughes, Ethel Turner and others. My first memorable experience of Australian literature was Patrick White's *The Tree of Man* in high school. I had a violent reaction against its portentous seriousness and refused to study it, choosing instead Joseph Heller's *Catch-22*. I then elected to study Australian literature in my second year at the University of Sydney, where as a field of study it was separate from English literature.

At the time I knew very little about the literature of my own country, having found in the literature of elsewhere the books that fired my imagination and taught me the beauty and power of words: the works of the ancient Greeks and Romans; French,

German and Russian literature, English, Irish and American. And so I will never forget the shock of hearing in one of my first Australian literature classes a poem by John Shaw Neilson. I had never heard of him. As the words of 'Song Be Delicate' sounded through the room I wondered how it could be possible that such exquisite lyrics had been created in the Australian bush somewhere. I was astonished. I experienced similar astonishment several times during that first year of Australian literature as its secrets were revealed—and I became so obsessed with Patrick White that of all the literature in the English-speaking world, I chose to write my English honours thesis on White's novel *The Twyborn Affair*. So Australian writing has long preoccupied me, first as something I rejected, in the form of *The Tree of Man*; then as a subject for study at university, where I was seduced by its poetry and the novels of White, especially *Voss* and *The Twyborn Affair*; and later as the object of my work as an editor.

With the same outward-looking gaze that had led me to the literature of Europe and America before Australia's, after leaving university I travelled straight to London and Venice without a backward glance. It never once occurred to me to voyage through Australia—or not until 1988, when a friend told me he was buying a motorbike and leaving the next week to travel around Australia. This seemed like the most bizarre idea in the whole world and within moments I had decided to leave my job and go with him. So we bought an old Holden panel-van, borrowed a tent and drove west from Sydney through the Blue Mountains, heading for Bourke and then up into the gulf country of Queensland. We took several months and travelled through the centre to Uluru, north to Darwin, around the coast of Western Australia and across the Nullarbor. It was one of the most extraordinary experiences of my life. Just as I had earlier been staggered by John Shaw Neilson, so I was awed by the natural beauty of Australia, by the breathtaking variety of rock and earth and water and sky, and by the many remarkable people we met along our way. Falling in love with the land of my birth opened me more deeply to its literature—and made me realise that it was their profound engagement with the world of Australia, with the soul of its landscape bush and urban, that I had been responding to all along in its poets, from Neilson to Slessor, and later Gordon, Judith Wright, Les Murray, and that I had found in *Voss* and *The Twyborn Affair*: the passionate response of these writers to place.

Because of my experience of Australian poets—and their concern with the Australian landscape and attempt to 'know' it in the way that its painters have—I knew *Australian Classics* would have to encompass not just novels but poetry. I then realised that to give as full a picture as possible of Australia's written word, I would also have to include non-fiction and children's literature. And so I set to work on the hardest task of all: choosing fifty Australian books that would reflect both some generally recognised set of 'Australian classics' as well as my own idiosyncratic literary tastes. The first book in *Australian Classics* is one of the earliest novels written in Australia to be designated a 'classic': Rolf Boldrewood's *Robbery Under Arms*, first published in serial form from 1882 to 1883. The fiftieth book is Tim Winton's *Cloudstreet*, published in 1991, which has already gathered the weight of a 'classic'. Between these two novels are twenty-seven more novels, two short stories, ten poems, three histories, three memoirs and three children's books.

So, based on this selection of fifty works, what does a literary portrait of Australia look like? It is wild and riotous, interspersed with quieter moments; it is often located beyond the law, probing the boundaries of geography, family, culture, race and identity. *Robbery Under Arms* takes up the theme of outlaws and convicts that rings through Australian literature and led one 1891 commentator to muse: 'What a curious comment it is on Australian history that the heroes of our best novels are convicts and bushrangers.' Other motifs in *Robbery Under Arms* that echo through Australia's literature are the horse; the bush; and movement, flight from the law or from Australia itself, or travels on the road like Tom Collins's *Such is Life*, AB Facey's *A Fortunate Life*, Norman Lindsay's *The Magic Pudding* and Eve Langley's *The Pea-pickers*. Writers from AB 'Banjo' Paterson and Henry Lawson to Judith Wright and Les Murray are deeply preoccupied with the bush—and when Australian poetry first moves beyond the bush, it does so with a determined awareness that it writes to the exclusion of the bush, such as Slessor's discovery of mountain streams in neon lights reflected in rain and pastures on the pavements of Kings Cross; and Christopher Brennan and AD Hope's turning to the literature and myths of Europe to write erotic poetry and a poetry of the mind. An obsession with the nature of art and the artist is also present in the work of White, Wright, Elizabeth Jolley, Thea Astley, David Malouf and Gerald Murnane.

This turning from the bush to the literature of Europe—the flight from Australia to the northern hemisphere—is another facet of Australian writing, and reaches from Gordon and Brennan to Martin Boyd and Shirley Hazzard. And sometimes this flight is literal, among Australian women writers in particular: Henry Handel Richardson, Christina Stead and Hazzard all fled Australia; even Barbara Baynton and Miles Franklin, whose best-known works are so focused on the bush, lived overseas for much of their lives. The theme of Europe and Australia also works the other way: the exile in Australia of Europeans sounds through writers from Gordon to Marcus Clarke's *His Natural Life* and Robert Hughes's *The Fatal Shore*, to White's *Voss*, Jolley's *Milk and Honey* and Geoffrey Blainey's *The Tyranny of Distance*. In the 1960s Donald Horne's *The Lucky Country* focused on suburban life and located Australia in its geographic vicinity of Asia and the Pacific; in *The Man Who Loved Children* Stead relocated her entire Sydney childhood to Washington and Baltimore. And Australia has not only been on the receiving end of colonialism: from after the First World War to 1975 it governed the territories of Papua and New Guinea, a realm Randolph Stow explores in *Visitants*.

Colin Thiele's *Storm Boy* and the work of Tim Winton turn from the bush to Australia's beaches, oceans and water. In *Lilian's Story* by Kate Grenville, Lilian Singer's urge to flight is from the life of affluent suburban womanhood to freedom; similarly in Jessica Anderson's *Tirra Lirra by the River* and Helen Garner's *Monkey Grip* women escape their tradition-ordained lives and voyage into new worlds where work, life, love, relationships and households are improvised and haphazard.

Robbery Under Arms introduces another great theme of Australian literature: false or assumed identities—imposture, disguise, pseudonyms—which continues in *Such is Life*, where it is extended to women with male names and moustaches, and ambivalent gender and sexuality. Disguise and fluid identity recur again and again in Australian writing, in *The Pea-pickers*, Frank Moorhouse's *Grand Days* and Peter Carey's impersonation of Ned Kelly in *True History of the Kelly Gang*. And so it is most fitting that for his tale of exile—*An Imaginary Life*—David Malouf chose to draw on the life of Ovid, the Ancient Roman poet famed for *Metamorphoses*, his epic work on shape shifting, transformation and the creation of gods.

For a nation that honours sport above almost all else, there is a marked absence of Australian classics about sport, but it does appear as a means to power in Frank Hardy's *Power Without Glory* and as one of life's most sacred callings in David Ireland's comic novel *The Glass Canoe*. More common are its close relatives gambling and horse-racing, to which Gerald Murnane believes all art aspires. I have included from the annals of cricket—Australia's national game and the one sport renowned for the literature it has spawned—the autobiography of Arthur Mailey, who rose from slums to mansions courtesy of his skill with a red leather ball.

As I worked through the literature of Australia I was reminded again and again of the obvious: that it was introduced to the continent in 1788; that before British colonisation there was no written literature in the land and so to write about Australia's literary heritage means working to the exclusion of Aboriginal voices—whose rich storytelling tradition was an oral one—until the mid twentieth century. The earliest literary engagement with Aboriginal Australians comes through the eyes of white writers like Katharine Susannah Prichard and Xavier Herbert, whose great novels *Coonardoo* and *Capricornia* are considered classics but whose attempts to enter into the experience of another people can seem fraught in the twenty-first century. In 2001 Thomas Keneally spoke of his own discomfort with his novel *The Chant of Jimmie Blacksmith*, written in the 1970s mostly from the point of view of Jimmie Blacksmith, born of an Aboriginal mother and white father. Keneally believes 'It would be insensitive to write from that point of view now.' Not until the 1960s did Oodgeroo Noonuccal publish her first volume of poetry, the first book of verse by an Indigenous writer. In it she speaks of suffering and dispossession, and of a rich ancient culture severed from its land, themes echoed in Sally Morgan's *My Place*.

The history of Australian literature is a story of writers attempting to engage with a land they found alien, then claimed and celebrated; of writers engaging with modern Australia's criminal origins and their legacy, as well as the impact of European settlement on Indigenous Australians, their land and culture; and of writers dealing with the fact that Australia's language—English— was imported from elsewhere and that the literary font of this language lies in the green fields, soft light, low skies and delineated social structures of a small island on the other side of the world. There are many broken lives in the corridors of Australian literature—several early deaths, some madness, poverty, alcoholism, disappointment, frustration with the nation's philistinism—and yet many have answered the call to write. It seems to me that Clive James's words capture well the pain and enormity of their literary achievement: 'Culture builds itself like a coral reef and like a reef it entails much sacrifice.'

Because any selection of fifty books necessarily excludes many wonderful books, I have invited a number of writers and readers to contribute lists of their own favourite Australian books to *Australian Classics*. The enthusiasm with which these writers and readers responded to my invitation and the trouble they took to choose only ten from among their many favourite Australian books inspired me as I read and wrote, and reminded me over and over how deeply loved are the books of this land.

I

ROBBERY UNDER ARMS:

*A story of life and adventure in the bush
and in the Australian goldfields*

Rolf Boldrewood (1826–1915)

Rolf Boldrewood's bushranging tale *Robbery Under Arms* was one of the first novels written in Australia to be considered a classic. Reviewing the book in 1889 on its publication, the *Age* called Boldrewood 'the Homer of the Bush' and his novel, with its 'unmistakable air of verisimilitude', second only to *Jane Eyre* (1847) as fictional autobiography. The following year, the Melbourne *Argus* hailed *Robbery Under Arms* as an 'Australian classic'.

First published in serial form by John Fairfax & Son's *Sydney Mail* from 1882 to 1883, *Robbery Under Arms* caused an immediate sensation. Its instalments became so eagerly awaited that when floodwaters prevented the latest issue of the *Sydney Mail* from reaching one outback town, its residents arranged for the whole chapter to be telegraphed from nearby Dubbo.

Robbery Under Arms is narrated by condemned bushranger Dick Marston, who tells his story in a rhythmic vernacular with such engaging directness that it feels alive more than one hundred years after its first telling: 'My name's Dick Marston,' he begins,

'Sydney-side native. I'm twenty-nine years old, six feet in my stocking soles, and thirteen stone weight. Pretty strong and active with it, so they say.' Dick's escapades on the wrong side of the law start with his introduction to crime by his father, Ben Marston, who was transported to New South Wales for poaching, and his corruption of his younger brother Jim. Their sister Aileen, who shares her brothers' high spirits and gift for horse-riding, attempts over and again to persuade them to stay home and work the land honestly, like their dull but upstanding neighbour George Storefield. But they can't resist the call of freedom and easy money.

The brothers' reckless adventures escalate when their father introduces them to the notorious, enigmatic bushranger Starlight, who is as charming and gentlemanly as he is lawless. As Dick recalls from his father's hideout Terrible Hollow, while anticipating his first meeting with the mysterious Starlight: 'I began to be uneasy to see this wonderful mate of father's, who was so many things at once—a cattle-stealer, bush-ranger, and a gentleman.' After successful episodes of cattle-duffing, prison-escape and armed robbery—interrupted by a lawful stint of mining on the Turon goldfields near Bathurst—Starlight and the Marstons soon become the colony's most wanted men.

And so Dick confesses his incorrigible ways from a prison cell, addressing the reader with a frank and easy familiarity: 'it's all up now; there's no get away this time; and I, Dick Marston, as strong as a bullock, as active as a rock-wallaby, chock-full of life and spirits and health, have been tried for bush-ranging—robbery under arms they call it—and though the blood runs through my veins like water in the mountain creeks, and every bit of bone and sinew is as sound as the day I was born, I must die on the gallows this day month.'

Boldrewood's novel was so popular that it was serialised a second time, from 1884, and was published in three volumes in London in 1888. While the British reviewers criticised *Robbery Under Arms* for its focus on criminals and its 'slang and rough language', they conceded that it made gripping reading. They were torn between their concern for the book's immoral subject matter and its irresistible storytelling. The *Guardian* called *Robbery Under Arms* 'a capital story full of wild adventure and startling incident' but worried that it was possible to 'feel some admiration' for the bushrangers, 'even to entertain real sympathy for their fate'. As the *Spectator* lamented: 'The fact is that the book is too fascinating.' And so it is. *Robbery Under Arms* has rarely been out of print since 1888.

Today the novel is still striking for its uncanny truthfulness, its 'air of verisimilitude' so noted by contemporary readers. As one Sydney journalist recalled in 1889 of his first reading *Robbery Under Arms* on the Monaro, the reason he 'loved the story years ago', was that 'even then I knew how true it all was. I knew the very landscape; I believed I had met men and women that might have served for originals of those distinct copies; the whole story came to me as clear, as distinct, as personal, as if it had been part of mine.'

Boldrewood's use of the 'colonial vernacular' has been compared to Mark Twain's use of the vernacular in *Huckleberry Finn*, published in 1884, two years after *Robbery Under Arms* first appeared. As with Twain's novel, it is the brilliant vitality and intimacy of Dick's narrative voice, as well as the wild adventures he has with his brother Jim, Starlight and the women they love, that make *Robbery Under Arms* such lively reading. And at times Dick's voice, with its conversational ease, evokes JD Salinger's twentieth-century misfit, Holden Caulfield: Kate 'had a way of talking to me and telling me everything that happened, because I was an old friend she said—that pretty nigh knocked me over, I tell you.' Through his Antipodean tale-teller, Boldrewood weaves together many of the true tales he heard in the courts while travelling across western New South Wales as a magistrate, and later as Goldfields Commissioner and Coroner.

Rolf Boldrewood is the pseudonym of Thomas Alexander Browne, who took the name from 'Marmion', a poem by Sir Walter Scott. Browne was born in London in 1826. Five years later, he sailed for New South Wales aboard his father's ship *Proteus*, which carried a cargo of convicts. Captain Brown (Thomas added the distinguishing 'e' in 1875) established a whaling business in Sydney and gave his son Thomas a gentleman's education. After a stint as a squatter in western Victoria and New South Wales, which he abandoned in 1870 because of drought, Thomas Browne returned to Sydney with his wife and children. The following year he became Police Magistrate in Gulgong. It was then—'as an overburdened paterfamilias', as he put it—that he turned to writing to supplement his income. Boldrewood's stories of squatting life appeared in weekly newspapers and his first book, *Ups and Downs: a Story of Australian Life*, was published in 1878.

In 1882, at the suggestion of a friend, Boldrewood began a novel on bushranging, a subject that continued to fire the public imagination. Bushrangers had terrorised the colony during the 1860s and 70s; Boldrewood himself had been held up in 1867 and never forgot the feeling of having a pistol held to his head. He became so intrigued by the bushranging phenomenon that he later interviewed one of his assailants in Wagga Wagga gaol. By 1882, two sensational bushranging stories had gripped the nation: the 1879 capture of the notorious Captain Moonlight (said to be Starlight's original; although there was also a real Captain Starlight: Frank Pearson) and Ned Kelly's capture and execution in 1880.

The novel that resulted from his friend's suggestion was *Robbery Under Arms*. But despite the public's fascination for bushrangers, Boldrewood initially struggled to find a publisher for his novel because of its criminal heroes. Once published, however, his story of three fearless bushrangers was an immediate hit. As one critic observed in 1891: 'What a curious comment it is on Australian history that the heroes of our best novels are convicts and bushrangers.' The success of *Robbery Under Arms* established Boldrewood as a writer and he wrote fifteen more novels, but none was as popular as his great bushranging tale. After his retirement Boldrewood lived mostly near Melbourne, where he died in 1915.

Since it first appeared, *Robbery Under Arms* has inspired scores of adaptations, including a popular stage version in 1890. *Robbery Under Arms* was made into one of the first Australian feature films, in 1907, and four years later was adapted for screen a second time as *Captain Starlight*. In the publicity brochure for the popular 1907 film, the producers were keen to distinguish their film from a recent film on the Kelly gang: 'The story of the Marstons is not the story of the Kellys. The Kellys, however you may gild them, remain brutal realities . . . But the Marstons were always in a certain glamour of the ideal . . . Their story is the story of men of nominally good instincts, twisted by heredity and weakened by insidious elements of circumstantial environment.' In 1957 an English film version of *Robbery Under Arms* starring Peter Finch as Starlight was made in an attempt to compete with Hollywood's Westerns. Its publicity promoted Finch as Captain Starlight, 'the notorious robber whose most potent weapons were a polite phrase and a disarming smile'. The most recent adaptation of *Robbery Under Arms* was made for screen and television in 1985, starring Sam Neill as the charming Starlight.

Gold

Halfway through *Robbery Under Arms* the Marstons read the following news:

> WONDERFUL DISCOVERY OF GOLD AT THE TURON. We have much pleasure in informing our numerous constituents that gold, similar in character and value to that of San Francisco, has been discovered on the Turon River by those energetic and experienced practical miners, Messrs. Hargraves and party . . . It is impossible to forecast the results of this most momentous discovery. It will revolutionise the new world. It will liberate the old. It will precipitate Australia into a nation.

And so it did—the wealth of gold transformed Australia almost immediately. The *Sydney Morning Herald* announced the discovery on 15 May 1851 and two weeks later a thousand diggers had crossed the Blue Mountains for the goldfields. In *Robbery Under Arms*, Dick and Jim Marston join the rush. When they reach the Turon, they have never seen anything like it in all their solitary bush days: 'Upon that small flat, and by the bank, and in the river itself, nearly 20,000 men were at work, harder and more silently than any crowd we'd ever seen before . . . My word, we were stunned, and no mistake about it.' There, in country 'like we'd seen scores and scores of times all our lives and thought nothing of' were men everywhere digging up gold, 'just like potatoes'.

In February 1851, Edward Hammond Hargraves and his guide, bushman John Lister, had travelled west from Sydney and followed a tributary of the Macquarie River, where Hargraves was sure he would find gold. Hargraves had just returned from the Californian goldfields convinced that they resembled the country around Bathurst west of Sydney. He was right. When four of the five pans of gravel and earth he sifted revealed gold, he exclaimed to his astonished companion: 'Here it is. This is a memorable day in the history of New South Wales. I shall be a baronet, and you will be knighted, and my old horse will be stuffed, put into a glass case, and sent to the British Museum!'

In August that same year gold was found in Ballarat, in the new state of Victoria. News of the flood of gold spread quickly round the world and thousands headed for the Australian goldfields. As Dick says: 'One thing's certain; Jim and I would never have had the chance of seeing as many different kinds of people in a hundred years if it hadn't been for the gold.'

Although gold had reputedly been discovered several times in the Bathurst region before 1851, the news had been suppressed in order to prevent the convicts rebelling and labourers abandoning their work. But with the announcement of gold in 1851, the colony's purpose was completely redefined in the eyes of the British government. It soon became clear that the transportation of convicts to eastern Australia was no longer a punishment—for, as the British Secretary of State made plain, the convicts were being sent 'to the immediate vicinity of those very goldfields

which thousands of honest labourers are in vain trying to reach.' So in August 1953, after 65 years, the last vestige of convict transportation to eastern Australia was abolished. (Transportation to New South Wales had been abolished in 1840, but had continued in Van Diemen's Land. Transportation to Western Australia continued until 1868.)

Gold also heralded technological change, including the first steam train in Australia, in 1854, and the first telegraph line, between Sydney, Melbourne and Adelaide, in October 1858. And most memorably, gold proved a powerful agent of democracy. As one visitor to the Victorian goldfields put it, Victoria had become 'an equalising colony of gold and beef and mutton'. This was recognised by British parliament with the granting of self-government on local matters and responsible government to the Australian states: Victoria in 1855; New South Wales, South Australia and Tasmania (formerly Van Diemen's Land) in 1856; and the new state of Queensland in 1859.

But the most potent expression of the new democratic spirit came in 1854 at Eureka, on the Ballarat goldfield. Here the miners, already frustrated by their poor conditions, were provoked to rebellion by the murder of a fellow digger and subsequent release of those accused of his death. They responded with mass meetings and demands for reform, the focus of their agitation being the costly mandatory miner's licence. After mass burnings of licences, the miners erected a stockade at the end of November, which was stormed by troops on the morning of Sunday 3 December. The brief and bloody battle that ensued left twenty-two diggers and five troops dead. As a result, the Victorian government granted the miners' requests for better conditions and replaced the licence with a 'miner's right', which gave miners the right to vote. The rebellion became one of Australia's most rousing symbols of the power of workers, stimulated the eight-hour day movement, and left as its emblem a new flag with southern-hemisphere stars. As Henry Lawson put it in 'Eureka':

> But not in vain those diggers died. Their comrades may rejoice,
> For o'er the voice of tyranny is heard the people's voice;
> It says: 'Reform your rotten law, the diggers' wrongs make right,
> Or else with them, our brothers now, we'll gather in the fight.'

The gold rush of 1851 also brought an influx of Chinese immigrants—by 1861 the Chinese population on the Victorian goldfields was 24,062—and this sparked racial tension among the diggers. The New South Wales and Victorian parliaments responded by legislating to restrict the number of Chinese immigrants permitted into the colony, but the racial conflict eventually led to outbreaks of violence. There was a riot on the Buckland River in Victoria in 1857; and in 1860 at Lambing Flat in New South Wales the diggers attacked the Chinese quarter, leaving several people dead and others wounded. In June 1861 there was a second and more violent attack at Lambing Flat, with more than a thousand men marching on the Chinese quarters.

In response, the New South Wales Legislative Council passed the Chinese Immigration Act in November 1861, to control the arrival of Chinese gold seekers. (The act was repealed in 1867, once the rush for gold had waned.) And so the goldfields not only inspired the spirit of brotherhood among the workers, but also provoked racial animosity, another continuing theme in Australian life.

2

'THE SICK STOCKRIDER'

Adam Lindsay Gordon (1833–1870)

During his seventeen years in Australia, Adam Lindsay Gordon became famous for his unrivalled skill as a horseman. He was a fearless brumby breaker in South Australia; he rode three horses to three victories in a single afternoon at Flemington racecourse in Melbourne in 1868. He even wrote poetry on horseback, hooking his leg over the saddle and smoking his favourite pipe while scribbling verses. But only after his tragic death at thirty-seven did Gordon become famous as a poet, known as 'the National Poet of Australia'. A single Australian poet is commemorated in Poets' Corner at London's Westminster Abbey. It is Adam Lindsay Gordon: poet, horseman, boxer, mounted policeman, South Australian Member of Parliament and gentleman scholar.

There are stories told about Gordon's feats of learning—he could memorise in a single sitting long passages in Greek and Latin from Homer, Horace and Virgil—but there are many more told of his wild ways and spirited recklessness. When living at Brighton, Victoria, the sea-loving Gordon would swim, summer and winter, half a mile out into the bay, regardless of sharks. And Gordon's escapades on horseback were legendary. He once jumped a horse over a fence onto a slim ledge above Mount Gambier's Blue Lake, which lay two hundred feet below, and jumped it back again. The leap was considered impossible. No other rider dared attempt it. In 1887, an obelisk was erected on the spot in memory of 'Gordon's Leap'.

But perhaps the story that best illustrates Gordon's potent combination of restless energy and poetic learning is told by one of his few close friends, the Reverend Julian Woods. Late one night Woods and Gordon were riding from the coast to a station near Mount Gambier when they were caught in a ferocious storm. Unable to see their way, they sheltered under a tree. Here as the weather raged Gordon recited all the storm poetry he knew, concluding with the whole of the tempest scene from *King Lear*. When the sky cleared, they continued, reaching the station by midnight. Woods was exhausted. But Gordon, exhilarated, paced the supper room reciting Byron's *Childe Harold* almost till dawn.

Gordon published three volumes of poetry in his lifetime: *Sea Spray and Smoke Drift* and *Ashtaroth* in 1867; and *Bush Ballads and Galloping Rhymes*, published on 23 June 1870. The following day Gordon rose early, kissed his wife, took his rifle, walked down to the beachside scrub and shot himself. Dreams of death's sleep had always charged his poetry; melancholy had always suffused his passion for life and fast adventure. But by 1870 Gordon had also suffered the death of his beloved daughter and only child at eleven months; a series of damaging riding accidents; and crippling debt. Gordon's friend the poet Henry Kendall put it well when he said (in 'In Memoriam, AL Gordon') that beneath his 'sturdy verse' with its 'ringing major notes' was a mournful 'undersong / Which runs through all he wrote'.

This mournful 'undersong' runs through 'The Sick Stockrider', one of Gordon's most loved and celebrated poems. First published in Marcus Clarke's *Colonial Monthly* in 1869, it was then reprinted in the *Australasian*. Its popularity was immediate and it was considered by Gordon's Melbourne friends Clarke and Kendall to be one of his greatest poems.

'The Sick Stockrider' was written in February 1869 at Yallum Park, the Mount Gambier property of John Riddoch, who had invited Gordon to leave Brighton to spend the summer in the bush. It proved to be the most productive poetic period of Gordon's life. Every morning he would disappear across the paddock to climb his favourite gum tree, known as 'Gordon's tree', and spend the day draped along a bough, smoking and writing.

Descended from an illustrious Scottish family, Gordon was born in the Azores in 1833, where his family had moved for his mother's mental health. They soon returned to England, where the dreamy, athletic boy was sent to school, first at Cheltenham and then Worcester. Gordon later told his friend Julian Woods that he'd been expelled from school for riding in a steeplechase; although there is no record of this, the dashing Gordon did spend his teenage years racing horses, mixing with racetrack identities, courting girls and running up massive debts. He captures his zest for horseback speed in his poem 'Ye Weary Wayfarer': 'Oh! The vigour with which the air is rife! / The spirit of joyous motion; / The fever, the fullness of animal life, / Can be drained from no earthly potion.'

To curb his errant ways, Gordon was packed off at nineteen to South Australia to join the mounted police. When he arrived in Port Adelaide in November 1853, Gordon was an accomplished horseman who loved the heroic poetry of Byron, Browning, Tennyson, Shakespeare, Homer, Virgil and Horace. His poetry reflects his two passions. It is devoted to horses—racing across English fields or through the crackling bush—or to heroic tales of old. Gordon loved best among his poems 'The Rhyme of Joyous Garde', his moving verses about Lancelot and his fated passion for his king's wife: 'And I grew deaf to the song-bird—blind / To blossom that sweetened the sweet spring wind— / I saw her only—a girl reclined'. His poem 'Podas Okus' (meaning swift-footed, Homer's favourite epithet for Achilles) is the dying farewell of the great warrior Achilles to his lover Briseis: 'I am ready, I am willing, / To resign my stormy life; / Weary of this long blood-spilling, / Sated with this ceaseless strife.'

'The Sick Stockrider' is also a dying farewell. And like Achilles, the sick stockrider addresses a mate, recalls past glories and lost comrades, and goes willingly to his fate. 'Hold hard, Ned! Lift me down once more, and lay me in the shade' the poem begins, launching immediately into the action. 'Old man, you've had your work cut out to guide / Both horses, and to hold me in the saddle when I sway'd / All through the hot, slow, sleepy, silent ride.' True to its subject, the poem rocks to the rhythm of horses' hooves and radiates the heat of the bush. The unnamed stockrider remembers his days in the saddle—'Oh! the hardest day was never then too hard!'—galloping after cattle and bushrangers. He concludes by asking Ned to 'Let me slumber in the hollow where the wattle blossoms wave, / With never stone or rail to fence my bed'. This exhortation was taken literally by Lindsay's many admirers after his death, who planted wattles by his unfenced grave in Brighton Cemetery.

Although Gordon's poetry is notoriously uneven—he wrote as the moment seized him, swiftly and spontaneously without revising—there are several great poems among his work, including 'The Sick Stockrider'. Gordon's English champion Douglas Sladen, of Trinity College, Oxford, called 'The Sick Stockrider': 'the best poem of its kind in the language. It is very beautiful . . . and the genius of Australia sits brooding over every line, for it is the

Bushman's *requiem*. All through it we hear the voice of manhood, the burden and heat of a warrior's day.'

Gordon's poem 'The Swimmer', composed on his favourite cliffs at Victoria's Cape Northumberland overlooking the Southern Ocean, was used by the English composer Edward Elgar as the libretto for the fifth movement of his song cycle *Sea Pictures*, first performed in 1899. And Queen Elizabeth, at the end of her 'annus horribilis' (1992), quoted Gordon's well-known lines from 'Ye Weary Wayfarer' in her Christmas Message: 'Life is mostly froth and bubble, / Two things stand like stone, / KINDNESS in another's trouble, / COURAGE in your own'.

Before Banjo Paterson and Henry Lawson, Gordon was Australia's bush poet, and his rhythms and loneliness resonate through their work. Kendall's words best capture Gordon's achievement as a poet: 'Yea, he who flashed upon us suddenly, / A shining soul with syllables of fire, / Who sang the first great songs these lands can claim / To be their own'. Oscar Wilde concurred. In 1888 he wrote: 'Through Gordon Australia found her first fine utterance in song.' And perhaps Gordon's own lines, from 'Ye Weary Wayfarer', best convey the aptness of his posthumous title 'National Poet of Australia': 'For what's worth having must ay be bought, / And sport's like life, and life's like sport, / "It ain't all skittles and beer".'

Helen Garner's favourite Australian books

The Journey of the Stamp Animals by Phyllis Hay
Seven Little Australians by Ethel Turner
Penguin Book of Australian Verse edited by Harry Heseltine
Romulus, My Father by Raimond Gaita
My Father's Moon by Elizabeth Jolley
The Getting of Wisdom by Henry Handel Richardson
Collected Poems by Les Murray
Mahjar by Eva Sallis
Evil Angels by John Bryson

Helen Garner is an award-winning writer of fiction and non-fiction. Her fiction includes *Monkey Grip* (1977), *The Children's Bach* (1984) and *Cosmo Cosmolino* (1992). Her non-fiction works include *The First Stone* (1995) and *Joe Cinque's Consolation* (2004). She wrote the screenplay for the film *The Last Days of Chez Nous* (1992), directed by Gillian Armstrong.

3

SUCH IS LIFE
Tom Collins (1843–1912)

Such is Life, tales from eight days in the life of Tom Collins, was first published by the *Bulletin* in 1903. It is an eccentric and defiant novel, a rebellion against the 'flowery pathway' of romantic fiction in favour of the rambling ways of the bush, packed with the learning of its author, Joseph Furphy. Published just before his sixtieth birthday, *Such is Life* was Furphy's first novel and his life's work. As his literary champion AG Stephens wrote when recommending its publication: 'This book contains all the wit and wisdom gathered in Furphy's life-time: it is his one book—it is himself.'

So who was Furphy, if his book was 'himself'? Furphy once described himself as 'half bushman and half bookworm'. It is an apt description, perfectly fitting both his life and his magnum opus, *Such is Life*. Born in 1843 in Victoria, Furphy was brought up by his Irish parents on the Bible and Shakespeare, and by the age of seven could quote entire passages from both. As a boy he was known for his voracious reading and his witty verse, mostly variations on the classics by 'Josephus Australianicus', as he styled himself.

After marrying in 1868, Furphy spent several years unsuccessfully working a selection in the Goulburn River Valley. He soon
sold it and bought a bullock team—the nineteenth century's
heavy transport vehicle—to carry loads of wool, oats and hay
through the bush. This adventurous life on the road proved to be
Furphy's ideal employment: he roamed the Victorian border and
Upper Riverina by day, read pocket editions of Shakespeare by
firelight at night and saw 'all that was to be seen'.

When drought eventually forced him to abandon his open-air
life, Furphy moved with his family to work at his brother's foundry
in Shepparton (which is still run by the Furphys today). Here
he was introduced to the republican, pro-working class *Bulletin*
with its motto 'Australia for the Australians', which appealed to
his temperament and clarified his democratic political thinking.
Encouraged by friends, in 1889 Furphy submitted a story to the
Bulletin, 'The Mythical Sundowner', under the name 'Warrigal
Jack' (he later took the pen-name 'Tom Collins', a bush expression
for a tall story or rumour). His story was accepted for publication.

Heartened, Furphy resumed his writing, working in a shed
he built behind the family cottage on the Goulburn River in
Shepparton. By 1897 he had amassed 1125 pages of loosely linked
stories gathered from his days as a bullocky and shaped into a
single work. He wrote to the *Bulletin*'s editor, JF Archibald: 'I have
just finished writing a full-sized novel, title *Such is Life*, scene,
Riverina and Northern Vic; temper, democratic; bias, offensively
Australian.'

The *Bulletin*'s literary editor, AG Stephens, immediately requested
the manuscript and on reading it declared it an Australian classic:
'It seems to me fitted to become an Australian classic, or semi-
classic, since it embalms accurate representations of our character
and customs, life and scenery, which, in such skilled and methodi-
cal forms, occur in no other book I know.' Stephens persuaded

Archibald to publish it, arguing that the *Bulletin*, as the national Australian newspaper, owed it to the nation. But even Stephens was aware that this idiosyncratic book would appeal only to a limited readership—'intelligent bushmen . . . [and] those city-men who can appreciate it'—and Furphy had to wait six long years to receive the first three bound copies of *Such is Life* in June 1903.

Such is Life opens with the famous words: 'Unemployed at last!' Tom Collins, ex-government official, has lost his job as a Deputy-Assistant-Sub-Inspector. Directly addressing the reader in his bookish prose, Collins tells us that with this new time on his hands 'I purpose taking certain entries from my diary, and amplifying these to the minutest detail of occurrence or conversation. This will afford to the observant reader a fair picture of Life, as that engaging problem has presented itself to me.' And so he randomly takes a volume of his Letts diary and opens it at Sunday 9 September 1883. He then proceeds in the first chapter to tell the stories of that day, which begin with a group of bullockies paused on the road, drinking tea and discussing the most pressing question of the day: where to find grass for their beasts, 'a vital question in '83, you may remember' (it was a year of drought). Collins intersperses his road stories with ruminations on literature, science, history, religion, politics, music—and any other subject that crosses his omnivorous and opinionated mind.

Collins's original intention has been to write seven chapters, one for each day of the week. But when he comes to chapter two, he suddenly realises that the conversation he had on Monday 10 September with 'a party of six sons of Belial' (sheep drovers) was so full of swearing it is unprintable. And so for decency's sake he decides to write the remaining chapters on the ninth day of every month. This he does until he reaches chapter seven, 9 March 1884. This he finds is not 'a desirable text', so gives us instead, apparently arbitrarily, the stories of 28 and 29 March.

Like the mirages that so frustrate Collins ('the mirage is one of Nature's obscure and cheerless jokes'), nothing in *Such is Life* is quite what it seems. The spirited Jim turns out to be a woman; Collins's horse Cleopatra is male; his kangaroo dog Pup (real name 'The Eton Boy') is not a faithful hound nor even a good kangaroo hunter, but a cosseted, thieving wastrel whose good looks allow him to do as he pleases. And so with its mercurial narrator, moustached women and tricksy world, Collins's bush tale takes on the complex, refracted hue of Cervantes' *Don Quixote*, with its multi-layered narrative. And just as Cervantes rebelled against the popular tales of chivalric romance when writing his road story *Don Quixote*, so Collins rages against one Henry Kingsley (1830–1876) and his popular novel *The Recollections of Geoffrey Hamlyn* (1859), which happened to be one of Rolf Boldrewood's favourite novels.

Born in England, Henry Kingsley spent five years in Australia, and wrote a bestselling bush romance, complete with bushrangers, noble squatters, bushfires and drought. Collins has a low opinion of Kingsley: 'Those whose knowledge of the pastoral regions is drawn from a course of novels of the *Geoffrey Hamlyn* class, cannot fail to hold a most erroneous notion of the squatter'. There are all sorts of squatters in the world, Collins tells us, 'except the slender-witted, virgin-souled, overgrown schoolboys who fill Henry Kingsley's exceedingly trashy and misleading novel with their insufferable twaddle.' Collins writes in protest against Kingsley's 'false' fictional bush.

Such is Life, like life, is both funny and sad. It contains witty throwaway lines—'some men, by their very aspect, seem to invite confidence; others, insults; others, imposition; but Dick seemed only to invite arrest'—and entire episodes of high farce, most notably an escapade when Collins loses his clothes in the Murray River and scrambles naked onto the wrong shore, into Victoria instead of New South Wales. The novel is also deeply poignant, with its stories of lost love and lost children. And yet despite his skill as a maker of tales, Collins fails to notice the way the stories he tells and is told are connected, and therefore he fails to see the full picture beyond the fragments. That is left for the reader to see: the reader must shape the narrative. In this Furphy seems remarkably modern.

Like Herman Melville's *Moby-Dick* (1851) and James Joyce's *Ulysses* (1922), Furphy's novel is steeped in the great literature of the world, transposed through his own defiantly Australian imagination and planted firmly in the soil of the Riverina. *Such is Life* is a novel true to its time—Australia of the nationalistic 1890s—and yet transcends it. Furphy, a passionate democrat and 'state socialist', believed he was writing a new literature for a new land of free men and women thrown together from all walks of life, into the joys and hardships, the equalising unpredictability, of the bush.

Although very few copies sold, *Such is Life* was well received by critics on its publication. The Adelaide *Register* called Collins 'an Australian Fielding', remarking: 'Imagine a writer, who apparently has the whole range of literature at his fingers' ends, living the life of the bush, and caring for no other.' In London the *Athenaeum* wrote: 'one hesitates, in the interests of sweet justice, to admit that his madness is frequently both plausible and entertaining', noting that Mr Collins 'is in many ways a typical Australian writer, whose riotous tendencies in thought have been aggravated by the influence of the *Sydney Bulletin*.'

Soon after *Such is Life* was published, Furphy and his wife moved to Fremantle, Western Australia, to join their children. Although he continued to write and hope for publication, Furphy's move had apparently severed his ties to the literary world and he died suddenly in 1912 without having seen his cherished second novel, *Rigby's Romance*, in book form. *Rigby's Romance* was finally published in 1921 and a third book, *The Buln Buln and the Brolga*, in 1948.

After Furphy's death his friend Kate Baker vigorously promoted his work. In August 1928 an article on Australian literature appeared in the New York *Bookman* and to Baker's delight it focused on *Such is Life*. Written by C Hartley Grattan, who had visited Australia for his survey, it observed: 'Humor and hardship, denunciation and love, mingle in Tom Collins's *Such is Life*, a trite title for a superb book . . . Tom Collins (Joseph Furphy) is the nearest approach to a Herman Melville that Australia has produced'. Hartley Grattan continues: 'In spite of his undoubted intellectual superiority, Collins was an aggressive defender of the common man. He was for the bullock-driver and the station hands, and against the squatter . . . The aggressive insistence of the worth and unique importance of the common man seems to me to be one of the fundamental Australian characteristics'. This is a fitting tribute to the man who wrote: 'it is no way necessary that the manual worker should be rude and illiterate; shut out from his rightful heirship of the ages.'

In the 1930s and 40s there was a surge of interest in Furphy, encouraged by Miles Franklin and writer and critic Vance Palmer. In September 1934 Palmer unveiled a plaque to Furphy on the wall of Victoria's Yarra Glen State School (the public building closest to Furphy's birthplace). In 1944 Angus & Robertson published Miles Franklin's *Joseph Furphy: The Legend of a Man and his Book*. More recently, following the centenary of *Such is Life*'s publication, Furphy's great-grandnephew Andrew Furphy commemorated his forebear in 2005 with a monument in Shepparton: a statue of Furphy and a stone engraved with the story of how *Such is Life* was written.

The *Bulletin*

'In its way, it is the most scathing, most daring, the wittiest, the most impudent and best edited paper I know. Nothing quite so audacious exists, even in America, where all sorts of journalistic audacities are permitted.' So wrote French writer Paul Blouet of the *Bulletin*. (Blouet (1848–1903) was the author of the bestselling *John Bull and Co.* (1894), written under the pen-name Max O'Rell.)

This audacious weekly news magazine was founded in 1880 in Sydney by the journalists JF Archibald and his partner John Haynes. The first edition was published on 31 January 1880 and it soon became one of the most influential journals in Australia. Along with news of politics and business, the *Bulletin* famously promoted Australian writing, especially short stories and verse, and the concise writing style championed by Archibald. Among its popular contributors were AB 'Banjo' Paterson, Henry Lawson, Mary Gilmore, CJ Dennis, Harry 'Breaker' Morant and Christopher Brennan. It also published Furphy's *Such is Life* (1903).

From 1886 Archibald ran the *Bulletin* with AG Stephens as his literary editor and together they nurtured a fervently nationalistic, bush-focused literature until the magazine became known as 'the bushman's Bible'. Its outlook was radical, democratic and progressive, picking up the nationalist feeling of the 1890s—a decade of nationalism recalled by Vance Palmer in his critical study *The Legend of the Nineties* (1954). The *Bulletin* supported trade unions

and a white Australia. It was also fiercely anti-imperialist, urging Australian independence from Britain. During the centenary celebrations of British settlement in Australia in 1888, the *Bulletin* protested: 'The day which inaugurated a reign of slavery and loathsomeness and moral leprosy—is the occasion for which we are called upon to rejoice with an exceeding great joy. Yet there might be a palliation even for this, if Australia could show that she had shaken off the old fetters and the old superstitions of that dark era ... [B]ut the old slavish taint still clings to her garments, and her chains of iron are merely exchanged for chains of gold.'

The *Bulletin*'s most vigorous years spanned the period from 1890 to the First World War. Following Archibald's resignation in 1903—his mental health broke down and he was committed to the Sydney asylum, Callan Park—the *Bulletin* became increasingly conservative, although it continued as a forum for Australian writing, publishing the work of later poets Kenneth Slessor, Judith Wright and Les Murray. In 1907 Archibald published *The Genesis of the Bulletin*, a history of his magazine. When he died in 1919, Archibald bequeathed money for a large fountain in Sydney's Hyde Park, to be designed by a French sculptor, commemorating the association between France and Australia during the First World War. (Always a Francophile, as a young man Archibald had changed his name from John Feltham to 'Jules François'.) Archibald was also a passionate supporter of Australian artists and left money to found a national portrait prize—the famed Archibald Prize, first held in 1921 and still run today.

4

HIS NATURAL LIFE

Marcus Clarke (1846–1881)

In his masterpiece *His Natural Life*, Marcus Clarke plumbs the depths of human depravity and the nineteenth-century British penal system. His hero Rufus Dawes, a gentleman condemned to death for a crime on Hampstead Heath that he did not commit, is transported instead to Australia for the term of his natural life.

Clarke's brutal saga of the outcasts of the British penitentiary system opens in London in the late 1820s then cuts to the convict ship *Malabar*, destined for Australia, becalmed on an infinite sea: 'It was the dreadful stillness of a tropical afternoon. The air was hot and heavy, the sky brazen and cloudless, and the shadow of the Malabar lay alone on the surface of the great glittering sea.' Aboard the stilled ship are many of the novel's central characters: Rufus Dawes; his nemesis the dashing and cruel Lieutenant Maurice Frere; the opportunistic forger John Rex; the heroine Sylvia Vickers; and her minder Sarah Purfoy, whose shipboard machinations involve seduction and mutiny.

Through the treachery of his fellow convicts, on arrival in the colony Dawes is condemned to serve his term at Macquarie Harbour, the high security gaol of Van Diemen's Land notorious for its hardship. And here Dawes finds himself utterly alone. 'Shunned and hated by his companions, feared by the convict overseers, and regarded with unfriendly eyes by the authorities, Rufus Dawes was at the very bottom of that abyss of woe into which he had voluntarily cast himself.' When goodness does appear before him, in the form of kind words from an innocent child, it sustains his gradually diminishing human core throughout his long incarceration, first at Macquarie Harbour, then at Port Arthur, and finally and most appallingly at Norfolk Island, the '*ne plus ultra* of convict degradation'.

His Natural Life is a haunting and compelling novel. Typical of much Victorian fiction, including the novels of Charles Dickens, George Eliot and Wilkie Collins, *His Natural Life* is filled with chance happenings, imposters, false names, disguises, unlikely coincidences, idealised characters and melodrama—and like most great nineteenth-century novels it is also a powerful, passionate outcry against social injustice, human cruelty and institutional corruption. Clarke tells his convict saga with great energy and emotion; his prose is laced with gothic flourishes and supernatural horror: 'Was this marvellous hiding place that he had discovered to be his sepulchre! Was he—a monster among his fellow-men— to die some monstrous death, entombed in this mysterious and terrible cavern of the sea?'

In June 1863, aged seventeen, Marcus Clarke arrived in Melbourne from London. He had grown up in affluent Kensington, received a good grammar school education, and anticipated a life of literature and gentlemanly leisure. Instead, after his father's lingering death had almost exhausted his inheritance, he found himself forced to move to Australia, where he had family. After work in a bank and on a station, Clarke became a journalist for the influential newspaper the *Argus* and settled into the bohemian milieu of Melbourne, which was newly rich, vibrant and teeming with exotica following the discovery of gold the previous decade.

Clarke became editor of *Colonial Monthly* in 1868 and there published his first novel, *Long Odds*, in serial instalments from 1868 to 1869. *Long Odds*—about horse-racing and mostly set in England—was criticised for having no relevance to colonial life. In return, Clarke argued that he had not wanted to compete with 'the best Australian novel that has been, and probably will be written'—Henry Kingsley's bestselling colonial tale *The Recollections of Geoffrey Hamlyn* (1859), the novel so detested by Joseph Furphy's Tom Collins. But in 1870 Clarke travelled to Tasmania—searching for an Australian subject for his new magazine *Australian Journal* and inspired by the Public Library of Victoria's convict records, Clarke had decided to write about Australia's penal past.

While in Tasmania, Clarke visited the rugged penal settlement of Port Arthur. Although convict transportation to Van Diemen's Land had ceased almost twenty years earlier (and the state had been renamed Tasmania to mark this), Port Arthur was still open and remained open until 1878 to house old and infirm convicts. Clarke later wrote of his visit: 'I know that there seemed to me to hang over the whole place a sort of horrible gloom, as though the sunlight had been withdrawn from it.' Taking that feeling of horrible gloom, Clarke returned to Melbourne and wrote the opening chapters of *His Natural Life*. They appeared in the *Australian Journal* the following month, in March 1870. Henry Lawson, reading the serialised novel as a boy, considered Clarke's style in these opening chapters as equal to Charles Dickens's. (Dickens was one of Clarke's favourite writers, along with Honoré de Balzac and Victor Hugo.)

Clarke intended his new novel to run over twelve instalments; instead it became an epic tale of twenty-seven. The last instalment appeared in June 1872, by which stage *His Natural Life* had lost many of its readers as well as its status as the *Australian Journal*'s lead story. Two years later, the significantly cut and revised book version of *His Natural Life* was published. In his dedication Clarke distinguishes his convict story from others, notably Hugo's *Les Misérables* (1862) and English writer Charles Reade's *It Is Never Too Late to Mend* (1856): 'no writer—so far as I am aware—has attempted to depict the dismal condition of a felon during his time of transportation.' Unlike Hugo and Reade, Clarke wrote not about a convict's life either side of incarceration, but about that incarceration itself. *His Natural Life* is the story of one man's gradual immersion in the irredeemable world of violence and moral degradation that is a penal colony.

His Natural Life was criticised by contemporary readers for exaggerating the depravity of the colonial penal system. To defend himself against such accusations—of 'exaggerating facts to create "sensation"'—Clarke noted in the June 1871 instalment, which involved cannibalism, that this episode was based on fact, on convict Alexander Pearce's escape from Macquarie Harbour and survival by cannibalism. Clarke drew much of his novel from history, including many of the central characters. Maurice Frere is based on the notorious Norfolk Island commandant, John Giles Price (1808–1857), who was later murdered by prisoners in Melbourne's Pentridge Gaol. Price's first words to his 'lambs' (as he called the convicts) on Norfolk Island in 1846 were: 'You know me, don't you? I am come here to rule, and by God I'll do so and tame or kill you.' And the Reverend James North, perhaps the most vivid and psychologically complex character in *His Natural Life*, is based on the Reverend Thomas Rogers, who attempted to oppose Price's sadism on Norfolk Island. Clarke used Rogers's

Correspondence Relating to the Dismissal of the Rev. T. Rogers from his Chaplaincy at Norfolk Island (1849) as a source for both the Reverend North and Maurice Frere. And conman John Rex is drawn from the mutineer James Barker and from Arthur Orton, the infamous Tichborne claimant (see box on page 38).

His Natural Life was published in Britain in 1875 and in the United States in 1876. The reviews were unanimous in acknowledging the novel's horror, but divided on its value and veracity. The Melbourne *Herald* considered it 'one of the most horribly fascinating books we have read for a long time' and observed that 'Mr Clarke has shown us that transportation may be made more terrible than death.' In Britain the *Examiner* wrote that it was 'a work of much power but more horror'. For in *His Natural Life* Clarke deliberately focuses on the extremes of convict Australia. Most of the novel's action takes place in secondary detention centres—Macquarie Harbour, Port Arthur and Norfolk Island—which were notoriously and deliberately harsh, intended for those convicts who had committed offences in the colony.

Britain's *Saturday Review* did not know why Clarke should 'depict every revolting detail of terror and abomination that belonged to the old convict system'. But Clarke intended *His Natural Life* as a protest against the possibility that such a penal colony should ever exist again, against 'allowing offenders against the law to be herded together in places remote from the wholesome influence of public opinion'. For although by 1870 Britain had ceased transportation to Australia, that 'method of punishment, of which that deportation was a part, is still in existence.' As Clarke argues, India's 'Port Blair is a Port Arthur filled with Indian-men instead of English-men; and, within the last year, France has established, at New Caledonia, a penal settlement which will, in the natural course of things, repeat in its own annals the history of Macquarie Harbour and of Norfolk Island.' Port

Blair remained a British penal colony until 1947; New Caledonia a French one until 1922.

In late nineteenth-century USA, so recently torn by the Civil War (1861–65), the reviews were more favourable. *Harper's* thought Clarke's portrayal of transportation rivalled 'in atrocity the terrible processes of the Inquisition' but 'the skill with which it is written goes far to redeem its repulsive features'. The novel was also published in German (1876), Dutch (1886), Swedish (1892) and Russian (1903). But its widespread readership and rapid acclaim as an Australian classic were too late for Clarke. Always under financial pressure—unable to earn an adequate living as a writer with a wife and children to support—Clarke lost his job at the Public Library of Victoria in July 1881. He died the following month, aged thirty-five.

But Clarke's great novel has lived on. Like *Robbery Under Arms*, *His Natural Life* has rarely been out of print since first published and is one of the most adapted Australian novels, for stage, film and television. There has even been a graphic version, published as *For the Term of His Natural Life*, as the novel is sometimes known. The first film version, *His Natural Life*, appeared in 1908; the second, *The Life of Rufus Dawes*, was released in 1911. A 1982 television miniseries starred Colin Friels as Rufus Dawes and Anthony Perkins as the Reverend North.

The Tichborne Case

The Tichborne case is one of the most famous and longest-running court cases of Britain. In 1865 a butcher from Wagga Wagga, New South Wales, claimed to be the missing, presumed dead, aristocrat Sir Roger Charles Tichborne of Tichborne Park, Hampshire, Great Britain. The ensuing drama enthralled the public of Britain and Australia for almost a decade. With its true story of imposture, contested claims to a title and a fortune, and a doting mother desperate to believe her son had returned from the void despite ample evidence to the contrary, the Tichborne case was as suggestive as any mystery novel. So it is not surprising that writers drew on this extraordinary tale at the time—and have continued to do so ever since.

The story concerned Sir Roger Tichborne, whose ship the *Bella* was wrecked off the coast of Brazil in 1854 and all on board were lost. Tichborne was presumed drowned. But on 25 December 1866 a butcher from Wagga Wagga— Arthur Orton, also known as Tom Castro—arrived in London in response to Lady Henriette Félicité Seymour Tichborne's worldwide quest for her son, claiming to be the missing heir. Despite the fact that he was nothing like Tichborne—was fair where Tichborne was dark, plump where Tichborne was lean, and spoke no word of French, the language with which Tichborne had been raised in Paris by his French mother—Orton was instantly recognised by Lady Tichborne as her son, and immediately treated as such.

Gradually Orton became accepted as Sir Roger Tichborne, and lived accordingly, racking up huge debts in the process. But many Tichborne family members were suspicious, and accused the butcher of imposture.

Lady Tichborne died in 1868 (her husband had died six years earlier) and the case was put to trial in 1871. The first court case lasted 102 days, with more than one hundred witnesses confirming Orton's identity as Tichborne. When the case closed in 1872, Orton was charged with perjury. A second trial, starting in 1873 and running for 188 days, convicted Orton and he was sentenced to fourteen years' imprisonment. He served ten years and died in poverty in 1898. Orton was buried as Sir Roger Tichborne and his grave still bears this name.

Marcus Clarke based one of the central dynamics of *His Natural Life*—the twin narratives of Rufus Dawes and John Rex—on the Tichborne case. And his third novel, serialised in the *Australian Journal* from 1874 to 1875, was called *Chidiock Tichborne* (the real-life poet ancestor of Sir Roger Tichborne). Anthony Trollope was another who used the story. Charles Reade—whose convict novel *It Is Never Too Late to Mend* Clarke alludes to in *His Natural Life*—also wrote a novel based on the Tichborne case: *The Wandering Heir*, published in 1875. The influence of this peculiar case has been felt into the twentieth century. Jorge Luis Borges wrote a short story based on the trial, 'Tom Castro, the Implausible Imposter', and numerous other books and several films have investigated Orton's story.

5

'The Chosen Vessel'

Barbara Baynton (1857–1929)

Barbara Baynton's chilling bush story 'The Chosen Vessel' was first published in the *Bulletin* in December 1896 as 'The Tramp'. It was the only one of Baynton's stories to appear in the *Bulletin*, and it was carefully cut and edited by AG Stephens before publication. 'The Chosen Vessel' falls into two sections, the first about a woman and child alone on a selection as night descends; the second about a man, Peter Hennessey, who sees a vision in the bush of the Virgin and Child swathed in moonlight. It was this second section, with its supernatural, religious overtones, as well as its powerful ironic punch, that Stephens cut for the *Bulletin* readers. The Hennessey section was reinstated when the story was published as 'The Chosen Vessel' in Baynton's collection of six stories, *Bush Studies*, published in London in 1902.

Stephens reviewed *Bush Studies* in the *Bulletin* in 1903. He praised it highly: 'So precise, so complete, with such insight into detail and such force of statement, it ranks with the masterpieces of realism in any language.' And yet he also noted that its emphasis on 'the predominantly obstetric quality of Bush life' had been '"shocking" to some city critics'. And perhaps reflecting the *Bulletin*'s failure to publish more of Baynton's stories, he remarked on their potential to offend Australian readers: their 'truthful glimpses of Australian life, graphically expressed, could not (would not) have been printed in any Australian paper, though they rank highly as literature and are circulated widely in book form when issued by an English publisher. We are too mealy-mouthed (in print) and stuff far too much "respectable" wadding in our ears.'

Baynton was born in 1857 in Scone, in the Hunter Valley north of Sydney, to carpenter John Lawrence and his wife Elizabeth. She worked as a governess in Quirindi, where she met Alexander Frater, whom she married in 1880 aged twenty-three. They lived on a selection near Coonamble and had two sons and a daughter before Frater left Baynton for a servant. With characteristic decisiveness and energy, Baynton then moved to Sydney with her three children, supporting them all by selling Bibles door to door. By the time her divorce came through in 1890 Baynton had already met her second husband, seventy-year-old Dr Thomas Baynton, and they married the next day. Thomas Baynton lived well in Woollahra, mixing in Sydney's literary and academic circles and collecting Georgian silver and antiques.

With her financial stresses relieved, Baynton was able to devote herself to writing. Over several years during her thirties, she wrote and painstakingly revised until she had perfected six short stories, including 'The Chosen Vessel'. Her love of Charles Dickens, Leo Tolstoy, Fyodor Dostoyevsky, Ivan Turgenev and Edgar Allan Poe is evident in her stories, with their deft characterisation, wry humour, haunted landscapes, suspense, terror and preoccupation with human relations, motherhood, death and violence. Baynton also admired the work of Henry Lawson, whose collection *While*

the Billy Boils (1896) had inspired her to see the bush as a potential subject of literature: 'I remember thinking, after reading *While
the Billy Boils*, that here for the first time a man had shown that
the Bush was worth writing about, and it was a great encourage-
ment to me when I started to write.'

After unsuccessfully sending her collection of stories, *Bush
Studies*, to publishers in Sydney, Baynton travelled to London.
Through a chance encounter with critic and editor Edward
Garnett—who also supported Henry Lawson, John Galsworthy,
Joseph Conrad and DH Lawrence—Baynton found a publisher
in Duckworth & Co., who published *Bush Studies* in London in
1902. The volume was well received and Baynton was celebrated
in London's literary world.

Following Thomas Baynton's death in 1904, Baynton invested
the money he left her wisely and became very wealthy. She spent
much of her time in London or Cambridge, dressing lavishly and
wearing layers of gigantic pearls, black opals and other jewels.
Encouraged by Duckworth's, Baynton wrote a novel, *Human Toll*,
which was published in 1907, but it was not successful. In 1914
the young Australian critic and writer Vance Palmer published an
article praising Baynton's work in London's *Book Monthly*. Baynton
was so moved by Palmer's encouraging words that she invited him
to lunch at her London club. Her only other published book was
a reissued volume of *Bush Studies* with two additional stories,
published during the First World War as *Cobbers* in 1917.

Baynton's bush is a place of fear, where dogs are more loyal
than people and seem more capable of conversation; where
women live with the threat of violence and are useful only for
their youth and good looks, or for their physical strength, and are
discarded the moment they lose these qualities. The only abiding
beauty to be found in *Bush Studies* is the vital bond shared by
mother and child, which in the opening story 'The Dreamer' is

held up like a talisman against the nightmare of a storm. It is also invoked against danger in 'The Chosen Vessel': 'Something had set her heart beating wildly; but she lay quite still, only she put her arm over her baby.'

'The Chosen Vessel' opens abruptly: 'She laid the stick and her baby on the grass while she untied the rope that tethered the calf.' The unnamed woman is alone on a selection with her baby and only a slab hut to protect her against the danger she senses all around. It is Monday, and her husband is shearing fifteen miles away and will not be back until the weekend. With her spare, sure strokes, Baynton conjures a threatening landscape of isolation and terror, into which walks a swagman: 'She feared more from the look of his eyes, and the gleam of his teeth . . . than from the knife that was sheathed in the belt at his waist.'

The two parts of 'The Chosen Vessel' each play in a different way on the title and the way in which women are used—or 'chosen'—as vessels. In the first part of the story the woman is a potential vessel for a man's sexual desire and satisfaction. In the second part, with Hennessey's vision of the Virgin and Child shining white in the bush, the vessel becomes woman as the chosen repository for the gestation and birth of the Son of God. With extraordinary economy and tension, 'The Chosen Vessel' tells a bush story of woman seen either as whore or Madonna, vessels both, for men's physical desires or their spiritual aspirations.

In 1921 Baynton married in London for the third time—her friend Lord Headley, who had spent many years building dams in Egypt and India, where he had converted to Islam. He was a sporting country squire and she was a dominating city woman, as her friend, the wartime prime minister Billy Hughes, described: 'My God she used to make me laugh! But you know you never wanted to argue with her. I haven't a very good reputation myself when it comes to verbal disagreement, but Barbara—she was bloody well impossible!' Baynton's marriage to Headley lasted eighteen months. She eventually returned permanently to Australia, to the house she had built in Melbourne's Toorak near her daughter, and spent her last years being chauffeured around town in her red Daimler. Baynton died suddenly in 1929.

Vance and Nettie Palmer

From the 1920s to the 1950s, Vance and Nettie Palmer were among the most influential voices in Australian literature, actively promoting Australian writers and working as writers and critics themselves.

Vance Palmer (1885–1959) was a novelist, dramatist and critic, whose study of the nationalist literature of the 1890s—*The Legend of the Nineties*, published in 1954—defined a decade. Born in Bundaberg in north-east Queensland, after leaving school Vance worked on a sheep station in western Queensland to experience the Australian outback. Determined to become a writer, he travelled to London, first in 1905 and again in 1910, to broaden his literary experience. He met Nettie in Melbourne in 1909 and they were married in 1914 in London, where their first daughter was born. The following year they returned to Melbourne and moved to Katharine Susannah Prichard's cottage in Emerald, where they had a second daughter. In 1920 Vance published his first novel. During the Second World War he published several non-fiction works, including *National Portraits* (1941), *AG Stephens: His Life and Works* (1941) and a study of the Australian theatre. After the war he wrote a novel trilogy based on the life of a Queensland politician, *Golconda* (1948), *Seedtime* (1957) and *The Big Fellow* (1959), the last of which won the Miles Franklin Award in 1959.

Nettie Palmer (1885–1964) was a poet, writer and Australia's most influential literary critic of the day. Born in Bendigo, Victoria, Nettie was a gifted linguist. After completing her degree at the University of Melbourne she travelled to France and Germany to study literature. Her landmark, award-winning study of Australian literature, *Modern Australian Fiction 1900–1923*, was published in 1924. She also published in 1950 the first major work on Henry Handel Richardson, *Henry Handel Richardson: A Study*, which established Richardson's reputation in Australia. Her book *Fourteen Years: Extracts from a Private Journal 1925–1939* was published by Meanjin Press in 1948 and is seen as her most important work.

Two Victorian literary awards are named after the Palmers: the Victorian Premier's Literary Award for fiction is the Vance Palmer Prize and the non-fiction award is the Nettie Palmer Prize.

away'. The famed Clancy of the Overflow is also there, and he takes a different view. The horse and boy ought to go along, for they are mountain-bred: 'And the Snowy River riders on the mountains make their home, / Where the river runs those giant hills between; / I have seen full many horsemen since I first commenced to roam, / But nowhere yet such horsemen have I seen.'

And so with his galloping rhythms and tall-story twist, Paterson spins out one of the most enduring and exciting ballads of the Australian bush, turning the mountain riders into legends and their land into mythical terrain: Kosciuszko, 'where the pine-clad ridges raise / Their torn and rugged battlements on high, / Where the air is clear as crystal, and the white stars fairly blaze'. The boy is the only rider who can keep up with the colt, 'Through the stringy barks and saplings, on the rough and broken ground', while the men look on, dumbstruck and defeated.

The Snowy River rises on Mount Kosciuszko in the Great Dividing Range, near the border of New South Wales and Victoria. It is rugged territory, testing the skills of its famed horsemen and -women: 'He sent the flint-stones flying, but the pony kept his feet, / He cleared the fallen timber in his stride, / And the man from Snowy River never shifted in his seat— / It was grand to see that mountain horseman ride.' It is said that Paterson based the 'Man' from Snowy River on Jack Riley, a fearless mountain horseman who came from Corryong, a small town on the western side of the range. In honour of this possibility, Corryong celebrates Paterson's poem every April with 'The Man From Snowy River Bush Festival'. Others believe that the celebrated Monaro horseman Charlie McKeahnie was the original 'Man', for in the late 1880s the young McKeahnie chased down a runaway horse through rugged country in the Snowy River region, just like the 'Man'.

With their wry humour and easy rhythmic vernacular, Paterson's ballads portray an Australia that captured the imagination of the

1890s—and his verse continues to resonate today. His ballads range from the Snowy Mountains across the back country of New South Wales to the Queensland border and bring to life a troop of unlikely bush heroes. His bushmen defy prejudice, combat toffs, battle banks, and ride tall in the saddle. There is the weedy horseman who brings in the pedigree colt against all odds; the team of rough riders from up country whose polo play against the city 'Cuff and Collar Team' is so keen that not one horse or rider is left standing at the game's end; drover Saltbush Bill, the 'King of the Overland', who fights the squatters for grass; and Kiley, who toils through drought, dreaming of overdrafts, until the bank takes his land and life away. And riding among them all, introduced in the popular 1889 ballad, is Clancy of the Overflow, singing as he goes, 'For the drover's life has pleasures / that the townsfolk never know'. Clancy also appears in 'The Man From Snowy River', as does Harrison, originally seen in 'Old Pardon, Son of Reprieve' (1888).

Banjo Paterson was born in 1864 near Orange, 260 kilometres west of Sydney. When he was five, he moved with his parents to Illalong Creek near Yass. These were golden days for Paterson. He became a skilled horseman and later took the name of a favourite Illalong horse as his pen-name, 'The Banjo'. But the Illalong property was not a financial success and Paterson's father, Andrew Bogle Paterson—who had arrived in Australia from Scotland aged seventeen—was forced to sell. The new owner employed Andrew Paterson as manager, where he remained until he took an overdose of opium aged fifty-six. (The apparent suicide was recorded as 'an overdose of opium accidentally self-administered'.)

Paterson grew up with the complete works of Charles Dickens and Sir Walter Scott, whose Scottish ballads shaped his poetic style. Thomas Carlyle became Paterson's favourite prose writer, and he admired Alfred Tennyson, Henry Wadsworth Longfellow and Algernon Swinburne. When he was ten, Paterson was sent to school in Sydney. In 1880 he left school to train as a solicitor, and also wrote poetry and journalism.

The first poem to appear under the name 'The Banjo' was published in the *Bulletin* in 1886: 'The Bushfire—an Allegory', written in support of Irish Home Rule. The same year his poem 'A Dream of the Melbourne Cup' appeared. It prompted a meeting with the *Bulletin*'s visionary editor JF Archibald, who wanted to find out if Paterson knew anything about the bush, a favourite *Bulletin* theme. When he heard Paterson had grown up in the bush, Archibald said: 'All right. Have a go at the bush. Have a go at anything that strikes you. Don't write anything like other people if you can help it.'

'The Man From Snowy River' was published in the *Bulletin* in April 1890 and its appeal was immediate. Five years later it became the title poem of Paterson's first collection of poetry, published in 1895. *The Man From Snowy River* became an instant bestseller and is still in print—the first edition sold out in a week and it went through four editions in six months. In London, the *Times* praised *The Man From Snowy River* and compared Paterson to Rudyard Kipling. In the same year, 1895, Paterson also composed 'Waltzing Matilda', now widely considered as Australia's unofficial national anthem.

In 1899 Paterson travelled with three horses to South Africa as a Boer War correspondent for the *Sydney Morning Herald*. While there he met Olive Schreiner (*The Story of an African Farm*, 1883) and Rudyard Kipling. In 1903 he became editor of Sydney's *Evening News*. With a secure job, he married and had two children. In 1908, suffering ill-health, Paterson resigned from the *Evening News* and sought refuge in the bush, moving to a sheep station near Yass. His bush venture lasted until 1914, when he returned to Sydney and resumed his work as a journalist. As writer Richard Hall says, 'It was something of an irony that Paterson, the man who spoke for the bush, spent only twelve of his 77 years living in the country.'

When war broke out in 1914, Paterson travelled to Europe hoping to find work as a war correspondent, but he was too old. Instead, he drove an ambulance in France before heading to Egypt, aged fifty-one, with the Australian Remount Unit. Back in Australia, Paterson became editor of the *Sydney Sportsman* in 1921 and spent his remaining twenty years in Sydney, where he was widely known although his career had peaked decades earlier. Patrick White's father, a cousin of Paterson's wife, brought 'The Banjo' to meet his young son. White recalled his father introducing him as 'Mr' Banjo Paterson and seeming proud of their relationship.

The legend of 'The Man From Snowy River' has lived on—almost literally, as the Victorian Premier Steve Bracks found in 2005, when he was accused of killing him. That year Bracks banned cattle grazing on Victoria's high plain country, the Snowy River territory, thereby ending a 170-year-old tradition. In protest, not only did three hundred mountain men and women ride their horses down Melbourne's Bourke Street, but the leader of Victoria's National Party declared that Bracks would 'go down in history as the man who killed the man from Snowy River.'

'The Man From Snowy River' has also inspired two films: the first, a silent film shot in the Snowy Mountains in 1920; the second, the 1982 blockbuster starring Tom Burlinson as the 'Man', Jack Thompson as Clancy of the Overflow, Kirk Douglas as Harrison and Sigrid Thornton as his daughter. There has also been a television series based on 'The Man From Snowy River', called *Snowy River: The MacGregor Saga*, which screened in the 1990s. Paterson's poem also spawned 'The Man From Snowy River: Arena

Spectacular'—a theatrical work that premiered in 2002, featuring super horseman Steve Jefferys, the lone horseman from the 2000 Olympic Games Opening Ceremony. The show proved so successful that it toured every capital city in Australia, twice.

Banjo Paterson and the words of his most famous poem, 'The Man From Snowy River', are commemorated on the Australian ten dollar note.

David Malouf's favourite Australian books

Such is Life by Tom Collins
Maurice Guest by Henry Handel Richardson
Poems by John Shaw Neilson
100 Poems by Kenneth Slessor
The Aunt's Story by Patrick White
Voss by Patrick White
Poems by Les Murray
The Road to Botany Bay: An Exploration of Landscape and History by Paul
    Carter
The Children's Bach by Helen Garner

There. Nine—so that I still have one place open for another ten
or more to move in and out of.

David Malouf is a celebrated, award-winning author of poetry,
novels, memoir, short stories and opera librettos. His novels
include *Johnno* (1975), *An Imaginary Life* (1978), *Remembering Babylon*
(1993) and *The Conversations at Curlow Creek* (1996).

7

'NATIONALITY'

Mary Gilmore (1865–1962)

Mary Gilmore was a woman of enormous vitality, who in her poetry and prose devoted her life to fighting numerous causes on behalf of the vulnerable and the voiceless. Everywhere in her poetry her acute empathy for the pain of others can be felt: 'There was no hunted one / With whom I did not run' ('The Baying Hounds'). During her ninety-seven years, which reached from the pioneering days of colonial Australia into the atomic age, her output was massive, amounting to over 3000 poems and fragments on hundreds of subjects, from love and motherhood and the early days of Australia, to the ruin of the environment and Aboriginal culture, to war and the atomic bomb. As her friend, the poet and critic RD Fitzgerald observed of her many callings, Gilmore was a 'lyricist, poet of enthusiasms, champion of neglected causes, crusader, pioneer, sympathetic human being, intense human personality—whose skilled craftsmanship in words has always been at the service of some case to be stated.'

While her profligate poetic energies may have left behind a

body of work that is uneven, at its best Gilmore's poetry seizes with dazzling precision on a particular event or emotion and condenses it into lyrics as direct and simple as the first words she was introduced to (aged eighteen months, by her grand-father)—the opening verses of Genesis. This is true of one of her most celebrated poems, 'Nationality', of which writer T Inglis Moore said: 'If any single poem should be taught throughout our schools, it should be this superb lyric'. Written in 1942, during the Second World War, 'Nationality' is a concentration of intense and conflicting emotion in two brief stanzas (as it first appeared in Gilmore's last serious collection, *Fourteen Men* (1954)). 'Nationality' expresses the emotional paradox that war poses for a loving heart like Gilmore's—the tension between its natural connection with every living being and a love most deeply rooted in its own people, its own son: 'I have grown past hate and bitter-ness, / I see the world as one; / But though I can no longer hate, / My son is still my son.' When she wrote this poem Gilmore was almost eighty. She spoke from a lifetime.

'Nationality' continues: 'All men at God's round table sit, / And all men must be fed; / But this loaf in my hand, / This loaf is my son's bread.' These lyrics, resonant with biblical allusion, play on one of Gilmore's favourite themes—the bread (or wheat) of life, a basic food and the sacrament, the flesh of Christ given from love. While Gilmore was an unconventional Christian, she remained a Protestant all her life. In 1910 she wrote to the *Bulletin*'s AG Stephens: 'Funny thing how one continues to be haunted by a hope & a belief in religion when the evidence is all so much against it.' With its compact images and direct rhythmic expres-sion, 'Nationality' has the force of truth. Travelling in Europe, writer Dymphna Cusack (1902–1981) met a French man who recited 'Nationality' to her, then said with tears in his eyes: 'How simple it is. And how profound.'

The poem attests to Gilmore's complexity—she was both an internationalist and a patriot, a socialist reformer deeply attached to family history and national traditions. She was ardently devoted to peace and yet fiercely determined that Australia's soldiers should protect their shores from enemies, a belief most clearly expressed in her popular wartime poem 'No Foe Shall Gather Our Harvest': 'And we swear by the dead who bore us / By the heroes who blazed the trail, / No foe shall gather our harvest, / Or sit on our stock-yard rail.' The rich multiplicity of her view is suggested by the fact that this same poem was published by both the mainstream family magazine *Australian Women's Weekly* in 1940 and by the Communist newspaper *Tribune* in 1957.

Gilmore's best poetry is lyrical, condensed, empathetic. She describes it well in her poem '*Los Heridos*': 'I have not written mad things, / For mad things do not enchant me; / But I have written the small and simple, / Lest the mad things haunt me.'

Born near Goulburn in a slab cottage in 1865, Gilmore spent long months of her childhood travelling through wild stretches of New South Wales with her family as her Scottish father followed the economic boom in search of building work. Her days spent alongside teamsters encouraged her passionate connection with pioneers and the poor: 'The real makers of our foundation history lived on possum legs, had no carriages and slept in slab houses. They were the mass of the people.' Her affinity with 'the mass of the people' can be felt in her poetry. As can her lifelong commitment to socialism and her celebration of the ordinary stuff of life, 'the wonderful things, so common, so cheap and so close to hand'.

Gilmore settled with her grandparents when she started school—and it was here that she first felt the urge to write: 'I was like something for whom the gates of the world had opened.

I had wings. I could not help writing.' She also read voraciously and later admired Thomas Hardy (1840–1928), Thomas Carlyle (1795–1881) and Victor Hugo (1802–1885). At twelve Gilmore became a pupil-teacher at her uncle's school in Cootamundra, the first of a series of teaching posts across New South Wales. She later contributed articles to country newspapers under various pseudonyms (teachers were not allowed to write for the press).

In 1890 Gilmore moved to Sydney, where she was swept up in the political and literary ferment of the time, becoming involved with the trade union movement and the writers who were forging a new literature focused on Australia, published in the *Bulletin* and the *Worker*. She befriended Henry Lawson and met the three people who 'most shaped my mind and life'. They were William Lane, the charismatic English journalist whose vision for a communist utopia eventually led to the experimental New Australia colony in Paraguay; the bush balladist John Farrell; and renowned editor AG Stephens.

Having been actively involved in the Maritime Strike of 1890 and the Shearers' Strike of 1891, Gilmore became the first woman member of the Australian Workers' Union (formed from the Shearers' Union). When the strikes were crushed, there was a surge of rebel support for William Lane's utopian vision and in 1893 he sailed with hundreds of supporters to set up a colony in Paraguay. Gilmore joined him there in 1896 and later wrote to Lawson: 'I'd give a lot to see you here. The place teems with copy, the life makes it. I wish to Heaven I could write it up.' In 1897 she married fellow colonist William Gilmore, a shearer from Victoria, and their only child, Billy, was born the following year. In 1899 Lane left the failing colony and the Gilmores left soon after, living separately in South America until 1902. When they returned to Australia—which felt to Gilmore 'like coming to the backyard of the world'—they moved to rural Victoria.

In 1907 Gilmore wrote to the editor of the Sydney *Worker*, Hector Lamond, suggesting he include a women's page in his paper. He agreed, so from 1908 until 1931, Gilmore wrote the *Worker*'s popular women's page, whose contents ranged from current affairs to recipes. Gilmore moved with her son Billy to Sydney in 1912 and William Gilmore went to work in Cloncurry, Queensland. Billy later joined his father and although Gilmore remained intensely loyal to them both, she rarely saw them again. Father and son both died in 1945.

In Sydney, Gilmore devoted herself to a range of causes—from old age pensions and equal status for women to baby health centres—and continued to write poetry. In 1910, aged forty-five, she published her first book, *Marri'd and Other Verses*. Her second, *The Passionate Heart*, described as 'the literary sensation of 1918', marked the beginning of a period of intense productivity for Gilmore, during which she published *The Tilted Cart* (1925), *The Wild Swan* (1930), *Under the Wilgas* (1932) and *Battlefields* (1939). In 1954 *Fourteen Men* was awarded the Gold Medal of the Australian Literature Society as best book of the year.

Gilmore became a popular, widely celebrated poet. In 1937 she was the first person to be made Dame Commander of the British Empire for contributing to literature, in acknowledgement of her position as 'a national poet' and 'one of the grandest personalities in Australia today'. For her ninety-second birthday in 1957, William Dobel painted her (controversial) portrait. Four years later her support of the labour movement was honoured when she was crowned May Queen for the May Day procession. When she died in 1962, Gilmore was given the first state funeral for an Australian writer since Henry Lawson. At her request, a copy of *Fourteen Men* was put in her hands as she lay in her coffin: 'I have put the best of myself into those poems and when I go I want them to go with me.'

Mary Gilmore is commemorated on the Australian ten dollar note.

LES MURRAY'S FAVOURITE
AUSTRALIAN BOOKS

Fresh Fields by Peter Kocan
Honk if you are Jesus by Peter Goldsworthy
To the Burning City by Alan Gould
The Glass Canoe by David Ireland
The Year of Living Dangerously by CJ Koch
Moral Hazard by Kate Jennings
Lucinda Brayford by Martin Boyd
Selected Poems by Kenneth Slessor
A Million Wild Acres by Eric Rolls
Hell and After: Four early English-language poets of Australia (McNamara,
    Gilmore, Neilson, Harford) edited with introductions by
    Les Murray

Les Murray is one of Australia's most celebrated poets. His
collections include *The Weatherboard Cathedral* (1969), *The Vernacular
Republic* (1976), *Translations from the Natural World* (1992) and *Subhuman
Redneck Poems* (1996), which won the TS Eliot Prize in 1996.
He has written two verse novels, *The Boys Who Stole the Funeral*
(1980) and *Fredy Neptune* (1998).

8

'The Drover's Wife'

Henry Lawson (1867–1922)

'The two-roomed house is built of round timber, slabs, and stringy-bark, and floored with split slabs. A big bark kitchen standing at one end is larger than the house itself, verandah included.' The opening of Henry Lawson's story 'The Drover's Wife' is no innocuous description of a typical nineteenth-century Australian bush hut. It contains the key to the story's drama—the split slabs—and is the theatre of its unfolding. In the story's few pages, Lawson conjures a tale with an ancient resonance: a woman—in a garden of 'stunted, rotten native apple trees'—is confronted by a snake. Her companion is not a man ('The drover, an ex-squatter, is away with sheep') but a dog, a 'big, black, yellow-eyed dog-of-all-breeds'; the only man by her side is her eldest son, 'a sharp-faced, excited urchin of eleven'.

In four lean paragraphs Lawson puts the drover's wife and her four children at play in their bush isolation, and sparks the action of the tale: 'Suddenly one of them yells: "Snake! Mother, here's a snake!"' The woman responds in an instant, snatching up the baby and grabbing a stick. But it is too late—the snake has fled under the house and will not come out. There is a storm coming but the woman will not take her children into the house, 'for she knows the snake is there, and may at any moment come up through the cracks in the rough slab floor; so she carries several armfuls of firewood into the kitchen and takes the children there.'

And so begins her night-long watch for the snake with the dog Alligator by her side. The children sleep, nestled on the kitchen table, the storm comes, and the woman thinks over her life. She remembers bushfire, flood, death, a mad bullock and cunning crows, good times and times so ludicrous she had to laugh.

'The Drover's Wife' has a beautifully measured tempo, maintained by Lawson's exact, understated prose, which slowly builds in intensity throughout the woman's vigil, from dusk till dawn, until the long awaited climax. Within this compact frame—one night—Lawson gathers a whole life, so that by the story's end a fully formed woman and her world have emerged. The London *Academy* captured the essence of the story's magic when it said of 'The Drover's Wife': 'the woman's thoughts reveal herself to you as she sits there, until by the time the climax is sighted you know her as you know yourself.'

The story was first published in the *Bulletin* in July 1892. Two years later it was included in Lawson's first collection, *Short Stories in Prose and Verse*, published by his mother Louisa Lawson on the press of her women's magazine *Dawn*. In his *Bulletin* review of the collection AG Stephens declared: 'Every Australian should invest a shilling in a copy—firstly because the book is well worth it; secondly because it is a characteristically Australian book, one of the few really original attempts towards an Australian literature'.

The story appeared again in 1896, in *While the Billy Boils*, Lawson's first collection published by Angus & Robertson. The book was an immediate success and Lawson became a celebrated literary star. The *Sydney Morning Herald* called it 'an unsparing picture of the realistic, unlovely side of life as lived in the Australian bush'. The *Review of Reviews* wrote that Lawson had transformed the characters and locales of the Australian bush 'whole into his pages, and there they stand, with the full glare of the Australian sun on them . . . always and unmistakeably alive'. In London the *Spectator* praised the collection—saying Lawson's stories had 'enough rough pathos, fire, and tragic realism to draw the eyes of literary men upon the author'—and called its author 'the greatest Australian writer'.

Lawson wrote 'The Drover's Wife' in 1892. His first story, 'His Father's Mate', had been published in the *Bulletin* in 1888, but at the time Lawson was better known for his verse. His close friend, the poet Mary Cameron (to whom he later proposed and who would become Dame Mary Gilmore), was among several people who encouraged Lawson to focus on prose: 'I told him his prose was better than his verse . . . I begged him to write Australia, and again Australia.' But in 1892 balladry still continued to consume Lawson's attention—this was the year he challenged 'The Banjo' to a famous verse duel in the *Bulletin* (see box on page 65).

Although Lawson drew on his own bush childhood for 'The Drover's Wife', Gilmore later claimed that the story was hers: that the drover was her father; that the boy in the story, Tommy, was her brother Hughie; and that Tommy's moving declaration at the end of the story was originally Hughie's. But Lawson insisted that his aunt, Gertrude Falconer, was the drover's wife; that the house was drawn from his boyhood home near Mudgee; and that many of the story's episodes, such as the shooting of a mad bullock, had taken place there.

Born in 1867 in Grenfell, west of Sydney, Lawson was the son of a Norwegian seaman, Niels Larsen (later Peter Lawson), who had arrived in Melbourne in 1855 and joined the gold rush. After his marriage to Louisa Albury the couple continued to move around searching for gold until Peter took up a selection at Pipeclay near Mudgee, when their eldest son Henry was six. Henry's three years of schooling ended in 1880 when he went to work with his father as a builder. Soon after, aged fourteen, Lawson suffered major, permanent hearing loss as a result of an earlier childhood illness.

In 1883 Lawson moved to Sydney with his mother, brother and sister. Louisa bought a share in a newspaper, the *Republican*, in 1887, which published Lawson's early writing, and the following year she established the feminist journal *Dawn*. Lawson's first published poem, 'A Song of the Republic', appeared in the *Bulletin* in 1887. Lawson, a fierce republican like his mother, charged its lyrics with nationalistic fervour: 'Sons of the South, aroused at last! / Sons of the South are few! / But your ranks grow longer and deeper fast, / And ye shall swell to an army vast, / And free from the wrongs of the North and Past / The land that belongs to you.'

Despite his success as a writer, Lawson drifted around, unable to concentrate on his writing and spending his time in bars. To focus his mind, the *Bulletin*'s editor JF Archibald, who had taken an interest in him, gave him a train ticket to Bourke and five pounds so he could write bush stories. In September 1892 Lawson set off for the drought-stricken west, where he remained for nine months, walking around the countryside with his swag. He was overwhelmed by what he found: 'You can have no idea of the horrors of the country out here, men tramp and beg and live like dogs.' Many of his best stories were inspired by these brief travels through western New South Wales, including 'The Bush Undertaker' and 'The Union Buries its Dead'.

In 1896 Lawson married Bertha Bredt, the same year Angus & Robertson published his *While the Billy Boils* and *In the Days when the World Was Wide and Other Verses*. After his marriage, Lawson continued his drinking and restless ways. The Lawsons spent a year in New Zealand and then, encouraged by British interest in his work, Lawson travelled with his wife and two children to London in 1900. Here he wrote the four Joe Wilson stories, which were published in *Joe Wilson and his Mates* by Edinburgh's highly regarded William Blackwood in 1901. Blackwood also published Lawson's *Children of the Bush* (1902).

But despite this measure of success, London was a disaster for Lawson ('that wild run to London / That wrecked and ruined me'): Bertha's mental health collapsed and so did their marriage. Shortly after his return to Sydney, in December 1902, Lawson attempted suicide by jumping off a cliff at Manly. Henry and Bertha were officially separated in 1903. Lawson spent the rest of his life struggling with alcohol, being periodically hospitalised and imprisoned for failing to pay his children's maintenance. His writing deteriorated into pastiche; his best work had been done by 1902. After his lonely death in 1922, Lawson was honoured with a state funeral at St Andrew's Cathedral in central Sydney, the first state funeral for an Australian writer.

Like its author, 'The Drover's Wife' is now legendary in Australian literature. It has inspired parodies, tributes and a painting by Russell Drysdale. The historian Manning Clark, who wrote a biography of Lawson, put his achievement simply: 'he had the gift . . . to use words that could make people cry.'

Lawson remains one of Australia's most acclaimed and widely known writers. He was commemorated on the original Australian ten dollar note when decimal currency was introduced in 1966. Since 1957 Lawson's life and work has been celebrated annually at the Grenfell Henry Lawson Festival of the Arts.

The Paterson–Lawson Duel

The famous Paterson–Lawson duel began in 1892, when Henry Lawson suggested to AB 'Banjo' Paterson that they battle out their very different views of the bush—in verse, in the *Bulletin*. Lawson thought a battle on this topical subject would increase their readership. (At the time he was one of the few people who knew the real identity of 'The Banjo'.)

As Paterson later recalled: 'Henry Lawson was a man of remarkable insight in some things and of extraordinary simplicity in others. We were both looking for the same reef, if you get what I mean; but I had done my prospecting on horseback with my meals cooked for me, while Lawson had done his prospecting on foot and had had to cook for himself. Nobody realised this better than Lawson; and one day he suggested that we should write against each other, he putting the bush from his point of view, and I putting it from mine. "We ought to do pretty well out of it," he said . . . so we slam-banged away at each other for weeks and weeks; not until they stopped us, but until we ran out of material.'

Lawson, as spokesman of 'the people', made the first strike with 'Borderland' (later 'Up the Country'), which he wrote before he had travelled out west to Bourke: 'I'm back from up the country—very sorry that I went— / Seeking for the Southern Poets' land whereon to pitch my tent; / I have lost a lot of idols, which were broken on the track, / Burnt a lot of fancy verses, and I'm glad that I am back.'

And Paterson replied with 'In Defence of the Bush': 'So you're back from up the country, Mister Lawson, where you went, / And you're cursing all the business in a bitter discontent; / Well, we grieve to disappoint you, and it makes us sad to hear / That it wasn't cool and shady—and there wasn't whips of beer.'

Lawson then taunted back with 'In Answer to "Banjo", and Otherwise' (later 'The City Bushman'). Unbeknownst to them both, Archibald had invited other balladeers to contribute to the debate. One, Edward Dyson, replied with a ballad against 'The Banjo' and others subsequently joined in with 'The Overflow of Clancy' and 'Banjo, of the Overflow'. Then Lawson parodied Paterson with 'Grog-an'-Grumble Steeplechase' and Paterson hit back with 'An Answer to Various Bards', followed by 'The Poets of the Tomb'.

Archibald then dropped the debate. But Lawson had been right—readers were captivated by the fiercely contested duel, which seemed to support the *Bulletin*'s view that the bush was the shaping force of Australian identity in the 1890s. Although interestingly, for two poets so closely associated with voicing and imagining the Australian bush, Lawson and Paterson spent most of their lives in the city.

9

'LILITH'

Christopher Brennan (1870–1932)

Christopher Brennan was born in Sydney in 1870, three years after Henry Lawson. Although the lives of both men traced out the same tragic arc of early success and rapid decline into literary pastiche and alcoholism, the focus and style of their endeavours could not have been further apart. While Lawson was immersed in the nationalist fervour of the 1890s and held his vision on the Australian bush and its vernacular, Brennan turned his mind to Europe, in particular to the French Symbolist poet Stéphane Mallarmé (1842–1898), and used a mannered poetic diction of nineteenth-century England. As Brennan said in an interview in 1909: 'I'm afraid I'm very unpatriotic. I've written nothing about the horse or the swagman. As far as "national" traits go, I might have made my verse in China.'

More accurately, Brennan turned his gaze inward: 'I only know that I allow something in me to speak that gazes for ever on two heavens far back in me: one a tragic night with a few aspiring stars, the other an illimitable rapture of golden morn over innocent waters and tuneful boughs.' Almost exclusively, it is the tragic night that Brennan draws on for his longest poem, 'Lilith', one of his most acclaimed works. The poem is named after the mythical first woman, who in Jewish legend was created equal to Adam and was his wife before Eve: '*This is of Lilith, by her Hebrew name / Lady of the Night: she, in the delicate frame / that was of woman after, did unite / herself with Adam in unblest delight*'. The poem is composed of twelve fragments that vary in length from two to 183 lines, and in the tenth fragment Lilith speaks, claiming her rightful place as man's bride: 'I am his bride and was and shall be still'.

Brennan began to consider 'Lilith' in 1897, three years after his return from Germany, where he had taken postgraduate classical studies at the University of Berlin on a travelling scholarship and fallen in love with the beautiful Anna Elisabeth Werth, his landlady's daughter. In Berlin he became fluent in German, read Gustave Flaubert and discovered Mallarmé's *Vers et Prose* in 1893, the year of its publication. He returned to Sydney the following year without a further degree, but with a vast vocabulary of German and French, and an obsession with Mallarmé, with whom he later corresponded. Inspired, Brennan devoted himself to poetry.

Mallarmé's view of poetry as 'a mystery to which the reader must search for the key', and his vision of the poet as priest who alone can give form to the essence of things, whose task is 'to paint, not the thing, but the effect that it produces', are reflected in 'Lilith'. The poem weaves an erotic mythology that designates Lilith as that lost perfection ('the round of nothingness') for which all on earth long, especially those who live beyond the mundane: 'Warrior and prince and poet, thou that fain / over some tract of lapsing years wouldst reign / nor know'st the crown that all thy wants confess / is Lilith's own, the round of nothingness.'

Brennan's work has its roots in the esoteric traditions of Europe which inspired the Romantic and Symbolist poets, such as alchemy, Neoplatonism and the Kabbalah, as can be seen in his allusions to 'divine incest', 'bleeding rose', 'love occult', 'O priest and poet, thou that makest God'. The figure of Lilith had first appeared in nineteenth-century European literature in Goethe's *Faust Part I* (1808) and later became a favourite subject of the Pre-Raphaelite painter and poet Dante Gabriel Rossetti; both writers re-imagined her to emphasise her role as a seductress with ensnaring hair.

In Brennan's poem Lilith is to the poet narrator a symbol of both terror and ecstasy: 'all the ways of night converge / in that delicious dark between her breasts'; 'What terror clutch'd me, even as ecstasy / smote dire across transfigured mystery?' Brennan also plays on her 'flung hair that is the starry night', which entraps those susceptible to her charms. In one of the poem's most beautiful passages, all that humans hold dear is caught up in Lilith's hair: 'All mystery, and all love, beyond our ken, / she woos us, mournful till we find her fair: / and gods and stars and songs and souls of men / are the sparse jewels in her scatter'd hair.'

'Lilith' appeared in *Poems [1913]*, Brennan's most acclaimed work, published in 1914. All but twelve of the poems had been written between 1894 and 1902, which was Brennan's most intense period of poetic creation.

Born the eldest child of Irish parents in Sydney's Haymarket, where his father was a brewer, Brennan was an outstanding scholar with a gift for languages, especially Latin. He received a scholarship to Riverview on the understanding that he was destined for the priesthood, but instead he went to the University of Sydney to study classics and philosophy. In 1889 he suffered a devastating crisis of faith before finding in poetry what had eluded him in Catholicism. He described himself in 1890 as 'a ripe agnostic, already beginning to elaborate a special epistemology of the Unknowable, which was the Absolute.'

XXI Poems, Brennan's first collection, was published in 1897. The same year Anna Elisabeth Werth moved to Sydney from Berlin and she and Brennan were married at St Mary's Cathedral. Their marriage, which produced four children, was increasingly strained, exacerbated by Brennan's excessive drinking, financial problems and the arrival in Sydney of Anna's mother and disturbed sister. In 1909 Brennan found a position lecturing in French and German at the University of Sydney. He became a legendary figure in Sydney's literary world, known as a charismatic speaker in the lecture hall and over the lunch table. As his friend AR Chisholm recalls, Brennan had 'a great voice, a great head, a great human bulk. That voice, especially when it intoned Latin, fascinated several generations of students: that leonine head dominated all the artistic and bohemian circles that mattered in the Sydney of the early twentieth century.'

Brennan was given a Chair of German and Comparative Literature at the University in 1921, but his marriage fell apart soon after and he was dismissed for adultery in 1925. The same year his great love, Violet Singer, who had inspired some of his best poetry in the 1920s, was killed by a tram. Brennan sank into despair and poverty, and died of cancer in 1932.

An accomplished scholar and ambitious poet, Brennan never quite achieved his poetic vision. As one of Brennan's most ardent promoters, HM Green, observes: 'Brennan never fully realised himself, and this was his essential tragedy.' He is remembered as the first Australian poet to engage deeply with the European poetic tradition and inspired later poets like RD Fitzgerald, AD Hope and Judith Wright. In her poem 'Brennan', Wright tells of Brennan's towering ambition—'Self-proclaimed companion / of prophets, priests and poets'—with his cloak of 'old philosopher-kings' and his ruined face 'reddened with drink'. She dedicates her poem to Brennan with the following words: 'poor hero / lost looking for yourself— / your journey was our journey. / This is for you.'

Federation

Writing in the University of Sydney magazine *Hermes* in 1902, Christopher Brennan celebrated the newly federated Australia as a sign that 'We have got rid of the so-called nineteenth century', both in Australia and internationally. Among the things that Brennan hoped to leave behind with the new century were the fervent nationalism and provincialism of 1890s Australia.

The movement towards the federation of the Australian colonies in 1901 gathered pace from the 1880s, when the colonies' common interests in defence, a 'White Australia' and economic concerns fueled the urge to unity. In his famous 'Tenterfield Address' in 1889, Henry Parkes (1815–1896), Premier of New South Wales and 'Father of Federation', called for a federal government to ensure the proper defence of the colonies. As the *Sydney Morning Herald* reported, Parkes believed 'that it was essential to preserve the security and integrity of these colonies that the whole of their forces should be amalgamated into one great federal army, feeling this, and seeing no other means of attaining the end, it seemed to him that the time was close at hand when they ought to set about creating this great national government for all Australia.'

Parkes proposed a federal conference of representatives from the six colonies and New Zealand, which met in 1890 and agreed to a convention in Sydney in 1891 to draft a federal constitution. But it turned out that defence was not a strong enough motive to create agreement among the states. The prevention of immigrant labour from Asia and the Pacific Islands was. As Alfred Deakin (1856–1919) put it in 1901: 'No motive power operated more universally . . . and more powerfully in dissolving the technical and arbitrary political divisions which previously separated us than did the desire that we should be one people and remain one people without the admixture of other races.'

After a series of meetings during 1897 and 1898, fifty delegates—ten from each of New South Wales, Victoria, South Australia, Tasmania and Western Australia (but not Queensland)—agreed that there should be a federation, to be called the Commonwealth of Australia, and that the colonies should be called states. They drafted a constitution and put it to eligible voters (which excluded Aborigines, the poor, those of Indian and Chinese descent, and most women) in the referendum of June 1898. It was not passed, so the proposed constitution was amended. It was put to a second referendum in 1899, which attracted immense public interest. New South Wales, Victoria, Tasmania, South Australia and Queensland voted yes, and the following year Western Australia also voted in favour.

In July 1900, six months before her death, Queen Victoria signed the Bill passed by the British parliament and the following December Edmond Barton (1849–1920) was called to form the first Commonwealth cabinet. Elections for the inaugural members of the first federal parliament were announced for March 1901. The Commonwealth of

Australia was inaugurated on 1 January 1901. Thousands thronged the streets in celebration of the new nation and 'Federation Arches' were opened in each state. Barton became the first Prime Minister of Australia and the first federal parliament was opened on 9 May 1901 in Melbourne, where it remained until it moved to the new capital of Canberra on 9 May 1927.

10

SEVEN LITTLE AUSTRALIANS
Ethel Turner (1870–1958)

On 18 January 1893, Ethel Turner wrote in her diary: 'I *do* want *Fame*—plenty of it.' Six days later, on her twenty-third birthday, she sketched out the story that would bring her just that—*Seven Little Australians*. Already the author of tales published by magazines like the *Bulletin* and her own sixpenny monthly the *Parthenon*, Turner hoped her new work would be published as a book. So, after finishing the manuscript in October (having written much of it in an apple tree), she sent it off to the Melbourne office of Ward & Lock. Seven days later, on 9 November 1893, the publisher replied: 'I wish to negotiate for the immediate publication of it.'

In consultation with the *Bulletin*'s JF Archibald, Turner negotiated the deal and *Seven Little Australians* was published in London in 1894. The first edition sold out in weeks. The publisher's literary advisor in London had written: 'Here is the Miss Louisa Alcott of Australia—here is one of the strongest, simplest, sweetest, sanest and most beautiful child-stories I have read for years.' And this was how Turner was presented to her eager public—as an Australian Louisa May Alcott, whose novel *Little Women* had found the same immediate success almost three decades earlier in 1868.

Seven Little Australians is, as its title suggests, boldly Australian and centres on the lives of seven Australian children, the Woolcot siblings Meg, Pip, Judy, Nell, Bunty, Baby and the General. The warm and lively narrative begins with a warning to any reader who might expect an ordinary moral tale of childhood: 'Before you fairly start this story, I should like to give you just a word of warning. If you think you are going to read of model children, with perhaps a naughtily inclined one to point a moral, you had better lay down the book immediately . . . Not one of the seven is really good, for the very excellent reason that Australian children never are.' Then the reader is swept into the nursery of the Woolcot family home, fittingly known as 'Misrule', where the seven rowdy children are assembled at tea.

Turner was born in Yorkshire in 1870 and left England aged eight with her widowed mother and two sisters for New South Wales. Soon after their arrival in Sydney, Turner's mother married for the third time. The family settled in inner-eastern Sydney and Ethel went to Sydney Girls' High. At thirteen she began to write stories and planned to be a novelist, so when her school magazine failed to publish her work, she set up a rival magazine, *Iris*, whose motto was '*Dum vivo, canto*'—'While I live, I sing'. The motto perfectly captures not only Turner's own joyful disposition but the spirited-ness of her first novel, *Seven Little Australians*.

In 1891 Turner's family moved to Lindfield, where the railway had recently opened. Turner, who enjoyed a busy social life, dreaded this move away from the heart of the city: 'We have decided to go to Lindfield. I have named it Sepulchre but mother objected so I shall call it the Catacombs.' But she fell in love with her new house, with its large garden and surrounding bush, and it inspired her to write: 'red lonely roads running up hill and down dale; silent bushland everywhere filled with towering gums and wattles and the songs and flittings of birds; sunrises and sunsets uninterrupted by houses—of course one wrote a book!' In *Seven Little Australians* Turner writes of the influence of this vivid natural world on the new breed of Australian children it nurtures: 'There is a lurking sparkle of joyousness and rebellion and mischief in nature here, and therefore in children.' Her pleasure in her new environment can be seen in her evocations of the land round 'Misrule': 'The dusk had fallen very softly and tenderly over the garden, and the paddocks, and the river. There was just the faintest wind at the water's edge, but it seemed almost too tired after the hot, long day to breathe and make ripples.'

Turner loved children and captures the lives of the seven Woolcots—'my seven select spirits'—with a dazzling vitality. She easily conjures sixteen-year-old Meg's introduction to love and flirtation ('Just now, under her friend's tutelage, she was being inducted into the delightful mysteries of sweethearting, and for the time it quite filled her somewhat purposeless young life'); six-year-old Bunty's compulsive lying and incorrigible greed; and the tall, handsome Pip, devoted to his beloved younger sister Judy, whose spontaneous appetite for life and disregard for rules he finds impossible to resist. Judy's 'brilliant inventive powers plunged them all into ceaseless scrapes'—one of which ends with her severe punishment by Captain Woolcot, 'a very particular and rather irritable father', which leads eventually to the novel's tragic climax.

The *Sydney Morning Herald* thought *Seven Little Australians* 'too heavily charged with sentiment and the human tragedy for children'. But it is Turner's refusal to paint life in sweet hues that has ensured her novel's enduring popularity. *Seven Little Australians* takes in a wide view of life, including the 'exquisite misery' of first love, the complex dynamics of family, the thrill of forbidden adventure, the distractedness of a young mother, the inflexibility of a distant father, the torments of an alcoholic, and death.

Seven Little Australians was accepted for publication on the condition that Turner write a sequel. This she did, writing *The Family at Misrule* in five months, for publication in 1895. Turner wrote two other Woolcot stories: *Little Mother Meg* (1902) and her last novel, *Judy and Punch* (1928). Over the course of her long life, Turner wrote more than forty books, including children's books, short stories and poems. During the First World War she co-edited *The Australian Soldiers' Gift Book*, published in 1917.

In 1896 Turner married the lawyer Herbert Raine Curlewis. Their four-year courtship had been tumultuous, discouraged by her autocratic stepfather and at times by Turner's own reluctance to give up her freedom for marriage. But their marriage was happy, spent with their two children in a house they built overlooking Sydney's Middle Harbour. Turner continued to write prolifically. She also surfed, ice-skated, played tennis and golf; and supported other writers, including Henry Lawson (like Lawson, Turner struggled with deafness). She died in Mosman in 1958.

Seven Little Australians has been in print since it was first published over a century ago. It was translated the year after its publication, making it the first Australian children's story to earn foreign currency, and it has since been translated into more than a dozen languages. Its continuing appeal has ensured numerous adaptations: the first theatre version in 1915; an Australian feature film released for Christmas 1939; two television series, the first by the BBC in 1953, and the second by the ABC in 1973; and a musical in 1988.

Laura Moss's favourite
Australian books

My choices are both personal and academic. As my list shows, I am particularly drawn to texts that rework history from a variety of perspectives.

The Man Who Loved Children by Christina Stead (because I read it over fifteen years ago and it still haunts me)

Storm Boy by Colin Thiele (one of my favourite books when I was growing up)

Visitants by Randolph Stow (I love the use of language in this novel)

My Place by Sally Morgan (this is probably the most often taught Australian book in Canada)

Oscar and Lucinda by Peter Carey (because it got me hooked on his writing)

Joan Makes History by Kate Grenville (I enjoy the Australian Everywoman in history)

Master of the Ghost Dreaming by Mudrooroo (a gripping novel of colonialism and its legacy)

The Orchard by Drusilla Modjeska (I like the mixture of genres and stories)

Conversations at Curlow Creek by David Malouf (it is difficult to settle on just one book by Malouf)

Gould's Book of Fish by Richard Flanagan (because of its esoteric beauty)

The Book Thief by Markus Zusak (because it is a book about death that makes you feel grateful for life)

The Arrival by Shaun Tan (a wordless graphic novel that can make you weep and smile).

Dr Laura Moss is Associate Professor of Canadian, African and Australian literatures at the University of British Columbia in Vancouver, Canada. She is the editor of *Is Canada Postcolonial? Unsettling Canadian Literature* (2003) and the book review editor of the academic journal *Canadian Literature: A Quarterly of Criticism and Review*.

II

THE GETTING OF WISDOM
Henry Handel Richardson (1870–1946)

The Getting of Wisdom opens with a blissful summer idyll: four children sprawled out in a garden, the eldest telling a story about a prince who finds a beautiful lady in a glade. The storyteller, known to her siblings as 'Wondrous Fair', is making up the romance as she goes along: 'Well, as I said, the edge of her robe was all muddy—no, I don't think I will say that; it sounds prettier if it's clean.' When her brother protests about this revision—for these muddy marks indicate that the lady has been travelling—Wondrous Fair exclaims: 'Donkey! haven't I said they weren't there? If I say they weren't, then they weren't. She hadn't travelled at all.'

This opening fragment contains the essence of Henry Handel Richardson's novel: Wondrous Fair—or Laura Tweedle Rambotham—is a compulsive spinner of stories, improvised to suit whatever mood or desire takes her. Laura's easy tale-telling eventually wins her the first admiration she ever receives at her new boarding school, where most of the novel's action is centred, but it also becomes the source of her greatest agony. But worst of all, for this twelve-year-old girl who desperately wants to fit in at The Ladies' College, it marks her out as different from her schoolfellows. Laura's flimsy grasp of the truth and her facility for elaboration prevent her from developing the robust sense of right and wrong, truth and lie, appropriate and inappropriate behaviour, that is so crucial to being accepted by the group. Her storytelling proves to be a double-edged sword: it produces the greatest humiliation of her school life but it eventually opens the way to a future beyond it.

The Getting of Wisdom is Richardson's portrait of the writer as a young schoolgirl in 1880s Melbourne. It is a riveting, beautifully constructed novel, simultaneously hilarious and painful to read. Richardson writes with sharp irony and penetrating psychological insight, delicately teasing out the complex dynamics of schoolgirl life, of adolescence, of sexual awakening, of group behaviour and its abhorrence of difference (for Laura quickly learns that 'the unpardonable sin is to vary from the common mould'). The young adventuress, so filled with her own brilliance and self-importance while secluded in the haven of her family home and surrounded by admiring siblings who attend her every word, goes out into the world only to meet its crushing indifference.

With its entrance like a prison, its foyer like a dentist's ante-room, the architecture of The Ladies' School is as unwelcoming as its stately Lady Superintendent, Mrs Gurley. When Laura asks Mrs Gurley about her luggage, 'she might as well have spoken to the hatstand: Mrs Gurley had sailed off and was actually approaching a turn in the hall, before Laura made haste to follow her and to keep further anxiety about her box to herself.' The girls are equally intimidating: 'Fifty-five heads turned as if by clockwork, and fifty-five pairs of eyes were levelled at the small girl in the white apron, who meekly followed Mrs Gurley down the length of the dining room.'

Laura soon discovers her abilities count for nothing at this school: 'it was not the least use in the world to her, to have seen the snowy top of Mount Kosciuszko stand out against a dark blue evening sky, and to know its shape to a tittlekin. On the other hand, it mattered tremendously that this mountain was 7308 and not 7309 feet high.' And yet when Laura is offered the chance to shine—to display her skill on the piano—she is equally shunned. She has failed to understand another unspoken code: 'if you had abilities others had not, you concealed them, instead of parading them under people's noses.'

Published in London in 1910, *The Getting of Wisdom* was Richardson's second novel. Her first, *Maurice Guest*, a tragedy strongly influenced by German literature and music, especially Nietzsche and Wagner, and based on her experience as a music student in Leipzig, had been published in 1908 under the pen-name 'Henry Handel Richardson'. Richardson began her second novel in Bavaria in 1903, partly as an escape from writing the last harrowing chapters of *Maurice Guest*. Although *The Getting of Wisdom* is based on Richardson's own difficult years boarding at Melbourne's Presbyterian Ladies' College from 1883, its opening pages are drawn from the happiest days of her childhood, those spent in Maldon, Victoria. Twenty-one years after *The Getting of Wisdom* was published, Richardson wrote that of all her novels, 'It will always remain my favourite, &, I think one of my better if not the best.'

While some contemporary reviews praised *The Getting of Wisdom*, such as this from the *Academy* in November 1910: 'for the first time in English fiction as far as we know, it gives us a manifestly truthful account of life in a girls' school . . . its clever-ness is astonishing', many more were shocked by Richardson's frank treatment of adolescent sexuality. An Australian writing in the London journal *The Young Woman* wrote that her first thought on reading *The Getting of Wisdom* was 'to send it back as unfit for review . . . The book is coarse and sordid both in outlook and in expression, and is a libel on girlhood in general, and Australian girlhood in particular.' Acclaim for the novel came slowly. In 1924, fourteen years after *The Getting of Wisdom* was published, Richardson wrote, 'I rubbed my eyes to see Gerald Gould refer to it [in the *Observer*] as "the best of all contemporary school stories".'

Born Ethel Florence Lindesay Richardson in Melbourne, Richardson spent only the first eighteen years of her life in Australia before departing for Europe in 1888. Her parents had both migrated to the Victorian goldfields in the 1850s, where they met and married. Her Irish father Walter Richardson, a medical graduate from Edinburgh, moved with his family between the goldfields and Melbourne while his health slowly deteriorated. He was eventually committed to an asylum, where he was diagnosed with 'general paralysis of the insane' related to syphilis, from which he died in 1879. Walter's slow, horrific demise traumatised the young Richardson and she later drew on his life for her acclaimed trilogy *The Fortunes of Richard Mahony*, first published in one volume in 1930.

After leaving school, where she excelled in music, Richardson travelled with her mother and younger sister to Europe to study piano, arriving in Leipzig in 1889. Here she met John George Robertson, a brilliant science graduate from Glasgow studying philology at Leipzig University, who introduced her to Wagner and the literature of Germany and Scandinavia. They became engaged in 1891 and married four years later. Richardson graduated in 1892 but abandoned her musical career and her plans to become a concert pianist, and turned to writing instead. Her first publication was a translation (from German) of the influential Danish novel *Niels Lhyne* (1880) by JP Jacobsen, published in London in 1896 as *Sirens' Voices*. The novel, about an idealistic young poet, profoundly influenced Richardson's own work. The couple continued to live in Germany until Robertson was given the Chair in German and Scandinavian studies at London University in 1903 and they moved to London.

Richardson wrote four more novels: the three books that became the trilogy *The Fortunes of Richard Mahony*—*Australia Felix* (1917), *The Way Home* (1925) and *Ultima Thule* (1929), the last of which brought her international fame and won the Australian Literature Society's Gold Medal. Her last completed novel, *The Young Cosima*, was published in 1939. Richardson died in 1946, having spent the last years of her life with her companion Olga Roncoroni after the death of Robertson in 1933.

A comic film of *The Getting of Wisdom*, directed by Bruce Beresford, was released in 1978.

Jeffrey Smart's favourite Australian books

Maurice Guest by Henry Handel Richardson
The Fortunes of Richard Mahony by Henry Handel Richardson
The Tyranny of Distance by Geoffrey Blainey
Immortal Boy: A Portrait of Leigh Hunt by Ann Blainey
For Love Alone by Christina Stead
The Tree of Man by Patrick White
Riders in the Chariot by Patrick White
Unreliable Memoirs by Clive James
The Fatal Shore by Robert Hughes
Harland's Half Acre by David Malouf

Jeffrey Smart is one of Australia's best-known painters.
He is acclaimed for his iconic paintings of urban landscapes.

'THE GENTLE WATER BIRD'

John Shaw Neilson (1872–1942)

John Shaw Neilson, one of Australia's greatest lyrical poets, was born in 1872 in Penola, near Mount Gambier, where Adam Lindsay Gordon had first been stationed on his arrival in South Australia. Like Gordon, Neilson was a bush poet. He spent his days roaming the reaches of Victoria and parts of New South Wales in search of work, and with old Celtic songs running through his head he often found his rhymes on horseback. But unlike Gordon, Neilson was Australian-born, he spent less than three years at school, and he found a consolation in the bush and its creatures, especially birds, that had forever eluded the earlier poet. One of Neilson's most beautiful poems, 'The Gentle Water Bird', dedicated to his friend and admirer Mary Gilmore, is about his silent exchange with a crane, 'a calm soldier in a cloak of grey', who 'did commune with me for many a day / Till the dark fear was lifted far away.'

In the first of the poem's sixteen three-line verses, the poet invokes this old fear: 'In the far days, when every day was long, / Fear was upon me and the fear was strong, / Ere I had learned the recompense of song.' He is afraid of the God he has been taught about by his devout Presbyterian mother as a child; a God who is 'terrible and thunder-blue', able to instil terror in him even in daylight, 'even in my play'. But through his communion with a bird, the poet discovers a gentle face of God. For in the poem's sixth verse, something new appears from the sky, dropping into the water: 'There was a lake I loved in gentle rain: / One day there fell a bird, a courtly crane: / Wisely he walked, as one who knows of pain.' This wise bird who knows of pain also knows of joy, and communicates the whole of this wisdom to the poet. 'Gracious he was and lofty as a king: / Silent he was, and yet he seemed to sing / Always of little children and the Spring.' Through his silent song of life, the gentle water bird mystically transforms God, until 'God was not terrible and thunder-blue: / —It was a gentle water bird I knew.'

Neilson, who never married, lived in poverty in the bush for most of his life, close to the seasons, the sky, and the plants and animals of the earth. His poetry resonates with a deep understanding of this world, which speaks to him not in a voice but from a singing heart ('The Gentle Water Bird'), or with light ('The Orange Tree') or colour ('You, and Yellow Air'), and in silence ('Love's Coming'). With their evocative simplicity and purity, Neilson's poems seem to have been received from some timeless poetic source. This sense that Neilson's poetry was 'received' is echoed in writer James Devaney's description of Neilson in the throes of composition: he 'would sit with his eyes closed, his lips moving as they shaped silent words, his head sometimes shaking as though he were rejecting words or phrases. But sometimes when he had found the words he would look up with a strange intentness. Then he had a beautiful direct look . . .' (Neilson suffered for most of his life from increasingly poor eyesight and eventually, unable to read or write, he was forced to dictate his poems to friends, Devaney among them.)

For his poetry's natural purity and rapport with the earth, Neilson has been compared to Scottish bard Robert Burns (1759–1796) and the English 'peasant poet' John Clare (1793–1864). Perhaps academic and linguist AR Chisholm came closest to capturing the essence of Neilson the man when he compared him to Francis of Assisi (1182–1226), for their shared love of animals, especially birds; their modest living close to nature; and their 'benevolent simplicity'. Chisholm also noted the uncanny similarity between Neilson's poetry, with its ability to evoke realms of inner experience through simple, concrete images like the strange light in an orange tree at sunset, and the theory and practice of the French Symbolist poets, especially Stéphane Mallarmé (1842–1898), even though it is most unlikely that Neilson was familiar with their work.

The eldest of six children, Neilson was born in 1872 to a Scottish father, who was a selector, farm labourer and published bush poet, and an Australian-born mother of Scottish ancestry. In 1881 his family moved from South Australia to Victoria to take up a selection near Lake Minimay. And they continued to move, as they struggled first to earn a living from poor land and then to find work when Neilson's father was forced to labour as a hired farmhand. In 1889 they moved to Nhill. There Neilson sent his poetry to the local newspaper, the *Nhill Mail*, and was published. Four years later, in 1893, both Neilson and his father won prizes for their verse in the Australian Natives Association poetry competition. Forced out to work at fourteen, Neilson had little schooling (eighteen months at Penola and less at Minimay) and his reading was confined to what he found at home: the Bible, Robert Burns, Thomas Hood (1799–1845) and Samuel Taylor Coleridge (1772–1834).

Neilson soon began sending his work to AG Stephens at the *Bulletin*, who published his first poem in 1896: 'Marian's Child', which Mary Gilmore took with her to Paraguay the same year, having been moved by its 'passion of pity'. Following the death of his mother in 1897, Neilson had a nervous breakdown and wrote very little poetry, publishing nothing more until 1901. Though they met only once (in Sydney in 1926), Stephens became Neilson's mentor and editor, and when he revived his magazine *Bookfellow* in 1911 Neilson became a regular contributor. Stephens also prepared Neilson's poetry for a book, which eventually appeared in 1919 with the title *Heart of Spring*. In his introduction Stephens praised some of Neilson's verse as being 'unsurpassed in the range of English lyrics' and compared him to Shakespeare and William Blake. A second volume of Neilson's poetry, *Ballad and Lyrical Poems*, was published in 1923, with the financial assistance of music publisher and energetic patron of the arts, Louise Dyer. Neilson's other volumes include *New Poems* (1927), *Collected Poems* (1934) and *Beauty Imposes*, published in 1938 with Devaney's assistance (Stephens had died in 1933).

By the 1920s, Neilson was becoming too old to continue his hard physical labouring, but his poor eyesight severely restricted the range of work he could do. Through the efforts of his Melbourne supporters, he was given a pension by the Commonwealth Literary Fund, established in 1908 to support impoverished elderly writers, families of deceased writers, or established writers too poor to continue writing (speaking for the Fund in parliament, Labor member for Parramatta Joseph Cook noted: 'It is our first recognition—and a very small one—of Australian literature and as such we should pass it unanimously'). In 1928 Neilson was given a job with the Victorian Country Roads Board in an office in Melbourne's Exhibition gardens, where he worked until 1941. He died the following year of a heart attack.

AR Chisholm praised the gentle beauty of Neilson's lyrics when he wrote in 1965 of 'Song Be Delicate', one of his best-known poems: 'I have carefully and lovingly read a great deal of poetry in some five languages, and say without hesitation that I have never read any lyric (even in Verlaine's work) more quietly beautiful than the five short stanzas of "Song Be Delicate".' Critic HM Green found Neilson's legacy in his mystical quality, calling Neilson 'perhaps the most notable of all Australia's mystic poets.' His poetry has inspired many poets and musicians, including Judith Wright and composer Margaret Sutherland (1897–1984), who set 'The Gentle Water Bird' to music. Sutherland's only opera, *The Young Kabbarli* (1965), based on the life of Daisy Bates, also drew on Neilson's poetry (and the poetry of Judith Wright).

Louis Nowra's favourite Australian books

A Complete Account of the Settlement at Port Jackson 1788–1791 by
    Watkin Tench
The Langton Quartet by Martin Boyd
Lucinda Brayford by Martin Boyd
Eucalyptus by Murray Bail
Collected Poetry by John Shaw Neilson
100 Poems by Kenneth Slessor
The Man Who Loved Children by Christina Stead
Wild White Man of Badu by Ion Idriess
Vaudeville by Ronald McCuaig
Diaries by Donald Friend

Louis Nowra is an acclaimed playwright, screenwriter, novelist
and non-fiction author. His many works include the bestselling
memoir *The Twelfth of Never* (1999) and the plays *Cosi* and *Radiance*,
which were also adapted for the cinema in 1995 and 1997
respectively.

13

My Brilliant Career

Miles Franklin (1879–1954)

Miles Franklin began writing stories when she was twelve years old. Having left behind her beloved 'Brindabella', the Monaro station of her early childhood, for Goulburn, Franklin turned her mind to creating thrilling romances like those she read in the *Goulburn Evening Penny Post*, where she sent her stories hoping for publication. But the editor declined to publish them, suggesting instead that Franklin focus her literary attention on her local scene. This was just the stimulus she needed: 'The idea sprouted. Huh! I'd show just how ridiculous the life around me would be as story material, and began in sardonically humorous mood on a full-fledged novel with the jibing title *My Brilliant (?) Career.*' And so *My Brilliant Career* was born, from a challenge to make a story from the ordinary and unromantic life that Franklin found around her.

She began *My Brilliant Career* on 20 September 1898, just before her nineteenth birthday, and finished it six months later, when she immediately posted it off to Angus & Robertson in Sydney. The urgency of its creation charges through its exuberant pages. *My Brilliant Career* is an irreverent story told by a boisterous young girl afflicted by the need to write and a deep resistance to the idea of marriage and any other thing offered to her that might threaten her freedom: 'Marriage to me appeared the most horribly tied-down and unfair-to-women existence going.' Its spirited narrator, Sybylla Penelope Melvyn, also agonises over her self-perceived ugliness, which she believes makes her unfit for marriage—and alternately longs to be an ordinary girl suited for marriage and to escape from her perceived destiny in wifedom as an impoverished woman in the nineteenth-century Australian bush. But above all, Sybylla remains true to her deepest desire—to write: 'I arose from bed the next morning with three things in my head—a pair of swollen eyes, a heavy pain, and a fixed determination to write a book.'

Sybylla declares of her story: 'This is not a romance—I have too often faced the music of life to the tune of hardship to waste time in snivelling and gushing over fancies and dreams; neither is it a novel, but simply a yarn—a real yarn.' And yet despite this declaration, Sybylla's yarn becomes a poignant love story, even though she fills it with as much comedy as passion: 'On making my first appearance before my lover, I looked quite the reverse of a heroine . . . On the contrary, I much resembled a female clown.' The novel is also a tale of several faces of rural Australia at the end of the nineteenth century—from the desperate poverty of Sybylla's family at Possum Gully, Goulburn, reduced to the incessant daily round of dairy farming, to the frugal industry of their neighbours, the M'Swats; from the genteel comfort of her grandmother's Caddagat Station, to the vast wealth of the neighbouring Five-Bob Downs.

'Given to writing stories', Sybylla worships the bush poets, lauding Adam Lindsay Gordon, Henry Kendall, Henry Lawson and Banjo Paterson—'The pleasure, so exquisite as to be almost pain, which I derived from the books, and especially the Australian poets, is beyond description. The weird witchery of the mighty bush, the breath of wide sunlit plains, the sound of camp-bells and jingle of hobble chains, floating on soft twilight breezes, had come to these men and had written a tale on their hearts as had been written on mine.' Sybylla is fiercely patriotic and equally as fiercely determined to find a life that is hers alone. She refuses, despite all temptation, to be drawn into any bond that would compromise her unrealised future, regardless of how impossible that future might seem from Possum Gully.

My Brilliant Career first appeared in 1901, the year of Australia's federation, and was called by the *Bulletin*'s AG Stephens the 'very first Australian novel to be published'. And yet it could not find a publisher in Australia. Rejected by Angus & Robertson and returned to the author by the *Bulletin*, the manuscript soon found a local champion in Henry Lawson. After glancing over the manuscript, Lawson wrote immediately to its author: 'I believe that you have done a big thing.' Comparing it to Charlotte Brontë's *Jane Eyre* and Olive Schreiner's *Story of an African Farm*, Lawson took Franklin's manuscript with him when he sailed for London in April 1900. There Lawson's agent found a home for *My Brilliant Career* with the noted Edinburgh publisher, William Blackwood.

Although *My Brilliant Career* received immediate critical acclaim in Australia and England on its publication, in 1910 Franklin removed her great novel from sale. She prevented it from being reprinted during her lifetime and on her death left instructions that it not be published for a further ten years. Why did she take such ruthless steps to suppress her own work? Franklin had written her rebellious story of a young girl under the assumption that her authorship would remain secret, and that her novel would not be mistaken for a teenage girl's autobiography. On receiving Blackwood's offer, Franklin had written to him in February 1901 outlining her conditions for publication. Among them was her specification that the 'note of interrogation' in the title be kept, making it *My Brilliant (?) Career*. She also demanded that her identity remain secret, 'as I do not wish it to be known that I'm a young girl but desire to pose as a bald-headed seer of the sterner sex.' Hence her use of the male pseudonym.

But Franklin's letter with its conditions arrived in London too late to be acted upon. The novel was published without the title's mocking question mark and Lawson revealed the author's identity as a young girl in his preface to the book. Shocked by the literalness with which *My Brilliant Career* was subsequently read and dismayed by 'the absurdity of girls from all over the continent writing to tell me that I had expressed their innermost lives and emotions', in 1902 Franklin wrote a feisty sequel as 'a corrective', *My Career Goes Bung*, but this was not published until 1946.

Born Stella Maria Sarah Miles Franklin in 1879 at Talbingo, now in the Kosciuszko National Park, Franklin was the eldest child of John and Margaret Franklin, whose great-grandfather had been a convict on the First Fleet. After a childhood spent at Brindabella Station on the Monaro, Franklin moved with her family to a small holding near Goulburn in 1889. After leaving school, Franklin worked as a governess near Yass and following the publication of *My Brilliant Career*, she attempted to live from her writing. She eventually travelled to America in 1906 and settled in Chicago, where she worked for the National Women's Trade Union League for nine years. In 1915 Franklin resigned from the League and moved to London. During the First World War she worked as a volunteer with the Scottish Women's Hospitals for Foreign Service in Macedonia.

In 1925 Franklin returned to Australian subject matter in her writing, for which she used a new pseudonym: 'Brent of Bin Bin'. From 1928 to 1931, Blackwood published three volumes of her proposed nine-volume pastoral saga under this new name. Franklin returned permanently to Australia in 1932 after her father's death in 1931, where she devoted herself to writing and to Australian writing and writers generally. In 1935 Franklin was awarded King George V's Silver Jubilee Medal in recognition of her services to Australian literature. By the time of her death in 1954, Franklin had written twelve novels as well as critical essays, a biography of Joseph Furphy (1944) and the story of her early years, *Childhood at Brindabella* (published posthumously in 1963). In her will Franklin left money to found an award for Australian literature, which became the annual Miles Franklin Award. In 1957 Robert Menzies presented the inaugural award to Patrick White for his novel *Voss*.

Margaret Fink's internationally acclaimed award-winning film adaptation of *My Brilliant Career* was released in 1979, launching the careers of star Judy Davis and director Gillian Armstrong. Franklin's novel, with its vision of a young girl's determination to pursue her career over marriage, had changed Fink's life, and fifteen years after first reading it, she brought *My Brilliant Career* to the screen.

Nikki Gemmell's favourite
Australian books

My Brilliant Career by Miles Franklin
Capricornia by Xavier Herbert
Translations From the Natural World by Les Murray
The Moving Image by Judith Wright
The Riders by Tim Winton
My Place by Sally Morgan
The Man Who Loved Children by Christina Stead
The Stolen Children: Their Stories edited by Carmel Bird
A Fringe of Leaves by Patrick White
Tracks by Robyn Davidson
And my (very young) kids have begged me to include: *Diary of a Wombat* by Jackie French.

Nikki Gemmell is the author of the bestselling *The Bride Stripped Bare: A Novel* (2004); novels *Shiver* (1997), *Cleave* (1998) and *Love Song* (2001); and *Pleasure: An Almanac for the Heart* (2006).

14

THE MAGIC PUDDING

Norman Lindsay (1879–1969)

The Magic Pudding is a mad, offbeat story that opens with the narrator directing readers' attention to a drawing of two koalas in 'frontways view'. One is a 'fine, round, splendid fellow' called Bunyip Bluegum and the other is Uncle Wattleberry, 'more square than round', who has whiskers. The whiskers are crucial, because 'these very whiskers were the chief cause of Bunyip's leaving home to see the world'—for as Bunyip often says to himself: 'Whiskers alone are bad enough / Attached to faces coarse and rough / But how much greater their offence is / When stuck on Uncles' countenances.'

And so with its crazy logic, the story proceeds. Bunyip is launched into the world, but by lunchtime he realises that despite all his many preparations he has forgotten the most important thing—food. Magically, just as he is musing on this, he happens upon two characters eating a pudding for lunch—a sailor called Bill Barnacle and Sam Sawnoff the penguin. When Bunyip asks if there are onions in the pudding, before anyone can reply the pudding itself answers angrily in rhyme. The Puddin', known as Albert, is a rude, temperamental pudding much given to escape, but, marvellously for a pudding, he is 'always anxious to be eaten'. In fact, Albert has a mania for being eaten, he can be whatever sort of pudding you like, sweet or savoury, and 'The more you eats the more you gets'. As Bill explains, 'Me an' Sam has been eatin' away at this Puddin' for years, and there's not a mark on him.' He is a Magic Pudding, stolen from a cook called Curry and Rice during a storm off Cape Horn.

Eventually Bunyip is invited to join the Noble Society of Pudding Owners, whose members are required 'to wander along the roads, indulgin' in conversation, song and story, and eatin' at regular intervals at the Puddin'.' But being pudding owners does not make for an easy life on the road. The pudding has treacherous habits and escapes if he is not carefully watched. '"The trouble is," said Bill, "that this is a very secret, crafty Puddin', an' if you wasn't up to his games he'd be askin' you to look at a spider an' then run away while your back is turned."' Pudding owners are also plagued by professional puddin' thieves—a Possum and a boozy-looking Wombat—whom they must regularly fight for the return of their pudding.

The story, told in four 'Slices', is interspersed with rhymes, songs and Lindsay's vividly drawn illustrations, which record a range of bush types, larrikins and tall storytellers, including the three pudding owners; and a series of pompous and useless officials, including the Mayor, the Constable and the card-playing Judge. Lindsay made 102 pencil, ink and watercolour illustrations for the first edition of *The Magic Pudding*, which was published in 1918 as a high-priced limited-edition art book. The drawings are beautifully expressive. Albert the Puddin' is a cross little man with long skinny limbs and a pudding-bowl hat; Bunyip the koala—who has read all the best Australian poets and uses words (not violence) to combat the pudding thieves—is a dapper chap in a smart jacket with a bowtie and cane; and the thieving Wombat's hat is perfectly sloping and misshapen to mark him out 'as a man you couldn't trust in the fowl-yard'.

Lindsay wrote *The Magic Pudding* in 1917 to distract himself from the devastation of the First World War. Early that year he had heard that his brother Reginald had been killed on the Western Front, on the Somme. The idea for the story is said to have come from a discussion between Lindsay and the critic Bertram Stevens about what makes a good children's book. Stevens said that fairies were the most popular subject for children but Lindsay said that children liked food above all else. To prove his point Lindsay invented the Magic Pudding—a pudding that not only enjoys being eaten, but demands to be eaten, thrives on enormous appetites and can be whatever you want it to be. And best of all, although it runs away, it never runs out.

Born in 1879 in Creswick, north of Ballarat in Victoria, Lindsay was the fifth of ten children, many of whom were talented artists and writers. His father was a surgeon from Ireland who had arrived in Victoria in 1864. As a child Lindsay drew prolifically, having spent his first six years indoors with a blood ailment and been encouraged to draw by two of his elder brothers, artists Percy and Lionel (who would later work with Lindsay at the *Bulletin*). At seventeen Lindsay joined Lionel in Melbourne, where they worked as cartoonists and lived a bohemian life. His drawing was influenced by the baroque art of Peter Paul Rubens and fin-de-siècle illustrators like Aubrey Beardsley, as well as the classic literature of ancient Greece and Rome and the Renaissance. Lindsay was also profoundly affected by reading Nietzsche, whose rejection of Christianity and celebration of the ecstatic, Dionysian impulse shaped Lindsay's view of art and life.

In 1900 Lindsay married Kate Parkinson, with whom he had three sons. They moved to Sydney the following year when

Lindsay was offered a job at the *Bulletin* as a cartoonist and illustrator by JF Archibald. Editor AG Stephens had earlier judged Lindsay's drawings of Boccaccio's *Decameron* 'the finest example of pen-draughtsmanship of their kind yet produced in this country.' Lindsay worked with the *Bulletin* for over fifty years, visually expressing its editorial policy, including its nationalism, protectionism and racism. In Sydney Lindsay met Rose Soady, whom he later married (in 1920, having divorced his first wife) and in 1911 he moved with Rose to the Blue Mountains, where he bought a house in Springwood.

Lindsay became a prominent artist whose work scandalised religious and moral leaders, many critics and the public. In 1913 his 'Crucified Venus', which pictured a monk nailing a naked woman to a tree, caused such a public outcry in Melbourne that it was removed from display (and later rehung at the insistence of Julian Ashton). Lindsay also published eleven novels, including *A Curate in Bohemia* (1913); *Redheap*, published in London in 1930 but banned in Australia until 1959; *The Cautious Amorist*, published in New York in 1932 but forbidden entry to Australia; and two children's books. He also illustrated poet Hugh McCrae's *Satyrs and Sunlight* (1909) and Kenneth Slessor's *Thief of the Moon* (1924) and *Earth-Visitors* (1926).

But it was *The Magic Pudding*, which Lindsay called a 'little bundle of piffle', that became his most successful and enduring creation. When asked to name his favourite children's book, the author of the trilogy *His Dark Materials*, Philip Pullman (1946), replied: 'Without question it is *The Magic Pudding*.' In his introduction to an edition published in New York in 2004, Pullman called *The Magic Pudding* 'the funniest children's book ever written. I've been laughing at it for fifty years, and when I read it again this morning, I laughed as much as I ever did.'

The Magic Pudding, with its crazy humour and bizarre logic, has been compared to the work of Lewis Carroll and Roald Dahl, another writer who appreciated the irresistible appeal of food. In 2000 an animated film of *The Magic Pudding* was released, starring the voices of John Cleese as the Magic Pudding, Sam Neill as Sam Sawnoff, Hugo Weaving as Bill Barnacle and Geoffrey Rush as Bunyip Bluegum.

Sophie Cunningham's favourite Australian books

What struck me about almost all the Australian novels that have had a big impact on me is their powerful sense of place.

His Natural Life by Marcus Clarke. The landscape is the star of this gothic novel, which paints a devastating portrait of Australia's convict past.

The Fortunes of Richard Mahony by Henry Handel Richardson. It's tough-going at times, but I think this might be the best thing I've read on what it's like to grow up in a family ruled by mental illness. And Victoria's western district is strikingly recorded.

Coonardoo by Katharine Susannah Prichard. I haven't reread this novel in recent years, but when I was young its combination of a vivid portrayal of station life and interracial tensions and relationships made a big impact on me.

Voss by Patrick White. This novel had a bigger impact on me than any other Australian novel. I've read it several times and sometimes I love it, sometimes I hate it. Either way it looms large. There is the powerful north Australian landscape in its seeming prehistoric glory; the way White writes about the Wet Season and the flooding of the Northern Territory; the powerlessness of the explorers once the rain begins and their consequent entrapment; the mystical connection between Voss and Laura which I found intensely tragic and romantic. The romanticisation of the Aboriginal characters in the novel confused me—it's both problematic and compelling. It's an intensely visual novel, which I also loved.

The Vivisector by Patrick White. In this novel it wasn't the landscape that compelled me but the audaciousness of the sexual relationship between the ageing artist, Hurtle Duffield, and the young girl, Kathy Volkov. I was also riveted by White's evocation of Duffield's physical decay and his amorality.

Monkey Grip by Helen Garner. Again, *Monkey Grip* has a powerful sense of place: this novel is set in the suburb I've lived in most of my adult life, Fitzroy. I loved its unflinching depiction of the addictive nature of romantic love.

A Woman of the Future by David Ireland. This is another novel that I haven't reread in twenty years. But as someone wanting to be a writer, the novel's combination of Australian realism and surrealism broadened my sense of what was possible for an Australian writer.

Cloudstreet by Tim Winton. The rhythms of the prose in this wonderful family saga are just unlike any other novel I've read.

Holding the Man by Timothy Conigrave. I'm biased—I was the publisher of this memoir, but not only is *Holding the Man* a great love story, it nails what it was like to be a teenager in the seventies in Melbourne.

Gilgamesh by Joan London. A Western Australian novel. This novel is bleak in many ways, but it tracks Australia's complicated relationship with Europe and European history in a way that I found intensely memorable.

Sophie Cunningham is the author of *Geography* (2004). Her second novel, *Bird*, will be published in 2008. She has also had a successful career as a publisher, with McPhee Gribble, Penguin Books and Allen & Unwin.

15

COONARDOO

Katharine Susannah Prichard (1883–1969)

Katharine Susannah Prichard's novel *Coonardoo* is the story of an Aboriginal woman, the eponymous Coonardoo, and the struggle of white and Aboriginal Australians to live together and work the vast land of the Kimberley, where their worlds come into intimate contact. The novel opens with Coonardoo as a young girl at Wytaliba station: 'Coonardoo was singing. Sitting under dark bushes overhung with curdy white blossom, she clicked two small sticks together, singing'. Coonardoo grows up alongside Hugh Watt, the son of the station owner, Mrs Bessie Watt. The two children become deeply bonded through their shared love of the land and horses, but Hugh is sent away to school in Perth and they come to maturity hundreds of miles apart.

When Hugh is finally permitted by his formidable mother to return to his beloved Wytaliba, his old ease with Coonardoo has gone, but their rapport remains. When he eventually takes over Wytaliba, his need for Coonardoo has become so overwhelming, complex and fear-filled that he buries it: 'She was like his own soul riding there, dark, passionate and childlike. In all this wide empty world Coonardoo was the only living thing he could speak to, Hugh knew; the only creature who understood what he was feeling, and was feeling for him. Yet he was afraid of her, resented a secret understanding between them.'

The story of Coonardoo, inevitably, is told through her inter-action with the European world of the homestead and the three generations of the Watt family, and their neighbours, like Sam Geary, who do not share the Watts' respectful if proprietorial attitude to their Aboriginal companions and workers. Prichard was inspired to write *Coonardoo* after staying at Turee, an isolated cattle station in the Kimberley, in 1926. Filled with stories, 'delighted and quite mad with the beauty and tragedy of them', and prompted by the brilliant landscape and the Aborigines, Prichard determined to write a novel from an Aboriginal point of view. Her first-hand experience of Turee tells in the novel's rich detail of the daily round of station life—its food, clothing, yards, horse breaking, cattle work—and in her evocation of the immense beauty of the Kimberley.

Prichard's portrayal of the land and its people, black and white, is informed by DH Lawrence and CG Jung, who is mentioned by Mrs Bessie's granddaughter. The land is a monumental force, as are the prejudices and fears of the white men and women who attempt to live on it, and the novel is heavily loaded with symbolism. Coonardoo is beautiful, sensual and easy in the land, her wisdom is intuitive and of the earth. Hugh, rugged, virile and overwhelmed, thwarts his love for her through a misplaced sense of moral rectitude. He is white Australia; she is Aboriginal Australia. They are both doomed.

Like Lawrence, Prichard was deeply concerned with human sexuality as a shaping force not only of the health of individ-uals, but of the land and of nations. In *Coonardoo*, for the land to flourish, relations between men and women, between black and white, must be intimate and loving: 'It was very easy for a school-master to preach virginity in the playing fields of a boys' school; but here in a country of endless horizons, limitless sky shells, to live within yourself was to decompose internally. You had to keep with the flow of the country to survive. You had to be with it, and of it, in order to work, move as it did. After all what was this impulse of man to woman, woman to man, but the law of growth moving within them? How could a man stand still, sterilize himself in a land where drought and sterility were hell? Growth, the law of life, which brought beauty and joy in all the world about him? No wonder the blacks worshipped life, growth—sex—as the life source.'

First published in serial form in the *Bulletin* in 1928 and as a book in 1929, *Coonardoo* outraged contemporary readers with its story of a white man's unexpressed love for an Aboriginal woman. It was the first novel by a white Australian to attempt to see the world from an Aboriginal point of view—and it remains an extraordinary novel, powerful in its writing and its passions, fierce in its determination to explore what Prichard perceived to be an urgent question of the relations between European and Indigenous Australians and the relationship of both to the land. As Prichard wrote to scholar HM Green: 'I think that I know thoroughly every phase of life in Australia I write of; that I absorb the life of our people and country with love and an intense and intimate sympathy; I strive to express myself from these sources.'

In the twenty-first century, Prichard's view is necessarily anachronistic. Speaking in 2004 of Prichard's portrayal of Aboriginal women and men, Aboriginal lawyer, writer and academic Professor Larissa Behrendt called *Coonardoo* 'a story about white sorrow, not black empowerment. The book leaves out any possibility that

Coonardoo and her community could benefit from the assertion of their own authority or autonomy.'

Prichard was born in Fiji, the eldest child of Tom and Edith Prichard. Of her Fijian carer she later said: 'Maybe N'gardo is responsible for the instinctive sympathy I've always had for people of the native races.' Prichard's life was marked by poverty and tragedy, and great energy and intelligence that drove her achievements as a writer and as a tireless activist for Communism and the peace movement. Her family left Fiji as her father sought work as a journalist, eventually settling in Melbourne where at fourteen Prichard won a scholarship to South Melbourne College. She then worked as a governess in Gippsland and western New South Wales, and in 1903 won a prize for her story 'Bush Fires', which was published in *New Idea*. Four years later her beloved father committed suicide, which devastated Prichard and led to a crisis of faith.

The following year, in 1908, Prichard left for London to cover the Franco-British exhibition for the Melbourne *Herald*. She returned to London in 1912, aged twenty-nine, and in 1915 won the Australian section of Hodder & Stoughton's All-Empire novel competition for *The Pioneers* (1915), with a prize of 250 pounds. Here she met her future husband, Hugo Throssell, who was awarded the Victoria Cross for bravery at Gallipoli and whose father had briefly been the Premier of Western Australia. Back in Melbourne, Prichard's life was radically changed by news of the Russian Revolution and she became a committed Marxist: 'It was the answer to what I had been seeking: a satisfactory explanation of the wealth and power which controlled our lives'.

In 1919 Prichard married Throssell and moved to Perth. Their only child, Ric, was born in 1922. She wrote her first political pamphlet, on Marxism, in 1919 and in 1920 was a founding member of the Communist Party of Australia. During the

1920s she produced what are considered her best novels, notably *Working Bullocks* (1926), about timber workers in the karri forests of Western Australia, which Miles Franklin called 'the breaking of a drought' in the Australian novel; and *Coonardoo*. In 1933 Prichard travelled to Moscow to research her book *The Real Moscow* (1934). While she was away her husband committed suicide, traumatised by his experience of the First World War and suffering debts exacerbated by the Depression. Profoundly shocked and devastated, Prichard threw herself into political activism. Her only subsequent major literary work was the gold-fields trilogy, *The Roaring Nineties* (1946), *Golden Miles* (1948) and *Winged Seeds* (1950). Prichard was awarded the World Peace Council medal in 1959. She died in Perth in 1969 and was given a Communist funeral.

Gail Jones's favourite Australian books

Lines of Flight by Marion Campbell
The Scent of Eucalyptus by Barbara Hanrahan
Letters to Constantine by Joan London
The Great World by David Malouf
Working Bullocks by Katharine Susannah Prichard
The Fortunes of Richard Mahony by Henry Handel Richardson
Benang by Kim Scott
Visitants by Randolph Stow
The Man Who Loved Children by Christina Stead
The Aunt's Story by Patrick White

Gail Jones is an award-winning writer and Associate Professor of English and Cultural Studies at the University of Western Australia. Her novels include *Sixty Lights* (2004), *Dreams of Speaking* (2006) and *Sorry* (2007).

16

10 FOR 66 AND ALL THAT

Arthur Mailey (1886–1967)

In sport-obsessed Australia, cricket is the national game. It has been played here for over two hundred years, at least since 8 January 1804, when the earliest reference to the game appeared in the *Sydney Gazette*: 'The late intense weather has been very favourable to the amateurs of cricket who have scarce lost a day for the past month.' One of the most remarkable stories from early twentieth-century Australian cricket is told in *10 for 66 and all that*, the autobiography of Test cricketer and journalist Arthur Mailey, whose rise from the slums of inner Sydney to the green fields and opulent mansions of Great Britain came courtesy of his skill with a red leather ball, notably his mastery of the new 'freak' spin ball—the 'googly' or 'wrong 'un' or 'bosie', named after its English inventor, Bernard Bosanquet (1877–1936). As a spin bowler, Mailey played twenty-one Tests for Australia between 1921 and 1926, taking ninety-nine wickets for 33.9 runs each.

In 1921 against English county cricket side Gloucestershire, Mailey took all ten wickets of the match, conceding the opposition only sixty-six runs. Thirty-seven years later he used the numbers of this spectacular feat for the title of his autobiography *10 for 66 and all that*, a conflation of his best figures with the title of the bestselling satirical history of England *1066 and All That: A Memorable History of England, comprising all the parts you can remember, including 103 Good Things, 5 Bad Kings and 2 Genuine Dates* (1930). First published in 1958, *10 for 66 and all that* caused a sensation, becoming an instant bestseller despite the fact that Mailey had retired from the game thirty years earlier. It tells the story of his cricketing life, complete with his musings on the great players of the game; the captains, umpires and rules of cricket; and the value of cricket's rebels, who Mailey believed made an essential contribution to the broad appeal of the game. He writes with wit and strong conviction, and, like his bowling—which was once described as a mix of 'spin, flight and sheer fun'—his lively prose simmers with humour.

Mailey's story begins in the laneways of Sydney's Waterloo, where as a boy he tirelessly threw a cricket ball to anyone he could find to bat against him. Mailey loses one of his earliest opponents, a neighbouring boy, when the child is called away in the late afternoon to buy beer for his mother at the local pub. By the height of his career as one of the greatest right-arm leg-spin bowlers of the game, Mailey is at the centre of the cricket world, in London dressed in evening suit at 2 a.m. and bowling a 'wrong 'un' down Piccadilly to the celebrated English cricket writer Neville Cardus, who has bet Mailey a bottle of champagne he can pick his spin. Cardus, who was a great friend and admirer of the spin bowler, once wrote that Mailey, who started life as a pauper, 'bowled like a millionaire'.

That Mailey managed to rise from the backstreets of Waterloo to cricket's international stage was entirely due to his own determination, application and talent. His early life was hard, lived with 'sufficient poverty and frustration to destroy the germ of ambition in any form'. His parents had no interest in cricket whatsoever, but for some reason the young Mailey was obsessed with the game and practised his bowling incessantly. He grew up in a house made of wood and hessian designed by his uncle Sam, whose architectural aspirations were modest—or, as Mailey puts it in his typically understated fashion, alluding to the great seventeenth-century English architect Christopher Wren, uncle Sam 'seemed to do his best to avoid any of the Wren influence'. Each time a new Mailey baby was born, another room was tacked on to the back of the house and in winter the hessian walls 'bellied and flapped like the sails of a ship in distress'. Mailey, with his accompanying drawings, brilliantly conjures this hessian house and its peculiar capacity to bring to life his poster of his cricket idol, Australian batsman Victor Trumper (1877–1915): pinned to his bedroom's hessian partition, the poster was 'a replica of the one at Lord's which shows a beautiful off-drive. When the wind blew, Vic appeared to go through his repertoire of strokes.'

After leaving school at thirteen with two passions—art and cricket—Mailey worked at a succession of jobs including one as a glass blower, which enhanced his spin bowling capabilities by strengthening his wrist and fingers and expanding his lungs. Each evening after work he would practise his bowling in the nets at Redfern Oval then travel across the city to his art lessons with noted teacher JS Watkins. Mailey later made a career from his drawing as well as becoming a painter in oils. When he was invited in 1921 to draw cartoons for London's *Bystander* for an astonishingly generous annual remuneration, Mailey could hardly believe his luck: 'It was like an umpire giving me Jack Hobbs' wicket without an appeal.'

The young spin bowler was soon selected to play cricket for Redfern and the day inevitably came when he faced his hero down the pitch—the great Trumper, who played for Paddington. After being belted for a couple of boundaries, Mailey decided to try out on Trumper his new freak ball, the googly, 'this most undisciplined and cantankerous creation of the great B.J. Bosanquet', first brought to Australia around 1904, picked up by Mailey at Waterloo Park and polished in the Domain. Much to his own immediate dismay, Mailey bowled a perfect ball. Trumper was out. Instead of feeling elation, Mailey was shattered: 'There was no triumph in me as I watched the receding figure. I felt like a boy who had killed a dove.' But this bowling triumph marked the beginning of Mailey's career as a cricketer. Yet when the moment for which he had been waiting all his life finally arrived—his selection for his first Ashes series in the Australian summer of 1920/21—Mailey thought not of his own achievement but only of what this would bring to his beloved mother and invalid older brother: 'a measure of pride to a little hard-worked woman and her war-crippled son who watched the match from a public stand.'

As well as recounting his own experience of and opinions on cricket, Mailey includes in *10 for 66* entertaining diversions such as his pick of players for a world team to challenge the planet Mars and his description of an imaginary dinner party he hosts for legendary batsmen Donald Bradman and Victor Trumper, whom he calls the tiger and the gazelle. Mailey's observations of the game are astute, especially his insights into the crucial place of spin bowling in a team and the role of the captain in setting fields for spin bowlers: 'I think it is reasonable to ask that, all things being equal, an expert on spin bowling should be regarded as better qualified to captain his country than one who isn't.' If Mailey's view of the inviolable rule of the umpire seems to have come from the distant past—'if it comes to publicly doubting the umpire then we may as well pull up stumps for good'—then his understanding of the need for rebels and entertainers in the world of cricket rings true in an era that has witnessed the spin-bowling genius and antics of the 'Wizard of Oz': Shane Warne. As Mailey says, entertainment is 'the life-blood of cricket. Whether the entertainer be a clown or an artist doesn't matter. From an international point of view the game cannot survive without its personalities, its actors, its heroes, its tragedians.'

Mailey married in 1913 and had four children. He enjoyed successful careers as a cricketer, a cartoonist and a journalist. His cartoons appeared in the *Bulletin*, the Sydney *Arrow* and London's *Bystander*, and he worked for the *Sun* and later the *Daily Telegraph* as a cartoonist and cricket writer. In 1932/33 Mailey covered the controversial 'bodyline' Ashes tour and subsequently wrote an acclaimed book about the series: *And then came Larwood*, which was published in 1933. He spent his old age living on Port Hacking, in Sydney's south, where he spent his time painting, writing, fishing and playing golf. Mailey died in 1967.

10 for 66 and all that is now recognised as one of the classics of world cricket writing, celebrated for its story of Mailey's extraordinary life (his 'big jump from an ordinary working-class environment to a Lord Mayor's banquet or a personal invitation to a Royal function'), for his sharp insights into the game of cricket and for the thoughtful warmth and humour of his writing. The noted cricket writer and editor of *The Picador Book of Cricket*, Ramachandra Guha, has said of Mailey's book: 'The finest of all cricket autobiographies is unquestionably Arthur Mailey's *10 for 66 and All That* (1958), the tale of a lowly mechanic whose playing skills allowed him to meet kings and prime ministers and to befriend Sir James Barrie and Neville Cardus. Mailey was a natural wit and a gifted artist (the book carries his illustrations), and had strong views on the game besides.'

Jamie Grant's favourite
Australian books

The Langton Quartet by Martin Boyd
Aunts Up the Cross by Robin Dalton
Romulus, My Father by Raimond Gaita
Grass Script by Robert Gray
Snake by Kate Jennings
The Broken Book by Susan Johnson
Beware of the Past Diptych by Christopher Koch
10 for 66 and all that by Arthur Mailey
Fredy Neptune by Les Murray
The Visit by Amy Witting

Jamie Grant is the author of several collections of poetry,
including *Skywriting* (1989) and *Relativity* (1998).

17

LUCINDA BRAYFORD

Martin Boyd (1893–1972)

Martin à Beckett Boyd was born in Lucerne, Switzerland, in 1893, the fourth son of painters Arthur Merric and Emma Minnie Boyd. At the time the Boyds were touring Europe from Australia with their other three sons, two of whom would also become artists—potter Merric, father of painter Arthur Boyd; and painter Penleigh, whose son Robin Boyd would become an architect and writer of international renown. Also accompanying the family was Martin's grandmother Emma à Beckett, whose fortune inherited from her father, ex-convict John Mills, had allowed Martin's parents to live in comfort and devote themselves to art. (Mills had bought property in Melbourne's first land sales in 1837 and founded the Melbourne Brewery.) At six months, Martin was brought home to Australia, where Melbourne's financial crash of 1892–93 had halved the à Becketts' income and consequently reduced the Boyds' financial standing.

This potent mix of art, dynasty, travel between Australia and Europe, inherited wealth from commercial origins, and the vicissitudes of fortunes lost and gained, characterised Martin Boyd's life and lies at the heart of his great novel *Lucinda Brayford*. Boyd considered *Lucinda Brayford* to be his best novel and said of it, echoing Gustave Flaubert on Madame Bovary, '*Lucinda Brayford*— c'est moi.' But where Flaubert identified with a single fictional character, Boyd refers to his entire novel as himself—*Lucinda Brayford* was composed from the whole fabric of Boyd's being.

The novel tells the story of three generations of an Anglo-Australian family born from the unlikely union in Melbourne of the offspring of two Cambridge University students, William Vane and Aubrey Chapman. Written in Cambridge during the Second World War as Boyd turned fifty, *Lucinda Brayford* is also the story of the devastation of two world wars, the decay of European civilisation, and the possibilities for its regeneration, which lie in art and love and the simple power of hope.

Lucinda Brayford opens at Clare College, Cambridge, with a wine party in the rooms of Mr William Vane. Among Vane's drunken guests is a Mr Brayford of Trinity College who, 'while singing a roundelay, let his cigar butt fall on to a spot on the carpet where Mr Vane yesterday had dropped and broken a bottle of scented hair pomade.' The sweet smell of burning that ensues leads to a brief and comic intersection of the lives of three men—Vane, Brayford and Mr Chapman, who is tucked up in bed on the floor below—all of whom will play a part in the life of Lucinda Brayford.

As its title suggests, the novel's primary focus is on Lucinda, born with such grace and beauty that all around her know she is destined for greatness. Their prejudice seems confirmed, Lucinda's happy promise fulfilled, when she meets in Melbourne the debonair new aide-de-camp, Hugo Brayford, son of an illustrious aristocratic English family. But her subsequent life in England and two world wars throw Lucinda into an existence that is far more complex—and open to more beauty and more tragedy—than any she could have possibly imagined in the early 1900s as the favoured child of one of Melbourne's richest families.

Having experienced for himself the horror of trench warfare on the Western Front in the First World War, Boyd was moved to write *Lucinda Brayford* in 1942 and finished it three years later on the day the war ended. His deep-felt opposition to war and his concern about the future of civilisation can be seen in his novel's incisive, urgent debates on the politics of war: '"Hitler and Mussolini are only the counterpart of Bolshevism," he said. "They're all the same. Secret police, purges and a denial of the human values. We're witnessing the suicide of civilisation."' These words belong to Lucinda's brother-in-law Paul Brayford, who speaks for the threatened estates of art and love. 'The mysteries of the human heart are the mysteries of God. They can't be analysed and labelled like the contents of a sewer, whatever Herr Freud may say.' It is Paul who introduces Lucinda to the art and music that awaken her to life's possibilities, like Nijinsky in *Scheherazade*, or Palestrina's choral music, which consoles her in her many losses.

Boyd is also concerned with the rising tide of money, from its role in war—'Our army is the instrument used by our business men'—to its function in shaping the social structures of the new century: 'I can remember when no business man would be admitted to houses like Crittenden, but nowadays people boast of being business men as if it gave them some kind of status. The objection to them was not pure snobbery. It was because they would corrupt with commercial ideas the tradition of manners and culture.' Boyd also casts an ironic eye on the pretensions of colonial architecture and the role of wealth in Australian society: 'Julie, emerging from the middle classes into grandeur, was not quite sure how grand she ought to be. The decision was more difficult as money fixed no limit. She wished to go as far as possible towards an aristocratic ménage, but to stop short of the theatrical or ridiculous.'

After leaving Melbourne's Trinity Grammar School, Boyd considered a career in the church and studied theology for a year until he went to work for a firm of architects in 1913. When war broke out he travelled to England to join a British regiment. In 1917 he was sent to the trenches of France, which so horrified him that he transferred to the Royal Flying Corps and became a committed pacifist. In 1919 Boyd returned to Melbourne but two years later was back in England, where he joined a Franciscan order of Anglican friars as a novice. Disillusioned, he left the order, and his first novel, *Love Gods*, published in 1925 under the pseudonym Martin Mills, was based on this experience. Boyd's third novel, *The Montforts* (1928), won the Australian Literature Society's first gold medal in 1929.

But it was *Lucinda Brayford*—with its humour, intelligence, elegant prose and compelling family story of inheritance material, temperamental and spiritual—that brought Boyd fame, fortune and critical acclaim. First published in 1946 in London, *Lucinda Brayford* was called one of the three great novels of the century by English writer Richard Church. It became a bestseller in England and America and was translated into Swedish and Danish. But when Boyd returned to Melbourne in 1948, he discovered that his celebrated novel had gone largely unnoticed in Australia. Unable to find a place in Australian life, in 1951 Boyd left again for England, where he published the first three books of his acclaimed Langton tetralogy, based on his family history: *The Cardboard Crown* (1952), *A Difficult Young Man* (1955) and *Outbreak of Love* (1957). The fourth book, *When Blackbirds Sing*, was published in 1962. Boyd moved to Rome in 1957 and died there in 1972.

As a writer, Boyd has been compared to John Galsworthy, the author of *The Forsyte Saga*, and the two share many preoccupations—such as the influence of inherited wealth and various family traits, and the uneasy relation between art and commerce—as do Boyd and EM Forster. In her introduction to *Lucinda Brayford*, the critic Dorothy Green wrote of the enduring nature of Boyd's concerns: 'The disorientation which really preoccupied him was not the temporary nostalgias of traveling Anglo-Australians, but the fundamental estrangement of man from his true, human self, the eternal nostalgia for what Einstein called "reconciliation with God".'

In 1980 a television miniseries of *Lucinda Brayford* was made in Australia, starring Wendy Hughes as Lucinda.

Robin Boyd and
The Australian Ugliness

Born in 1919 in Melbourne, Martin Boyd's nephew Robin Boyd studied architecture after leaving school in 1935. Robin Boyd was the first to bring the Boyd name to prominence in Australia when he became widely known as the director of the Small Homes Service from 1947 to 1954, set up by the Royal Victorian Institute of Architects in association with the *Age* newspaper. The service provided inexpensive architectural advice to amateur builders and Boyd wrote a related weekly architectural advice column in the *Age*. In 1952 Boyd published his first book, *Australia's Home*, in which he criticised Australian domestic building as 'a material triumph and an aesthetic calamity'. His influential and scathing study of Australian architecture and design, *The Australian Ugliness*, was published in 1960. In it Boyd laments the 'shorn look' of modern Australian living: 'The countryside in which the suburb grows is shorn of trees. The plot in which the house builds is shorn of shrubs. The house itself is shorn of the verandas which the colonists knew, shorn of porches, shelter and shade. It sits in sterile shaven neatness . . .' A landmark account of Australian suburbia and its obsession with American materialism—for which Boyd coined the phrase 'Austerica'—*The Australian Ugliness* became a bestseller and is now considered an Australian classic.

18

A Fortunate Life

AB Facey (1894–1982)

A Fortunate Life is the story of a boy who grows up to experience directly many of the great milestones of late nineteenth- and twentieth-century Australia: the Western Australian gold rush of the 1890s; the settlement and development of its wheat belt; the First World War landing at Gallipoli; the rise of trade unionism; the Depression years, which struck particularly hard in Western Australia and forced many off the land; and the outbreak of a second world war just as the sons of many First World War veterans were reaching fighting age. Suddenly, through Albert Barnett Facey's eyes, a man who had been there and lived it, Australian history becomes real. *A Fortunate Life*, Facey's autobiography, is a beautiful story of a hard and well-lived life told simply and directly, without any sense of self-pity nor too much reflection; it is quintessentially Australian.

As he writes in his opening sentence, Facey was born in 1894 in Maidstone, a suburb of Melbourne. Within months of his birth his father had left with his two eldest sons for the goldfields of

Western Australia, 'where thousands believed that a fortune was to be made'. In September 1892 gold had been discovered 550 kilometres east of Perth in Coolgardie, and the following year more gold was found in nearby Kalgoorlie. Within days of the Coolgardie find, the Western Australian gold rush had begun. Eager to escape the depression in the eastern states sparked by the 1890 financial crash in Argentina and the subsequent failure of banks in Victoria, New South Wales and Queensland, thousands like Facey's father took the opportunity to head west for gold and fortune. But though some became rich, the chronic shortage of water on the goldfields also led to outbreaks of typhoid. In 1896 Facey's father succumbed to the bacteria and died, and Facey's mother decided to go west, to care for her two teenage sons left alone on the goldfields. All this happens in the first two paragraphs of Facey's autobiography, told with the succinctness and eye for telling detail of a practised storyteller. 'I was then nearly two years old.'

This beginning set the pattern of Facey's life, which would continue to be characterised by travel and abandonment and to resonate with the big themes of Australian history. In 1899 Facey sailed for Western Australia with his beloved grandmother, in search of his mother and brothers, before settling near Wickepin, a new farming district 214 kilometres south-east of Perth. Aged eight, Facey was sent out into the world alone, to work for strangers in the bush. It was the beginning of a lifetime of itinerant work: 'I have never ever felt like I was tied down to any one place or any one job. I have always felt that I could sell out or walk off at any time. It didn't matter.'

The gold rush in Western Australia peaked in 1903 and the government encouraged gold miners to stay in the west by opening up new tracts of land and providing favourable terms for new settlers. As the Western Australian agricultural minister James

Mitchell (1866–1951) said at the time: 'Gold brought these men to Western Australia, and superphosphate will keep them here.' Wheat farming in the low-rainfall, marginal land of regions like Wickepin was made possible by the introduction of super-phosphate fertiliser and a new variety of wheat resistant to drought and fungus, developed by William Farrer in Canberra in 1901. Aptly named Federation wheat after Australia's federation of the same year, the new strain became the dominant grain in Australia until the 1920s. After its introduction, the area of land under wheat trebled in Western Australia between 1906 and 1911 and Western Australia became a major wheat exporter. Facey was part of this development, clearing and working the new wheat and sheep holdings.

Facey's life continued to resonate with the broader life of his country when he found himself in Egypt in 1915, mobilised for war. One day in late April he was taken aboard a warship to cross the Mediterranean, heading for an unknown destination. It turned out to be Gallipoli, on the coast of Turkey. The soldiers in his division were to land and storm the beach: 'We thought we would tear right through the Turks and keep going to Constantinople.' But instead they found themselves engaged in drawn-out trench warfare, and 'Ex-goldminers were used a lot for this kind of work throughout the whole time Australia was at Gallipoli.' These gold-diggers were immortalised as the ANZAC 'digger', an enduring symbol of Australian manhood.

As well as touching on the key moments of Australian history, Facey also lived out many of the themes from the realm of Australian myth: the lone boy in the bush, the lost child, the cattle drover, dingo combatant, snake battler, the boxer, the unionist.

Having spent most of his life in the bush, often in solitude, Facey was attuned to its beauty and to its birds and animals: 'On Sundays, when we didn't work much, I would often go into the bush and watch the birds and they were lovely. In some ways they were like me—they had to fend for themselves as soon as the mother bird thought that they were old enough.' But despite his solitary ways and his shyness, Facey loved to talk and told stories all his life, as his book makes clear. During his travels, he often stops along his way to tell his story, while his companions 'just sat and listened and hardly said a word until I finished.' Facey's itinerant life, his adventures attuned to his times, his urge to tell his stories over and over until they are recorded at last, evoke the myth of Odysseus, the Greek warrior of Troy (near present-day Gallipoli); in many ways *A Fortunate Life* is an Australian *Odyssey*, with Facey as the wandering, storytelling Australian Odysseus. And like Odysseus, Facey learns an instinctive wisdom of people and things through his courageous roaming life.

Facey never went to school and struggled to teach himself to read and write. After the First World War he began recording his life in exercise books, scribbling at the kitchen table, encouraged by his wife. After his wife's death and as he neared his own, Facey sent his collection of books to the Fremantle Arts Centre Press, south of Perth, hoping simply to get them printed and bound for his children and grandchildren. But the editors soon realised that what Facey had written was an incomparable folk history of Australia's twentieth century, direct and unadorned. His exercise books were published as *A Fortunate Life* by the Fremantle Press in 1981. Nine months before his death in 1982, Facey found himself hurtled into Australia's literary limelight, feted by thousands as *A Fortunate Life* became an immediate bestseller and won the 1981 Banjo Award for Australian Literature and the New South Wales State Library Award. It has sold over 750,000 copies to date.

In 1985 a four-part television miniseries was made of the early years of *A Fortunate Life*, from 1894 to 1915 (the book ends in

Meg Stewart's favourite
Australian books

The Flyaway Highway by Norman Lindsay. Although I was brought
up on *The Magic Pudding* and loved it, I always had a soft spot for
The Flyaway Highway's mad adventuring with a satyr.

Seven Little Australians by Ethel Turner. I read and reread this,
crying every time about Judy's sad fate. I was also hooked
on a book called *January and August* by Elisabeth George, the
fictional tale of two children who travelled with their parents
around outback Australia in a van drawn by donkeys. I was
instantly intrigued by the names of the children—the girl was
called January and the boy, August. In fact, the whole book
seemed enticingly strange and again was not without a tinge of
unhappiness.

Selected Poems by Douglas Stewart. For obvious reasons, the
contents tell me what to treasure in life. [Douglas Stewart is Meg
Stewart's father.]

Poems by John Shaw Neilson. Individual poems by Kenneth
Slessor, Judith Wright and Ronald McCuaig are also absolute
favourites. Who could resist a poem with a title like McCuaig's
'The Wanton Goldfish'?

The Pea-pickers by Eve Langley.

Voss by Patrick White. I studied *Voss* at university and the
experience of reading the novel in that context has stayed with
me vividly.

Dark Palace by Frank Moorhouse. Of course, this novel wouldn't
exist without its equally compelling companion *Grand Days*.

The Diaries of Donald Friend. Any volume or all four, I especially like Volumes 2 and 3. (Paul Hetherington edited Volumes 2, 3 and 4 of the *Diaries*; Volume I was edited by Anne Gray.)

Joe Cinque's Consolation by Helen Garner. Because we do need to be reminded of what is disturbing. I admire all Garner's work, both fiction and non-fiction. Recently I found Mandy Sayer's memoir *Velocity* moving and also Peter Skrzynecki's memoir *The Sparrow Garden*.

The New McCulloch's Encyclopedia of Australian Art by Alan McCulloch, Susan McCulloch and Emily McCulloch Childs.

Meg Stewart is a filmmaker, journalist and author of the award-winning bestselling biography of Margaret Olley, *Far From a Still Life: Margaret Olley* (2005), and a biography of her artist mother, *Autobiography of My Mother* (2007).

19

PICNIC AT HANGING ROCK

Joan Lindsay (1896–1984)

Joan Lindsay wrote *Picnic at Hanging Rock* in 1967 while living at 'Mulberry Hill', her house on the Mornington Peninsula, south of Melbourne. The story came to her like a film. She would think about it all night long and each morning go straight up to her workroom, sit on the floor surrounded by papers and 'write like a demon'. The novel bears the marks of its visual, night-time origins—*Picnic at Hanging Rock* has the otherworldliness of a dream and the rich symbolic play of images, the plasticity of time and space, of film.

The novel opens on Saint Valentine's Day in the year 1900, at Appleyard's College for Young Ladies, a boarding school near Victoria's Mount Macedon. The students are charged with excitement by the morning's myriad declarations of love and the prospect of a picnic. In three chapters Lindsay sets up the mystery that will ripple through the lives of the schoolgirls, their teachers, headmistress, two young men also picnicking at the Rock, and into the local community and beyond into the wider world. Three schoolgirls and their maths teacher vanish. One is found a week later, unconscious and sprawled across a rock. She slowly recovers but remembers absolutely nothing of the long afternoon at the Hanging Rock. And nor does the only other girl who had been among the party of climbers and had run from the Rock 'stumbling and screaming'.

The first obvious sign that things are awry on Valentine's Day is the breakdown or absence of all time-keeping devices at the Rock. The only two watches that have been brought along have both stopped at midday. Miranda, one of the schoolgirls, no longer wears her diamond watch. The French governess has left her clock at the watchmaker. And so the party is launched into a timeless world—and into the Australian bush with a six-million-year-old rock, ancient, striated and crevassed, looming overhead. The Hanging Rock, fifty kilometres north-west of Melbourne, was formed from volcanic activity and the region is remarkable for its rich soil and lush garden estates. By 1900 it had become a popular holiday spot for Melbourne's wealthy families, including the Lindsays, and the Governor of Victoria had his official summer residence at nearby Mount Macedon.

Picnic at Hanging Rock is preoccupied by this uneasy imposition of contemporary European civilisation on the ancient Australian bush. The College is 'already, in the year nineteen hundred, an architectural anachronism in the Australian bush—a hopeless misfit in time and space.' At the Hanging Rock long violet shadows trace 'their million-year-old pattern of summer evenings across its secret face'; while at the 'exquisitely ordered world' of Lake View, the estate of Colonel Fitzhubert, 'the Hanging Rock and its sinister implications were a nightmare, thrust aside.' For the European settlers, their new country is an ominous and haunted place. As the Colonel's English nephew Michael says to one of the traumatised girls: 'Tell me. I'm an expert on nightmares since I came to Australia.' His adopted land is a gothic realm: 'Australia, where anything might happen.'

Lindsay sent off her finished manuscript to Melbourne's Cheshire Publishing, which had earlier published her auto-biography *Time Without Clocks* (1962). In consultation with Cheshire's editorial team, Lindsay made one significant change to the novel before it was published—the final chapter, 18, was omitted. This chapter contained a description of the girls' mysterious disappearance from supernatural causes. Lindsay preferred to leave the mystery unexplained: 'It's written as a mystery and it remains a mystery,' she said in 1974. Much to her surprise, after the novel's publication in 1967, Lindsay received letters from readers wanting to know the story's secret and wondering if it was true. Lindsay would only say: 'It's all terribly true for me.'

Three years after Lindsay's death, the missing chapter 18 was published in *The Secret of Hanging Rock* (1987). But the novel as Lindsay left it is not interested in explaining the vanishings. Instead it focuses on the impact of the losses as their effects spread through the school, to the local community and out into the wider world beyond Macedon: 'The reader, taking a bird's eye view of events since the picnic will have noted how various individuals on its outer circumference have somehow become involved in the spreading pattern . . . all of whose lives have already been disrupted, sometimes violently.' *Picnic at Hanging Rock* is concerned with the contagion of fear, with suggestibility and the behaviour of groups, and plays on the suppressed emotions and sexual yearnings of young girls isolated in the bush. And it is a ghost story, precise in its accrual of evocative and haunting detail.

Picnic at Hanging Rock creates an atmosphere and as Lindsay writes: 'An atmosphere can be generated overnight out of nothing or everything, anywhere that human beings are congregated in unnatural conditions. At the Court of Versailles, at Pentridge Gaol, at a select College for Young Ladies where the miasma of hidden fears deepened and darkened with every hour.' The reference to Versailles is telling. All her life Lindsay had been interested in time—she was able to stop watches just by being near them—and felt that time present, past and future coexisted simultaneously. This belief had been encouraged by a controversial account of time travel published in 1911 by two English academics, Anne Moberly and Eleanor Jourdain, from St Hugh's College, Oxford University. On 10 August 1901 the two women had visited the Petit Trianon near the Court of Versailles south-west of Paris, and claimed to have been transported back to 1792, where one believed she had seen Marie Antoinette sketching. Published under pseudonyms, their story *An Adventure* became a bestseller and caused a sensation in England, where debate about its truth lingered for decades. Among the many avid readers of this tale of 'retro-cognition' were poets WB Yeats and Ezra Pound, who had been investigating the paranormal at the time.

Interest in Lindsay's novel was further fuelled when the internationally acclaimed film *Picnic at Hanging Rock* was released in 1975. Conceived by producer Pat Lovell and directed by Peter Weir, the film was a critical and commercial success, and became a classic of Australian cinema. Weir deliberately played on the mystery—the unknown had become an essential part of the story's appeal. 'I did everything in my power to hypnotise the audience away from the possibility of solutions,' he said. Powered by the film's success, the Penguin paperback edition of *Picnic at Hanging Rock* sold 350,000 copies in its first fifteen years, becoming the publisher's bestselling title after AB Facey's *A Fortunate Life*.

Lindsay was born Joan à Beckett Weigall, into a Melbourne legal family related to the Boyds. She was educated at Clyde Girls School in St Kilda—which later moved to Woodend, near Hanging Rock—and studied painting from 1916 to 1920 at Victoria's National Gallery School of Art. In 1922 she married Daryl Lindsay, Norman Lindsay's youngest brother, on Saint Valentine's Day in London; she also took up writing. Lindsay's first book, the comic novel *Through Darkest Pondelayo*, was published in 1936 under the pseudonym Serena Livingstone Stanley. In 1941 Daryl Lindsay became the director of the National Gallery of Victoria. In 1950, during his directorship, the Gallery bought a painting called 'At the Hanging Rock', painted by William Ford in 1875, which shows a group of lavishly attired picnickers in the dappled light of the bush among rocks. In 1964 Joan Lindsay published *Facts Soft and Hard*, an account of her travels in the United States. She also wrote a children's book, *Sid Sixpence* (1983). Lindsay died in Melbourne in 1984.

Gideon Haigh's favourite Australian books

These aren't the ten best, most important or most influential Australian books; simply ten, in no particular order, that I have never forgotten reading, and would not want to be without.

The Middle Parts of Fortune: Somme and Ancre, 1916 by Frederic Manning
On the Beach by Nevil Shute
African Trilogy by Alan Moorehead
Conqueror's Road: An Eyewitness Report of Germany 1945 by Osmar White
The Unforgiving Minute: How Australia Learned to Tell the Time by Graeme Davison
Lion and Kangaroo: The Initiation of Australia 1901–1919 by Gavin Souter
Two Centuries of Panic: A history of corporate collapses in Australia by Trevor Sykes
Sacred Places: War Memorials in the Australian Landscape by Ken Inglis
Jock: A Life Story of John Shaw Neilson by Cliff Hanna
The Steelmaster: A Life of Essington Lewis by Geoffrey Blainey

Gideon Haigh is a sports and business journalist. He has written or edited over twenty books, including *The Battle for BHP* (1987), *The Cricket War* (1993), *The Vincibles* (2002), *Ashes 2005* (2005) and the award-winning *Asbestos House* (2006), about James Hardie.

Cross hangs upside-down in water.' Slessor was above all a poet of image—and it is no wonder that when commissioned to paint a mural for the Sydney Opera House, painter John Olsen paid homage to Slessor's harbour poem 'Five Bells'.

In the poem's opening stanzas Slessor rails against his stubborn memory that will conjure the dead: 'Why do I think of you, dead man?' He apprehends the totality of Joe's disappearance and yet he has not gone: 'You have gone from earth, / Gone even from the meaning of a name; / Yet something's there, yet something forms its lips / And hits and cries against the ports of space, / Beating their sides to make its fury heard.' He cries out to Joe: 'Are you shouting at me, dead man . . . ?' But violent anger is useless against death, 'I hear nothing, nothing . . . only bells'. In his wild despair the poet knows only Joe's absence, forever gone into the void, 'Nothing except the memory of some bones / Long shoved away, and sucked away, in mud'. Slessor's vision is unrelieved by faith and utterly beyond hope. And yet it is so fiercely human.

The poem then draws memories of the dead man. But even in recalled life Joe now appears insubstantial, and the poet cannot reclaim him: 'The night we came to Moorebank in slab-dark, / So dark you bore no body, had no face, / But a sheer voice that rattled out of air'. Slessor's vision leads inexorably to what poet and academic Dennis Haskell has called 'the most powerful evocation of death I know of in the English language': 'I felt the wet push its black thumb-balls in, / The night you died, I felt your eardrums crack, / And the short agony, the longer dream, / The Nothing that was neither long nor short; / But I was bound, and could not go that way, / But I was blind, and could not feel your hand.'

All that remains is the harbour, and the vivid beauty of Slessor's poem: 'I looked out of my window in the dark / At waves with diamond quills and combs of light / That arched their mackerel-backs and smacked the sand / In the moon's drench, that straight enormous glaze'. Slessor later wrote that 'Five Bells' suggested that 'the whole span of a human life can be imagined, and even vicariously experienced, in a flash of thought as brief as the interval between the strokes of a bell.'

'Five Bells' was published with drawings by Norman Lindsay in *Five Bells: XX Poems* in 1939, when Slessor was living in Sydney's Kings Cross. His inspiration came not from the bush but from the harbour and the city, from the lights and multitudes of its streets. In his poem 'William Street' Slessor writes of the Cross as a source of his poetry: its pawnshops and its smells; its lights 'Spilt on the stones, go deeper than a stream'; its 'dips and molls, with flip and shiny gaze / (Death at their elbows, hunger at their heels) / Ranging the pavements of their pasturage; / You find it ugly, I find it lovely.' Pavements are Slessor's pastures, neon lights his mountain streams. As he wrote of his territory: 'with its unending flux of lights and colours, its gaudiness and reticence, its sunsets and midnights, it seems (to me) a good deal more beautiful than the highly advertised stones and sand of Central Australia.'

In 1940, the year after 'Five Bells' was published, Slessor was appointed by the Commonwealth government as Australia's official war correspondent and he travelled to Britain in May 1940. He served in North Africa, Greece, Crete and Syria, and after 1943 in Papua and New Guinea. He resigned from the post in 1944. The same year Slessor published *One Hundred Poems, 1919–1939*, to which he added three more poems—including the war poems 'An Inscription for Dog River' and the haunting 'Beach Burial'—in 1957. From that year Slessor never published a new poem again, despite being active in Sydney's literary community until his death in 1971.

Born in 1901 in Orange, west of Sydney, Slessor moved with his family to Sydney when he was two. His father Robert Schloesser, born in London to a German family, had studied in Belgium and made his children speak French over breakfast. After war broke out in 1914, he changed the family name to Slessor. At fourteen, Kenneth was sent to the boys' school Shore, where he edited the school magazine. He began writing poetry as a child and his first poem was published in the *Bulletin* in 1917, while he was still at school. When he left school he became a journalist with the *Sun*, and continued to work as a journalist all his life.

In 1922 Slessor married Noela Senior. He met Norman Lindsay and his son Jack, and the poet Hugh McCrae the same year. Slessor later wrote of Lindsay's influence in his collection *Bread and Wine*: 'Lindsay's doctrine insists on the concrete image, and it is not without significance that most of the Australian poets whom he may be considered to have influenced show the same abhorrence of abstraction.' The following year Slessor joined with Jack Lindsay to edit *Vision: a Literary Quarterly*, whose object was to attack Australian parochialism and 'liberate the imagination by gaiety or fantasy'. *Thief of the Moon*, Slessor's first book of poetry, was published in 1924 with three Lindsay woodcuts; a second volume, *Earth-Visitors*, was dedicated to Norman Lindsay and published in 1926. His third major collection, *Cuckooz Contrey*, also illustrated by Lindsay, was published in 1932 and the following year *Darlinghurst Nights* appeared. In 1945 Slessor's wife died of cancer. He married again in 1951 and had a son, Paul, but divorced ten years later. Slessor was appointed an Officer of the Order of the British Empire in 1959.

Inspired by TS Eliot and particularly by Wilfred Owen's experiments with rhyme, Slessor brought a dazzling new voice to Australian poetry. As Haskell says of his early poem 'Marco Polo' (1920)—with its 'bridges cleft of serpent-stone' and 'fire-fish in the topaz fount'—it is 'a long way from the brumby-dusted tracks of Lawson and Paterson, the formal, intellectual poetry of Christopher Brennan'.

John Olsen's mural 'Salute to Five Bells' hangs in the northern foyer of the Sydney Opera House. It was commissioned in 1972 and completed in 1973.

MANDY SAYER'S FAVOURITE
AUSTRALIAN BOOKS

The Man Who Loved Children by Christina Stead
Illywhacker by Peter Carey
Eucalyptus by Murray Bail
100 Poems by Kenneth Slessor
At the Cross by Jon Rose
Vaudeville by Ronald McCuaig
The Shark Net by Robert Drewe
Bush Stories by Barbara Baynton
The Turning by Tim Winton
Aunts Up the Cross by Robin Dalton

Mandy Sayer is the author of seven books, including novels, short stories and the award-winning memoirs *Velocity* (2005) and *Dreamtime Alice* (1999).

21

CAPRICORNIA

Xavier Herbert (1901–1984)

Xavier Herbert was born in Geraldton, north of Perth, in 1901 and published his first story in 1926 under the pseudonym 'Herbert Astor'. The following year he moved from Sydney to Darwin, where he witnessed the devastation of the local Aboriginal people, the use of Aboriginal women by white men for sex, and the hard lives of their mixed-race children. In 1930 Herbert set out to conquer London (as he later said) with *Black Velvet*, a novel inspired by his experience of Darwin, but it was rejected by the English publishers. While in London, encouraged by his future wife Sadie Norden, Herbert reworked his material. The result was *Capricornia*, a satiric, exuberant, extravagant and ultimately tragic novel of the founding of Port Zodiac (Darwin), the settlement of the Gulf country—Capricornia—by white Australians and their impact on Aboriginal life. With a brutal metaphor, Herbert describes the permanent planting of 'Civilisation' in Australia's north: 'Nature is cruel. When dingoes come to a waterhole, the ancient kangaroos, not having teeth or ferocity sharp enough to defend their heritage, must relinquish it or die.'

The novel opens with the genesis of the white settlement: 'Although that northern part of the Continent of Australia which is called Capricornia was pioneered long after the southern parts, its unofficial early history was even more bloody than that of the others.' The early white settlers fight not only against the local inhabitants but against nature, which plunges the land into continual flux: 'the whole vast territory seemed never to be anything for long but either a swamp during the Wet Season or a hard-baked desert during the Dry.'

Eventually Port Zodiac is established on this protean land. The region attracts a wild and disparate range of characters, many with comical names—like policeman O'Crimnell, the Reverend Hollower, Magistrate Paddy Larsney and grazier Andy McRandy—but the story focuses on two brothers, Oscar and Mark Shillingsworth, and Mark's son Norman who is born to an Aboriginal mother. The Shillingsworth brothers head north to Capricornia in the early 1900s to take advantage of the spoils of the raw colonial outpost. Within hours of their arrival at Port Zodiac they have transformed themselves from lowly government clerks in serge suits into 'Potentates' clad in the tailored white linen of colonial masters and, 'Carried away by this magnificence, Oscar added a walking-stick to his outfit, though he had till lately been of the opinion that the use of such a thing was pure affectation.'

Herbert's novel embraces a vast range of Capricornia life—from Port Zodiac to the several-hundred-square-mile cattle stations, the Christian Mission, the Aboriginal reserve, the Compound, the fishing boats of the Gulf—but at its heart is Norman, christened with grog as Mark Anthony but called Nawnim, or No-Name, and later Norman. He lives a fractured life, first as a 'yeller-feller', and then as the supposed son of a Javanese princess taken in by his rich uncle Oscar. Only later does Norman learn of his Aboriginal heritage.

The fate of Norman and other children born of Aboriginal and white parents is one of Herbert's great concerns in *Capricornia*. In a debate between Oscar Shillingsworth and Herbert's spokesman Peter Differ about 'half-castes', Oscar says: 'I don't like this Black Velvet business. It makes me sick.' To which Differ replies: 'You're like the majority of people in Australia. You hide from this very real and terrifically important thing, and hide it, and come to think after a while that it doesn't exist. But it does! It does! Why are there twenty thousand half-castes in the country? Why are they never heard of? Oh my God! Do you know that if you dare write a word on the subject to a paper or a magazine you get your work almost chucked back at you?'

After returning from England, by 1935 Herbert was back in Darwin. He was appointed the Superintendent of the Kahlin Aboriginal Compound where he saw the effects of colonial settlement on Aborigines: 'I saw these starving, wretched people expected to die out at any time. And from a very early stage I felt that it was wrong.' His description of the food at the compound— sour porridge, weevils, bread like congealed glue—was included in the 1997 Human Rights and Equal Opportunity Commission's report on the Stolen Generation. In 1910 the *Northern Territory Aboriginals Act* had established an Aboriginal Department to 'provide, where possible, for the custody, maintenance and education of the children of Aboriginals', who were confined to reserves or institutions. But by the 1930s Australian governments had begun to debate the place of the growing population of 'half-caste' children in the current system. This led to the adoption in the late 1930s of the controversial policy of assimilation.

This was the atmosphere into which Herbert's novel was published in 1937 by PR Stephensen, a vocal promoter of Aboriginal rights. On its publication Stephensen called *Capricornia* 'an Australian masterpiece destined to become a classic'. (It was republished in 1938 by Angus & Robertson.) Herbert had written frankly and furiously about what he had experienced of Aboriginal existence in northern Australia, determined that his novel would bring change and improve the lives of Indigenous people. As he said in a letter to Patrick White in 1979: 'to you the written word is primarily artistic expression, whereas to myself it is merely a tool for use for a practical purpose, namely to effect social reform. While you are essentially an artist, practising for art's sake, I am a revolutionary, using my art to plead my cause.'

Herbert was born an illegitimate child which, according to his biographer Frances de Groen, 'gave him an insight into and appreciation of the position of Aborigines'. He was named Alfred Jackson by his mother but later adopted the surname of his father, a railway engineer. After school Herbert trained as a pharmacist before leaving Perth to study medicine at the University of Melbourne. In 1926 he turned instead to writing and went to Sydney. He then travelled across northern Australia, working as a sailor, miner, stockman and pearl-diver. After serving in the Second World War, Herbert moved to the Daintree in 1948 and then to Cairns. He published several more novels and an autobiography, *Disturbing Element* (1963). His acclaimed novel *Poor Fellow My Country*, which is longer than *War and Peace*, won the Miles Franklin Award in 1975. Six months before his death in 1984 in Alice Springs, Herbert, a passionate republican, rejected an Order of Australia from the Hawke government because it was granted by the Queen, not the people of Australia.

In 1988 *Capricornia* was adapted to the stage by Louis Nowra, who focused on the story of Norman and his discovery of his Aboriginal heritage. Alexis Wright's novel *Carpentaria*, published in 2006, evokes the title of Herbert's *Capricornia* and is written on the same epic scale about the same territory. *Carpentaria* was inspired by Wright's experience with her Waanyi people fighting the Century Mine in the Gulf of Carpentaria in the 1990s. When *Carpentaria* was shortlisted for the 2007 Miles Franklin Award, which it went on to win, Wright said of her novel: 'It is about Aboriginal sovereignty of mind. The last frontier we are fighting for is having control of our own imagination and how we define our future.' She told the story of *Carpentaria* in a way 'that might encourage Aboriginal people to read and understand the possibilities of literature to explain who we are'.

Tara June Winch's favourite Australian books

Here are THE ten of my favourite in no particular order:

Carpentaria by Alexis Wright
The Red Tree by Shaun Tan
Shadow Lines by Stephen Kinnane
Kayang and Me by Kim Scott and Hazel Brown
Surrender by Sonya Hartnett
Possum Magic by Mem Fox and Julie Vivas
Smoke Encrypted Whispers by Samuel Wagan Watson
Sister Girl by Jackie Huggins
Elders: Wisdom from Australia's Indigenous Leaders by Peter McConchie
Stories of Bird by Lucy Holt

Tara June Winch is the author of the short story collection *Swallow the Air* which won the David Unaipon Award for an Indigenous writer in 2004. She was one of the *Sydney Morning Herald*'s 'Best Young Australian Novelists' of 2007.

22

THE MAN WHO LOVED CHILDREN
Christina Stead (1902–1983)

In her great novel, *The Man Who Loved Children*, Christina Stead creates a family world that is intense, febrile, and wracked with brooding, seething passions. Its three central characters—husband, wife and child—are fatally locked within each other's orbit until the child breaks them free. Set mostly in 1930s Washington DC during the Depression, *The Man Who Loved Children* is the story of the Pollit family, particularly of the father Sam, mother Henny, and Louie, Sam's daughter from his sanctified first marriage. Stead's extraordinary evocative powers so sharply conjure these three and Henny and Sam's own six children, who spill endlessly through the Pollit house with assorted neighbouring children and relatives, that the book teems with a constant flux of life and the dynamic interaction of personalities.

Sam Pollit, a Washington bureaucrat and naturalist, is an eternally playful, childish, vociferous, domineering self-proclaimed visionary who speaks in baby language and believes in vast abstractions like 'the United States of Mankind'. He cannot be long without children. When confined to the company of adults during an eight-month field trip to Singapore, he is profoundly unnerved. For Sam Pollit is The Man Who Loved Children—or 'the Great I Am', as Henny calls him. Sam dreams he can engineer a perfect family, which he has attempted with his first wife, Louie's mother: 'I say frankly, Looloo, that I believed that I could remold her life and with my wife and children make a little nucleus of splendid men and women to work for the future. That was, is, my only dream, my life hope: for I am only a dreamer in realities.'

Henny, his second wife, is a southern belle who has married beneath her: 'When she had first come to Washington, she had come with no more sense of married life or of social life than a harem-reared woman, being then a gentle, neurotic creature, wearing silk next to the skin and expecting to have a good time at White House receptions.' But her lean dark beauty has been exhausted by poverty and the birth of six children in ten years, 'they were simply eating away at her flesh as they had when they were at the breast, no less.' Henny undermines Sam's puritan reign of health, wholesomeness and 'Sunday-Fundays'. She is chaotic and spiteful, in her ragged dresses, raging at Sam, at Louie, at her own children, at Sam's sister Bonnie, from her bedroom near the kitchen, where endless cups of tea are made.

Louie is a go-between in this hated marriage. She comes to see Henny and Sam as 'two selfish, passionate people, terrible as gods in their eternal married hate.' Louie is in disaffected puberty; she is dreamy and perverse and unhappy. Turning thirteen, she brims with unfocused love and passion which find their escape in poetry, diaries and writers like Nietzsche, from whom she takes her motto: 'By my faith and hope I conjure thee, throw not away the hero in thy soul.' She tells wild stories to the other children and has a nascent genius for verbal invention, but dreams of being an actress.

The Man Who Loved Children charts the decline of the Pollits' marriage and financial affairs, already so dire at the novel's opening, as they disintegrate further until there is almost nothing left of either. Stead began to write the novel in 1939, basing it on her own painful childhood in Watson's Bay, Sydney, where she had been the only child of her father's first marriage; he had then remarried and had six more children. Her portrait of the insidious influence parents can unleash upon children, of the damage their tempers and unrealised dreams can wreak as they leak into family life, has a dark and terrible truth. And Stead has a dazzling ability to evoke a family's multitude of views: 'What a dreary stodgy world of adults the children saw when they went out! And what a moral, high-minded world their father saw! But for Henny there was a wonderful particular world, and when they went with her they saw it: they saw the fish eyes, the crocodile grins, the hair like a birch broom, the mean men crawling with maggots, and the children restless as an eel, that she saw.'

As well as her remarkable gift for vital prose, Stead had a profound understanding of human psychology: 'My purpose, in making characters eloquent, is the expression of two psychological truths; first, that everyone has a wit superior to his everyday wit, when discussing his personal problems and the most depressed housewife, for example, can talk like Medea about her troubles; second, that everyone, to a greater or lesser extent, is a fountain of passion, which is turned by circumstances of birth or upbringing into conventional channels.'

First published in 1940 during the Second World War, *The Man Who Loved Children* disappeared almost without trace and was out of print for many years. But in 1955 the American poet Randall Jarrell wrote his now famous review for the *New York Times*, calling *The Man Who Loved Children* a great book: 'It has one great quality that, ordinarily, only a great book has: it does a single thing better than any other book has ever done it. *The Man Who Loved Children* makes you a part of one family's immediate existence as no other book quite does.' But still the novel did not find a wide readership nor acclaim in the United States until it was reissued there in 1965. Accounting for Stead's struggle to find an audience, her editor Clifton Fadiman said: 'Her humour is savage, her learning hard to cope with, her fancies too furious. Like Emily Brontë, she has none of the proper bearing, the reassuring countenance of a "lady author".'

Stead was almost unknown in Australia until she returned permanently to the land of her birth in 1974. She had fled her birthplace and family for London as soon as she could, aged twenty-six. Like Sam Pollit, her father was a self-taught naturalist and bureaucrat who became the general manager of the State Trawling Industry in New South Wales and was the co-founder of the Wildlife Preservation Society of Australia. Her mother died when Stead was two.

Having first trained as a teacher, Stead was so unsuited to teaching that she left after three years to become a clerk. Arriving in London in 1928, she began her first novel, *Seven Poor Men of Sydney*, which was accepted by her publisher on the condition that she wrote a more conventional novel for him to publish first. And so Stead wrote *The Salzburg Tales*, her first published book, which appeared in 1934. In London Stead also met the Marxist banker and writer William Blake, a married man with whom she moved to Paris in 1929 and whom she eventually married in 1952. Stead moved with Blake to New York in 1939 and began *The Man Who Loved Children* the same year, setting this story of her Sydney childhood in Washington and Baltimore. Stead was first recognised in Australia when she was awarded the inaugural Patrick White Literary Award in 1974—and White believed her to be Australia's greatest novelist. She wrote fourteen novels before her death in 1983, including her second autobiographical novel, *For Love Alone* (1945), one of her few books to be set in Australia.

GEORGIA BLAIN'S FAVOURITE
AUSTRALIAN BOOKS

The Man Who Loved Children by Christina Stead. It has a gothic, wild darkness that is completely unforgettable. The horror builds and builds to an appalling climax.

The Pea-pickers by Eve Langley. It's a wonderful book, absurd, hilariously funny, messy, anarchic; the kind of book that so rarely gets published.

The Fortunes of Richard Mahony by Henry Handel Richardson. *Richard Mahony* is such a relevant book today. Mahony is restless, dissatisfied and constantly searching for something else. He destroys any security he builds as he tries to find purpose and meaning to his existence, and his journey is both frustrating and admirable. Each time I reread this book I find myself reassessing Mahony, sometimes understanding him, at other times wanting to strangle him.

Georgia Blain is the author of the novels *Closed for Winter* (1998), *Candelo* (1999), *The Blind Eye* (2001) and *Names for Nothingness* (2004); and the forthcoming book of autobiographical essays *Births. Deaths. Marriages.*

23

THE PEA-PICKERS

Eve Langley (1904–1974)

The Pea-pickers is a passionate and exuberant novel about two sisters who set out in the late 1920s from their impoverished home in Dandenong to work packing apples in their mother's legendary territory of eastern Victoria—Gippsland, 'there's no place like it' she tells them. So vital is this journey to the lost land of their mother's birth that the sisters agree implicitly that it requires nothing less than a complete change of identity: 'Now that we're going to Gippsland, we said, we must put off our feminine names for ever.' And so the nineteen-year-old narrator becomes Steve, 'because the comic literature of the Australian bush has always had a Steve in it and, of course, we had always loved Steve Hart in that bushranging song'; and Steve gives her younger sister June the classic bush name of Blue. Steve and Blue dress in tailored trousers, silk shirts and ties for the train journey, and pack khaki overalls for work. As they travel, Steve becomes a Gippslander: 'At some part of the journey, my hereditary Gippsland mind awoke. It was a totally different apparatus to my Dandenongian mind.'

The hyperbole and elaborate play of the novel's opening scenes, with Gippsland as the promised land and the sisters transformed into men clad in red, gold and royal blue stroking their imaginary black whiskers, are maintained throughout Steve's narrative as she captures every nuance of her alternately ecstatic and melancholic response to life, to the bush, to the men and women the sisters meet along their way as they follow the seasonal crops and move from apples to hops, maize and pea-picking. Steve describes herself as a comical woman who longs to be 'a serious and handsome man'; and she is possessed by 'a desire, amounting to an obsession, to be loved. I suffered from it, as others suffer from a chronic delicacy of health. It haunted my sleep and impeded my waking hours.' Tormented by love, by the beauty of the Australian land and two of its men, and by the horror of her vanishing youth as she turns twenty, Steve pours her heart into words. Although she has had little education, she is a voracious and eclectic reader. She quotes Virgil in Latin; Keats and Verlaine are her poetic heroes; and she remakes the world around her with her elaborate, metaphorical speech: 'My first illness was that one most common to the children of the poor . . . a bad education and, like the bite of a goanna, it was incurable and ran for years. My early arnicas of Matthew Arnold, small balsams of Wilde, Rabelaisian cauterizers, Shavian foments and Shakespearean liniments have only added to it and spread the offence.'

The Pea-pickers is an extraordinary novel, a raucous romp through the Victorian countryside in praise of Australia, and a voyage through the passions of a young woman with the soul of a poet determined to live by her own elusive law. Steve is a complex, contradictory woman: she ardently desires love and yet flees from any possibility of intimacy; she invites a man to her bed only to send him away for snoring and not talking of Virgil's *Aeneid*. She embraces all humanity and yet, like Tom Collins in *Such is Life*, she is also wantonly racist: 'Intensely Australian, although despised by her sons, I scorned defilement by another race.' Above all Steve wants fame and freedom—and the company of sensual women.

Langley's writing is remarkable for its fluid ability to rise to the heights of Steve's joy and plunge to the depths of her sorrow: 'Yes, from the Greek lands had come the moon, full of the memory of Grecian art, and through the broken columns of the night I wandered in search of my love, while from the withered moonlit bush on each side of the road came a distressful watching, a sadness and a melancholy unspeakable.' And at times Langley's prose has the evocative power of poetry, such as when Steve looks back on her mother's garden, now lost to them, but captured alive in her mind and in her sister's and mother's minds: 'It is a thought as sweet as heaven to know that in the minds of each of us the may by the fence still blooms in an eternal springtime; that the snowdrop has in our hearts a triple birth, and blooms in three separate minds, faultlessly.'

Eve Langley was born in 1904 in Forbes, in mid-western New South Wales. Her father was an itinerant labourer and violinist, and both her parents came from Victoria. When her father died, her mother took her two daughters back to her birthplace of Gippsland, settling in Crossover, where she ran a hotel. They later moved to Dandenong, where Langley finished school. In 1924 Langley and her younger sister June travelled through Gippsland and the Ovens Valley finding work picking peas and hops. Defying the strict conventions of the day, the sisters dressed in men's clothing and renamed themselves Steve and Blue. Langley based *The Pea-pickers* on her diaries written during these years, from 1924 to 1928.

Langley's mother and sister moved to New Zealand and in 1932 Langley followed them. She lived in poverty, publishing her poetry in small magazines, writing journalism and doing domestic work. In 1937 she married a young art student, Hilary Clark, with whom she had three children. Between March and May 1940, while she was pregnant with her third child and living alone with her two elder children, Langley wrote *The Pea-pickers*. She entered it in Sydney's SH Prior Memorial Prize in 1940 and it won, with two other writers (one of whom was Kylie Tennant). By the time *The Pea-pickers* was published in 1942, Langley had been committed to the Auckland Psychiatric Hospital by her husband. She remained there for seven years.

On Langley's release from hospital in 1949 her sister looked after her. Langley was divorced three years later and in 1954 she changed her name by deed poll to Oscar Wilde. She returned to Australia in 1960, travelling the country, and in 1965 went to Greece for inspiration. When she returned to Australia she lived in a bush hut in Katoomba, in the Blue Mountains, where she continued to write and paint and to dress in men's clothes, wearing a pinstripe suit in winter and shorts and a singlet in summer. Although Langley wrote prolifically all her life and wrote ten more novels about Steve and her cross-dressing itinerant life, her only other published work was *White Topee*, about Steve's rebirth as Oscar Wilde, which was released in 1954. Langley died alone in Katoomba in 1974.

The New Zealand writer Ruth Park, who was a friend of Langley's, wrote of her: 'I never wanted to talk to or question Eve. To listen was enough. Her ideas were to me, dazzling. She opened doors in my mind in all directions. She would quote from Seneca, Montaigne, Epictetus, the Greek playwrights . . . It was she who, in this careless, drifting manner, filled my mind with treasure which still delights me.' In writing *The Pea-pickers*, Langley celebrated Australia and her own poetic vision. As Steve says to Blue: 'Some day, I shall write fully our life together, with its tragedy and

JANE MESSER'S FAVOURITE
AUSTRALIAN BOOKS

Only ten allowed! That's difficult. I opted for daring, tears, subtlety, and of course a fine ear for language; and the unique, sometimes provocative ways these writers speak of our country and the countries we come from. In random order:

M by Peter Robb—read it and discover not only Caravaggio but
    Shakespeare's 'Italy'
Jesus wants me for a sunbeam by Peter Goldsworthy
'Australia' by Ania Walwicz
Double Wolf by Brian Castro
Dead Europe by Christos Tsiolkas
'The Drover's Wife'—by Henry Lawson, and the stories of the
    same name it inspired by Murray Bail, Frank Moorhouse
    and Barbara Jefferis, all originally published in the *Bulletin*
    magazine
A Map of the Gardens by Gillian Mears
The Pea-pickers by Eve Langley
Come in Spinner by Dymphna Cusack and Florence James
Don't Take Your Love to Town by Ruby Langford

Jane Messer is the author of novels *Night by Night* (1994) and
Provenance (2007); and the editor of *Bedlam: An Anthology of Sleepless
Nights* (1996) and *Certifiable Truths: Stories of Love and Madness* (1998).
She is a lecturer in creative writing at Macquarie University.

24

'A LETTER FROM ROME'

AD Hope (1907–2000)

Like poet-scholar Christopher Brennan, AD Hope was an academic, a poet of the intellect and of erotic desire, and looked to the literature and mythology of Europe for his poetic inspiration. As Hope wrote in 'An Epistle from Holofernes': 'It is the meaning of the poet's trade / To re-create the fables and revive / In men the energies by which they live'. And as with Brennan, central to Hope's work are poetry and the poet, and their place in an increasingly uninterested, uncomprehending modern world, which produces 'Only the arts it can afford, / Stamped, sterilized and tinned and tested / And standardized and predigested' (as he wrote in 'Conversation with Calliope').

But unlike Brennan, Hope also directly addressed Australia and its poetic heritage in his verse, even if only to scorn or dismiss them both for their failure of intelligence. His famous poem 'Australia', written some time after his return from Oxford University, refers to Australia's river of 'immense stupidity' which floods 'her monotonous tribes', and dismisses Australia as a place

'Where second-hand Europeans pullulate / Timidly on the edge of alien shores.' And yet even in this most damning poem, Hope does not conceal his secret dream that something great might one day come from the land of his birth: 'Yet there are some like me turn gladly home / From the lush jungles of modern thought' to the 'Arabian desert of the human mind'—Australia—in the hope that it might one day also nurture prophets—or a revitalised poetry free from the burden of doubt that weighs on European civilisation.

Hope's childhood in Cooma, on the high plains of southern New South Wales, and in Tasmania, also prompted some later poems about the Australian landscape, including 'Beyond Khancoban' and 'Tasmanian Magpies', which recalls his Tasmanian boyhood, 'when each bird, / Stone, cloud and every tree that grew / Spoke and I had by heart all that I heard'. He also wrote a rollicking bush yarn, 'Teaser Rams'. But typical of Hope (whom American poet and critic John Hollander called 'one of the great poets of heterosexual eroticism of any time'), 'Teaser Rams' is not the story of a lone bushman on horseback conquering an inhospitable land-scape, but a comic, raunchy tale of a station-hand called Johnny, a pastoralist's wife, seduction and multiple orgasm.

And for his virulent, satirical outbursts against the modern world, his explorations of men's carnal desires and the poet's task, Hope employed a series of measured, ordered poetic forms, rhymes and meters drawn from eighteenth-century English poets like Alexander Pope.

Hope's belief that the poet's role is to reconnect with and revital-ise the myths and stories that spawned European civilisation is at the heart of his poem 'A Letter from Rome'. Dated 1958, the poem was written for Dr Leonie Kramer (who later became Pro-fessor and Chair of Australian Literature at the University of Sydney). Its epigraph from 'Roman Girl's Song' (1826) by nine-teenth-century British poet Felicia Hemans sets the tone of Hope's lament about the changing world of Rome and its languishing tradition: 'Rome, Rome! thou are no more / As thou has been!' As befits a letter, the poem is personal and conversational, and in true epistolary style its seventy-two eight-line stanzas range over a number of subjects, from the comic to the serious, from the impossibility of digesting the overwhelming feast of Rome's treasures to an overseas student's determination to find an Italian lover in Florence just to record the experience in her diary.

'A Letter from Rome' opens with a conversation between the poet and the Muse, who tells him to 'write a letter home'. Addressing the Muse as 'My dear, good girl', the poet replies that such a grand theme, a letter about Rome, 'needs eagle wings to soar' and 'Australian poets, you recall, prefer / The packhorse and the slip-rail and the spur.' The Muse replies that she 'never liked that pioneering strain' and protests that 'Australian poets, if they ever tried, / Might show at least a rudiment of brain'. And so the poet takes up her challenge.

The poem's observations about tourism and the prepackaging of the classical past in an age of 'plastics and alloys' into an offering for modern travellers are pithy, funny and true. For example, every night in bed 'I / have groaned, I must admit, as I recall / That on the morrow waits for me a fresh / Mountain of marble chiselled into flesh.'; 'The modern tourist pays a job-lot bill, / Takes one quick look and then is whisked away: / Next we see Titian's famous—Ah, too late!'; and his sharp observation about the tourists who spend their time taking photographs and 'must get home to find where they have been'. His allusions to mythology, European history and to other illustrious travellers to Rome, from Virgil to Ruskin, who come to pay homage to the 'womb' of European culture are typical of Hope's preoccupations.

But the poem also moves inexorably towards its more serious, hesitant, almost reluctant confession of a mystical experience at

Lake Nemi, south of Rome, where there was once a grove sacred to the goddess Diana—'I was possessed, and what possessed me there / Was Europe's oldest ritual of prayer.' In Italy the poet connects to the fount of civilisation and ultimately realises that 'The thing I came to find was lost in *me*'. The poem is also concerned with poetry and its place in Australia, and with Australia's connection to the European tradition. Australia's 'roots are European but the tree / Grows to a different pattern and design'. Antipodeans, divided and possessed of 'a doubt of what we are', must return to the source: to Italy, and Rome, where Europe's 'great venture of the heart began'.

The son of a Presbyterian minister, Hope was born in 1907 and grew up in Cooma and country Tasmania. After graduating from the University of Sydney in 1928, Hope was awarded a scholarship to Oxford University. He returned to Australia in 1931 and trained as a teacher. His academic career began in 1937 at Sydney Teachers' College and in 1945 he became Senior Lecturer in English at the University of Melbourne. In 1951 Hope was made the first Professor of English at the new Canberra University College, which later merged with the Australian National University (ANU). While at the ANU Hope helped to found with T Inglis Moore the first full university course in Australian literature.

Hope began writing poetry in the 1930s and 40s, but many of his early poems are so highly charged with sex and satire that they would have risked censorship if widely published. So not until 1955, when he was forty-eight, did Hope publish his first book, *The Wandering Islands*. During his life Hope published more than fifteen collections of poetry as well as celebrated essays and criticism. Married with three children, Hope was awarded an Order of the British Empire in 1972.

Writing in 1970, Clive James said of Hope: 'Against modernism and for classicism; against the bloodlessly refined and for the

FRANK MOORHOUSE'S FAVOURITE
AUSTRALIAN BOOKS

These are more 'books that have had an influence', but of course, I suspect (with the contemporary writers) that some of their work will become classical.

A Complete Account of the Settlement at Port Jackson by Watkin Tench
The Fortunes of Richard Mahony by Henry Handel Richardson
Henry Lawson's stories
The Persimmon Tree and Other Stories (including 'Dry Spell') by
    Marjorie Barnard
Voss and *Riders in the Chariot* by Patrick White
Bush Studies ('Squeaker's Mate' and other stories) by Barbara
    Baynton
Steele Rudd's stories
Murray Bail's stories
David Campbell's poetry
The Man Who Loved Children by Christina Stead

Frank Moorhouse is the author of acclaimed novels *Grand Days* (1993) and *Dark Palace* (2000), which won the Miles Franklin Award in 2001, short story collections, film scripts and *Martini: A Memoir* (2005).

25

VOSS

Patrick White (1912–1990)

Voss opens in the early spring of 1845 at the house of a Sydney merchant, Mr Bonner. His niece Laura Trevelyan, a 'flawless girl', is interrupted from her embroidery by the arrival of a visitor, who has come to see Mr Bonner. Her servant, Rose Portion, shows in a distressed, shabby German man with 'noticeable cheekbones and over-large finger-joints'. The man is Johann Ulrich Voss, whose expedition into the heart of Australia Mr Bonner is sponsoring. In one of Patrick White's most extraordinary acts of imagination, during the course of this novel of exploration the lives of these three outcasts of Sydney society—the bookish orphan Laura, the foreigner Voss and the emancipist servant Rose—will become bound with the Australian landscape and united in a mystical realm that only Voss and Laura can access.

The basic movement of *Voss* is straightforward. Voss and his party of oddly assorted men—including a poet, an ornithologist and an ex-convict—set out from Sydney via boat to Newcastle, from where they travel up through the Hunter Valley to the

Darling Downs. Equipped by several of the richest men in New South Wales, Voss intends to travel across the continent from east to west through its unknown interior, which may yet prove to be a 'veritable paradise', as one Sydney gentleman observes. 'But I am inclined to believe, Mr Voss, that you will discover a few blackfellers, and a few flies, and something resembling the bottom of the sea.'

It is quite clear from the beginning that on some level Voss is mad—and this is exactly how he is perceived by most of those who meet him in Sydney, to the increasing discomfort of Mr Bonner. To the general public, Voss has already passed into legend: 'What kind of man is he? wondered the public, who would never know. If he was already more of a statue than a man, they really did not care, for he would satisfy their longing to perch something on a column, in a square or gardens, as a memorial to their own achievement.' But Voss is not interested in what others think of him. He is only and utterly obsessed with his mission: 'I will cross the continent from one end to the other. I have every intention to know it with my heart. Why I am pursued by this necessity, it is no more possible for me to tell than it is for you, who have made my acquaintance only before yesterday.'

But the novel is also a strange and powerful love story, as befits its eccentric mystic-hero. Voss and Laura meet only four times in Sydney before his departure. Their meetings are cryptic and become increasingly charged, although they barely touch each other beyond the brush of an arm or the clutch at a wrist: 'In the passion of their relationship, she had encountered his wrist. She held his bones.' Laura cannot decide if she likes the peculiar arrogant man, but she begins to understand him and the purpose of his journey, and realises that they are twin beings. And so the novel cuts back and forth from Voss and his expedition as they move west through water-logged plains of plenty into the desert of rock and gullies and silence, to Laura, as she goes about her life in Sydney living more and more in her dreams and fevered wanderings among her uncle's camellias. They conduct a passionate affair through letters, dreams and telepathic conversations: 'Air joining air experiences a voluptuousness no less intense because imperceptible.'

White began writing *Voss* in Sydney in 1955, but the novel had come to him years before, during the Second World War, in London when he was reading Edward John Eyre's *Journals of Expeditions of Discovery into Central Australia*, and then in the western desert of Egypt where he was stationed as an Intelligence Officer with the Royal Air Force. Following his demobilisation, White returned to Australia with Manoly Lascaris, whom he had met during the war. It was only after some research in Sydney that White realised that the explorer Ludwig Leichhardt (1813–1848) was the historical figure most like the explorer of his imagination.

Voss is White's attempt to create and inhabit the Australian landscape; to fuse his European mythological imagination with the vast internal spaces of the continent he was born to and could not leave. As Voss says: 'in this disturbing country, so far as I have become acquainted with it already, it is possible more easily to discard the inessential and to attempt the infinite. You will be burnt up most likely, you will have the flesh torn from your bones, you will be tortured probably in many horrible and primitive ways, but you will realise that genius of which you sometimes suspect you are possessed, and of which you will not tell me you are afraid.' The desert of *Voss* is a symbolic landscape. White had never been to central Australia and his vision is drawn from painters like Sidney Nolan, and from the work of William Blake, Eugène Delacroix, Gustav Mahler and Franz Liszt. *Voss* is about the great effort and sacrifice required to enact a vision, whether of the explorer, the mystic or the artist. It is about the nature of genius, the following of a destiny beyond reason and the rational. It is also about White himself, and his Voss-like endeavour to bring a visionary art to a nation uncomfortable with the metaphysical: 'I was determined to prove that the Australian novel is not necessarily the dreary, dun-coloured offspring of journalistic realism.'

Published to critical acclaim in 1957, *Voss* became a bestseller and made White famous. It won the first Miles Franklin Award and the inaugural WH Smith & Sons Literary Award in London. As Robert Hughes noted, it also inspired the work of a number of Australian painters: 'Patrick White's *Voss* has given Australian artists a private goldmine. I do not like to think how many pictures I've seen in the last two or three years bearing titles like *The Death of Voss*, *Voss Triumphant*, *Voss Among the Elders* and *Voss Agonistes*.' The writer David Malouf collaborated with composer Richard Meale to write an opera based on *Voss* and there have been several unsuccessful attempts to bring *Voss* to the screen, including one by English director Ken Russell.

White was born in London in 1912. His parents returned with him to Australia when he was six months old but he was sent back to England, to boarding school, when he was thirteen. He returned to Australia to work as a jackeroo in the Monaro and the Darling Downs, but then went to Cambridge University, where he studied French and German. After university he settled in London and began to write. His first novel, *Happy Valley*, was published in 1939. After serving in the Royal Air Force during the Second World War, White returned to Australia with Lascaris and settled in Sydney, where he finished the novel he had been writing on the voyage out, *The Aunt's Story* (1947). During the course of his celebrated and controversial writing life, White wrote twelve novels and many short stories and plays. In 1973

Patrick White was awarded the Nobel Prize for Literature, for his 'epic and psychological narrative art which has introduced a new continent into literature'. With the Nobel prize money White created the Patrick White Literary Award, won by Christina Stead in its inaugural year.

GARTH NIX'S FAVOURITE
AUSTRALIAN BOOKS

My Brother Jack by George Johnston
The Magic Pudding by Norman Lindsay
Selected Poems by Philip Hodgins
The Official History of Australia in the War of 1914–1918 by CEW Bean
The Sea and Summer by George Turner
Midnite: The Story of a Wild Colonial Boy by Randolph Stow
African Trilogy (Mediterranean Front, A Year of Battle and *The End in
    Africa)* by Alan Moorehead

Garth Nix is the bestselling author of young adult fantasy
novels, including *The Old Kingdom* series, *The Seventh Tower* series
and *The Keys to the Kingdom* series. His books have been translated
into twenty-eight languages.

26

MY BROTHER JACK
George Johnston (1912–1970)

After an illustrious career as the 'golden boy' of Australian journalism, George Johnston left Australia in 1951 with his second wife Charmian Clift and their two children for the London office of the Sydney *Sun*. In 1954 he resigned and moved with his family to the Greek islands to devote himself to writing fiction. He published several novels, including a detective series, but it was not until after he had been diagnosed with tuberculosis in 1959 and was sinking into despair that he turned to his Melbourne childhood; on Hydra in 1962 Johnston wrote the first fragments of a story that would bring him immediate fame as a novelist, *My Brother Jack*: 'My brother Jack does not come into the story straight away. Nobody ever does, of course, because a person doesn't begin to exist without parents and an environment and legendary tales told about ancestors and dark dusty vines growing over outhouses where remarkable insects might always drop out of hidden crevices.'

Set in Melbourne, *My Brother Jack* spans the years from

Johnston's father's return from the First World War, through the Depression, to the close of the Second World War. The story, based on Johnston's early life, is told by David Meredith, whose formative years are shaped by war and the constant counterpoint of his brother Jack: 'The thing I am trying to get at is what made Jack different from me. Different all through our lives, I mean, and in a special sense, not just older or nobler or braver or less clever.' Three years older than David, Jack is interested only in girls, fighting, smoking, drinking and having a good time. He is 'a character born for ardent adventure'. David, on the other hand, is painfully shy, especially with girls ('it was on the question of girls that he most resented me'), and avoids at every opportunity the vital life his brother embraces: 'My feelings and attitudes were so totally opposed to his in every imaginable way that I would sometimes catch him looking at me and shaking his head in an utterly mystified way.'

The other great influence on David's life is the First World War, which is responsible for the walking sticks, wheelchairs and artificial limbs that clutter the front hallway of the Merediths' house. The war also brings the dozens of ex-servicemen who pass through their house, taken in by David's mother from the hospital where she is a nurse. While the war fills David with fear, it brings his brother Jack more alive. Jack dominates the local streets and advances into manhood with ease, having his first sexual experience at twelve. Meanwhile David lives in the shadows, furtively trying to avoid the adult responsibilities that Jack is so eager for. But unbeknownst to them both, and to the rest of the family, David is haphazardly following his own destiny, which will take him further from their suburban Melbourne working-class neighbourhood than any of them could ever have dreamed.

David's parents arrange for him to be apprenticed to a lithographic studio when he is fourteen. But while he passively allows them to decide the outward forms of his life, he is all the time secretly working towards his own independent future, which he discovers in an ecstasy of revelation by the wharves, when 'for the first time in my life I came to be aware of the existence of true beauty, of an opalescent world of infinite promise that had nothing whatever to do with the shabby suburbs that had engulfed me since my birth.' By the wharves David begins to sense some destiny that awaits him: 'I did not see it then as a way out of the wilderness, for the stuff of this material was too fragile to be considered as something which might be *used*, but I was quite sure that something important had happened to me.' Johnston writes beautifully and poignantly about David's coming to manhood, about his almost accidental discovery of his calling, his one thing in life.

Through his story of the disparate lives of David and Jack, the bookish career boy and the athletic Australian bloke, Johnston also draws a vibrant portrait of life in Australia between the two world wars; and of life in Melbourne in particular, from the Merediths' working-class suburb to the new middle-class suburbs built in mindless uniformity, with their colour-coded cocktail parties and pickled onions, blond-wood furniture, and manicured lawns with sterile borders of neat flowers.

Born in 1912 into a working-class family in Melbourne, Johnston was a child of the First World War. His father went to war in France in 1915 and his mother served as a nurse in the Caulfield Military Hospital. He left school at fourteen to be apprenticed to a lithographer and studied art at the National Gallery Art School. Johnston became obsessed with sailing ships and at sixteen he sent an article to the *Argus* on shipwrecks which was accepted for publication. In 1933 the *Argus* took him on as a cadet reporter. He married five years later and had a daughter in 1941, the year he was appointed to the prestigious role of Australia's first official war correspondent. In 1942 Johnston was sent to New Guinea and he travelled extensively during the war, to Britain, the United States, Asia and Europe, and was present for the signing of the Japanese surrender aboard the USS *Missouri* in 1945. He published several books during the war, including *Grey Gladiator* (1939), *Australia at War* (1942) and *New Guinea Diary* (1943).

On his return to Melbourne after the war Johnston became the first editor of the *Australasian Post*, where he met the writer Charmian Clift. Their passionate affair caused a scandal in conservative post-war Melbourne and Johnston resigned in 1946. The couple moved to Sydney, where they later married after Johnston's divorce, and had two children. In 1951 they moved to London and then to the Greek islands, where Clift wrote her celebrated books *Mermaid Singing* (1956) and *Peel Me a Lotus* (1959), about their life first on Kalimnos and then on Hydra, where their second son was born.

Johnston and Clift were a glamorous couple and received a constant flow of visitors in Hydra, including the Canadian musician Leonard Cohen, then a young poet. Cohen remembers the couple's mythic dimensions: 'They had a larger-than-life, a mythical quality. They drank more than other people, they wrote more, they got sick more, they got well more, they cursed more and they blessed more, and they helped a great deal more. They were an inspiration. They had guts.' Their big life and financial pressures began to tell on their marriage and on Johnston's health. In the midst of these pressures and in despair over his life, Johnston began work on *My Brother Jack*. Encouraged by Clift, he wrote the novel in seven months.

First published in London in 1964, *My Brother Jack* became an immediate bestseller. When Johnston returned to Australia in 1964 for the local launch he was celebrated as a literary star and the novel won the Miles Franklin Award. Clift returned to Sydney with the children soon after. As his health declined, Johnston spent months in hospital for lung operations and Clift was left to support the family. She wrote a popular column for the *Sydney Morning Herald* and the script for the ten-part television series of *My Brother Jack* which screened in 1965. During this time Johnston wrote the second book of his David Meredith trilogy, *Clean Straw For Nothing*, about his years in Greece. Clift committed suicide in 1969, a month before its publication. *Clean Straw for Nothing* won the Miles Franklin Award and Johnston was appointed Officer of the Order of the British Empire in 1970. Johnston was writing the final book in the trilogy, *A Cartload of Clay* (1971), when he died of tuberculosis in 1970.

My Brother Jack has continued to be one of Australia's most popular novels and has been twice adapted for television, in 1965 and as a two-part series in 2001. Since it was first published, the novel has enjoyed critical acclaim as well as commercial success, as Johnston's biographer Garry Kinnane points out: 'The staggering popularity of *My Brother Jack* should never be taken as evidence of its superficiality. It is without doubt one of the most richly detailed, deeply felt and strikingly penetrating accounts of Australian life ever written.'

CHARLOTTE WOOD'S FAVOURITE
AUSTRALIAN BOOKS

I thought of this list as a gift for someone newly arrived in
this country. It's a list not so much for a sense of who we are
now—a reader can soon discover that for themselves—as for
a kind of threading back to where our literature has come
from, and a sense of how our stories have grown out of and
alongside one another. My list is too short, of course, but once
the thinking starts, the writers and titles flood in (what about
Christina Stead? all of Robert Drewe? Christopher Koch? Not
to mention Oodgeroo Noonuccal, Kylie Tennant, Charmian
Clift, Kate Grenville, Tim Winton . . .). I know others
will make up for my lack—but these particular books, in no
particular order, are too precious to me to be forgotten.

The Magic Pudding by Norman Lindsay
Five Bells by Kenneth Slessor
Selected Poems by Judith Wright (a little blue Angus & Robertson
    Australian Poets paperback published in 1963)
The Tree of Man by Patrick White
The Solid Mandala by Patrick White
My Brother Jack by George Johnston
The Chant of Jimmie Blacksmith by Thomas Keneally
Johnno by David Malouf
A Descant for Gossips by Thea Astley
Postcards from Surfers by Helen Garner
Lilian's Story by Kate Grenville
The Shark Net by Robert Drewe

Charlotte Wood is the author of acclaimed novels *Pieces of a Girl*
(1999), *The Submerged Cathedral* (2004) and *The Children* (2007).

27

'WOMAN TO CHILD'

Judith Wright (1915–2000)

Judith Wright published her first book of poems, *The Moving Image*, in 1946 after the Second World War. Encouraged by her mother, she had been writing poetry since she was a small child and had published poems in *Hermes* while at the University of Sydney, and from 1938 in the *National Times*, *Southerly* and the *Bulletin*. After travelling to Europe in 1937, Wright worked briefly in Sydney before being called home by her father when the Pacific War broke out. Her brothers had gone to war and she was needed to help work the large family property near Armidale, on the bleak and rugged New England tablelands of northern New South Wales.

The poems in *The Moving Image* are drawn from Wright's return to New England and her discovery that she was intimately bound to this land: 'As the train panted up the foothills of the Moonbis and the haze of dust and eucalypt vapour dimmed the drought-stricken landscape, I found myself suddenly and sharply aware of it as "my country". These hills and valley were—not mine, but me;

the threat of Japanese invasion hung over them as over me; I felt it under my own ribs. Whatever other blood I held, this was the country I loved and knew.' *The Moving Image* was immediately and widely acclaimed. Douglas Stewart, poetry editor of the *Bulletin*, wrote that Wright's poems 'promise anything; everything; the world'. She was praised as an original and startlingly accomplished poet of the landscape. In her striking, compact poems, land and poet are inextricably fused, as the poem 'For New England' makes clear: 'and the long slopes' concurrence is my flesh / who am the gazer and the land I stare on; / and dogwood blooms within my winter blood, / and orchards fruit in me and need no season.'

Wright's second collection, *Woman to Man* (1949), was written after she had left New England for Brisbane in 1944 and then settled on Tambourine Mountain in the subtropical rainforest seventy kilometres to the south-east. By 1945 Wright had fallen in love with self-taught philosopher and married man Jack McKinney, a fellow contributor to Brisbane's new literary magazine *Meanjin*. McKinney changed Wright's life; as she wrote to him: 'I was never happy till I met you, just as I was never "me" till you made me.' Before McKinney poetry had been Wright's consolation, sustaining her through the trauma of her mother's death when she was eleven and the years that followed at boarding school in Armidale: 'the only thing I had to treasure was poetry and the knowledge that I was going to be a poet'.

The poems in *Woman to Man* come from the depths of Wright's passionate love for McKinney and give voice to her full sensual and procreative being. The title poem, 'Woman to Man', conveys the enormity and awesome exhilaration of the union of woman and man—'the blind head butting at the dark, / the blaze of light along the blade. / Oh hold me, for I am afraid.'—and celebrates its generative potential, the possible child: 'This is our hunter and our chase, / the third who lay in our embrace.' The poem 'Woman to Child', also published in *Woman to Man*, is about the creation of this 'third'.

In this powerful and taboo-breaking (for 1949) poem, Wright extends the sense of all nature blooming and fruiting within her evoked in 'For New England' to her pregnancy of 1949, a more literal blooming of nature within her as her unborn child grows in her womb: 'You who were darkness warmed my flesh / where out of darkness rose the seed. / Then all a world I made in me'. The poem forcefully captures in Wright's lucid, ecstatic images and sure rhythms the mystery of this growth and this unique love: 'There moved the multitudinous stars, / and coloured birds and fishes moved. / There swam the sliding continents. / All time lay rolled in me, and sense, / and love that knew not its beloved.' The closing stanza of 'Woman to Child' expresses precisely and emphatically the rootedness of a woman's procreative self in all of nature and her role as creative intermediary between being and non-being: 'I wither and you break from me; / yet though you dance in living light, / I am the earth, I am the root, / I am the stem that fed the fruit, / the link that joins you to the night.'

When Wright sent the poems of *Woman to Man* to *Meanjin*'s Clem Christesen (who had published *The Moving Image*), she wrote: 'I had better warn you, however, if you think of taking this lot on, that it will almost certainly not be as "popular" as *The Moving Image*'. He did not take them on. *Woman to Man* was published in 1949 by Angus & Robertson. Wright had been right—her frank treatment of sex and pregnancy in the opening poems of *Woman to Man* was shocking to many in conservative post-war Australia, and the critical praise and popular success of her first book did not immediately follow with her second. As WN Scott wrote in 1967 of the critical reservation about *Woman to Man*: 'These poems seem to have embarrassed many or most male readers . . . There was a facet of life which no male could experience.'

Woman to Man is above all else concerned with love, as its epigraph from British philosopher Francis Bacon (1561–1626) makes plain: 'Love was the most ancient of all the gods, and existed before everything else, except Chaos, which is held coeval therewith.' For Wright the very impulse to make a poem was 'a form of love'—and after McKinney's death in 1966 and Wright's extended mourning, her poetic impulse began slowly to wane. Although she continued to write and publish poetry—her last volume *Phantom Dwelling* was published in 1985—in the 1970s Wright turned her energies more and more to public issues, especially those concerning the environment, like her protest against drilling for oil on the Great Barrier Reef, and the rights of Aboriginal Australians, whose severance from the land she felt acutely. As she wrote in her poem 'Two Dreamtimes' to her friend, Aboriginal poet Oodgeroo Noonuccal: 'If we are sisters, it's in this— / our grief for a lost country, / the place we dreamed in long ago, / poisoned now and crumbling.' When Wright moved to Braidwood near Canberra in 1976, she joined with Nugget Coombs and others to establish the Aboriginal Treaty Committee. Wright's last public appearance before her death in 2000 was at a march for Aboriginal reconciliation in Canberra.

Veronica Brady, Wright's biographer, summed up her poetic achievement with the following comments: 'I think that Judith Wright's poetry speaks a sense of sacredness in the land, the sacredness of simple things like animals and plants, and the violation of that sacredness. She has a feeling not only for the land but also for the Aboriginal people.' In 1992 Wright became the first Australian to win the Queen's Medal for Poetry.

28

TIRRA LIRRA BY THE RIVER

Jessica Anderson (1916–)

In 1978 the little-known author Jessica Anderson won the Miles Franklin Award with her fourth novel, *Tirra Lirra by the River*. Her three previous novels had all been published in England between 1963 and 1975, and by 1978 they had gone out of print. *Tirra Lirra by the River* was Anderson's first book to be published in Australia and it rushed her into the literary limelight, selling over 100,000 copies. It is a measured and beautifully cadenced novel. Its intimate, haunting story is told in the first person by Nora Porteous, who returns to her family home in Brisbane for the first time in almost forty years. All her immediate family are dead— her father died when she was six, her brother in the trenches of France, her mother during the Second World War, and her older sister more recently. Alone in the large house and confined to bed with pneumonia, Nora's past comes trickling back to her, urged by familiar views and rooms, people whose names she remembers vaguely from many years before—including her doctor, whose mother had been a fellow misfit and lone walker when they were girls—and by the dreams that come with her fevered sleep. *Tirra Lirra by the River* ripples with memories and past recalled, and is as intense and compact as a poem.

The title—*Tirra Lirra by the River*—comes from 'The Lady of Shalott', one of the most popular poems of the nineteenth-century poet Alfred Tennyson (1809–1892). In his poem the Lady of Shalott is confined to a tower on an island in a river that flows to Camelot. She is cursed to sit alone watching in a mirror the bustling world of Camelot below and to record its reflection in the tapestry she works at. But one day her mirror shows her the dark-haired Sir Lancelot riding by—'"Tirra lirra," by the river / Sang Sir Lancelot.' The Lady of Shalott rushes to the window and looks down into the world, as she is forbidden to do. The curse is triggered; her life is done. She descends to the river where she finds a boat. After writing 'The Lady of Shalott' on its prow, she lies down in the boat and floats toward Camelot singing. She dies with the unfinished song on her lips.

The Lady of Shalott's sorrowful story reverberates through Anderson's novel. Like the Lady of Shalott, Nora has spent much of her life waiting, confined to houses or places that restrict her, places she feels she does not belong to, including her family home, the city of Brisbane, her husband's house, Australia itself. Her life has been a series of confinements and breakings away. Like the Lady of Shalott, Nora has long ago buried her sexual passion, and like her she uses an acceptably modest, female creative form—embroidery, like the Lady of Shalott's tapestry—to release in small gestures her thwarted creative gifts. For perhaps the greatest sorrow of Nora's story is that she is an artist born into a place—a conservative, conformist family in pre-Second World War Brisbane—with no idea that such exotic creatures as artists could exist in its midst; and so Nora cannot recognise herself for what she is. She feels instead only her acute difference.

In response to the harsh physical schoolgirl world around her in subtropical Brisbane, of sweaty tennis games and the fumbling groping of boys, Nora retreats to her window where she gazes out on the world through 'cheap thick glass', whose distortions 'gave me my first intimations of a country as beautiful as those in my childhood books'. She then drifts further away, into her inner dream world: 'And later, when I was mad about poetry, and I read *The Idylls of the King* and *The Lady of Shalott*, and so on and so forth, I already had my Camelot. I no longer looked through the glass. I no longer needed to. In fact, to do so would have broken rather than sustained the spell, because that landscape had become a region of my mind, where an infinite expansion was possible . . .'

Through a series of improvised, almost accidental decisions, Nora leaves Brisbane for Sydney, then Sydney for London. But we see her life in retrospect, pieced together with wit, irony and relentless probing, by Nora in her seventies as she lies in her sickbed. Her sharp perspective is apparent in the following episode: after evoking a moonlit scene in a paddock, where the teenage Nora has stripped open her bodice to lie on the earth, the present-day Nora remarks: 'in these times, when sexuality is so very fashionable, it is easy to believe that it underlies all our actions. But really, though I am quite aware of the sexual nature of the incident, I don't believe I was looking for a lover. Or not only for a lover. I believe I was also trying to match that region of my mind, Camelot.'

Anderson was born the youngest of four children in Gayndah, a farming town north-west of Brisbane, but her family moved to Brisbane in the early 1920s and she grew up near the Brisbane River. Her father worked for the Government Department of Agriculture and Stock, and died when she was sixteen. When Anderson finished school she went to the Brisbane Technical

College Art School, but she left to move to Sydney in 1935. She married young and had a daughter (who would later write the screenplay of Jane Campion's award-winning film *An Angel at My Table* (1990)). In Sydney Anderson found work as a writer, of racy short stories under a pseudonym, and then radio plays and radio adaptations of Charles Dickens, Henry James and Martin Boyd. She wrote her first original radio play in 1968 and many of her novels, including *Tirra Lirra by the River*, began as radio plays.

Anderson had always intended to write a novel, but she did not publish her first novel until she was in her mid-forties—*An Ordinary Lunacy* (1963), which was published in England because Anderson did not think she would be able to find an Australian publisher in the 1960s who would like her novel about 'how a utilitarian society treats those with unserviceable gifts'. Anderson has been a passionate reader all her life (the writer she most admires is English novelist Henry Green, for his 'poetic brevity') but it was not until she read *For Love Alone*, Christina Stead's novel based on her Sydney childhood and flight to London, that she realised 'there was an Australian background I could use: the urban background of *For Love Alone*.' Two more books followed, the psychological thriller *The Last Man's Head* (1970) and the historical novel *The Commandant* (1975), before Anderson found wide success with *Tirra Lirra by the River*.

By 1994 Anderson had published seven novels, including *The Impersonators* (1980), which also won the Miles Franklin Award, and a collection of short stories. Her lucid, compact prose and subtle, probing stories have been compared to the Canadian writer Alice Munro's short stories. In her study of Anderson, Elaine Barry astutely compares her to Jean Rhys when she says of *Tirra Lirra by the River*: 'It is a classic of its genre, making one think of Jean Rhys or Tillie Olsen, other clear-eyed recorders of emotional waste and modest affirmations.'

DELIA FALCONER'S FAVOURITE
AUSTRALIAN BOOKS

My favourites would be:

Riders in the Chariot by Patrick White
Tirra Lirra by the River by Jessica Anderson
The Watcher on the Cast-Iron Balcony by Hal Porter
The Tree of Man by Patrick White
Kenneth Slessor's poetry and prose, 'Five Bells' of course but
    also his journalism about Kings Cross
The Magic Pudding by Norman Lindsay
Grand Days and *Dark Palace* by Frank Moorhouse
The Road to Botany Bay by Paul Carter
The Children's Bach by Helen Garner
Summerland by Malcolm Knox

Delia Falconer is an acclaimed novelist, essayist and critic. She is
the author of novels *The Service of Clouds* (1997) and *The Lost Thoughts
of Soldiers* (2005). In 1998 she was a *Sydney Morning Herald* 'Young
Writer of the Year'.

29

POWER WITHOUT GLORY
Frank Hardy (1917–1994)

Frank Hardy's *Power Without Glory* opens with a telling scene: a young man is standing in a doorway on a bleak winter's afternoon spinning a gold coin. Opposite him is a tall policeman who is closely watching the coin's flight. As the two men—John West and the policeman—exchange words about an illegal totalisator allegedly being run out of West's tea shop, their eyes meet: 'As they did so, John West, as though reading a message in them, suddenly flicked the sovereign at the policeman, who reached quickly and caught the coin in front of his chest.' The policeman walks away, having given John West his first taste of power: he has effortlessly bribed the law. By the end of Hardy's massive novel, West will have similarly beguiled, bullied and bribed politicians, church men, businessmen, media men, his own family and inner circle on his rise to control the power structures of Australian business and politics.

Born into poverty in the fictional inner Melbourne suburb of Carringbush, West and his brothers are out of work. It is 1893, the land boom of the 1880s has long gone, the banks have failed, the economy is in decline—and the Wests have turned to crime. Having determined to 'rise out of the lower depths', when John West is eventually arrested for illegal gambling he enlists the services of a lawyer famed for his cunning and brilliance: David Garside, lawyer to Ned Kelly and a host of land speculators, businessmen, murderers and thieves. It is Garside who inducts West into the more sophisticated forms of power, advising him on how to use paid informers against the police and how to invest his money so others work for him. Most importantly, he explains how parliament works: 'any rich man can exert either direct or indirect influence over parliament, which exists to serve the needs of the rich.' When Australia is celebrating Federation in 1901, West is celebrating it as the year 'he turned to politics as a source of power'. He donates money to sports clubs and charities, he buys up entertainment venues, and soon turns to the Catholic Church and the media as further sources of influence: 'He did not want glory, he wanted power—power without glory'.

Power Without Glory is a brilliant story of one man's rise to dominate a city and a vigorous exposé of the structures of power and corruption in early twentieth-century Australia, the years in which the Australian Labor Party first came into being. Using the form of a history, *Power Without Glory* is told in three parts: 'Road to Power (1890–1907)'; 'Abuse of Power (1915–1931)'; and 'Decline of Power (1935–1950)'. And like a history, *Power Without Glory* was exhaustively researched, not only by Hardy in the streets and criminal underworld of Melbourne, but by a team of researchers backed by the Communist Party of Australia (CPA), which had been influential in Australian politics since the 1930s. Having returned to Melbourne from the Northern Territory at the end of the Second World War, Hardy renewed his relations with the CPA, which he had joined in 1939 after converting to Communism during the Depression.

In 1946 the CPA recruited Hardy, who had worked as a journalist, to write a novel that would expose the corruption of Melbourne gambling millionaire John Wren and his connections to the Australian Labor Party. Inspired by Balzac and possessed by a passionate vision of the political purpose of literature—'I will write under the light of the fundamental historical fact of our time—that the social order of capitalism, having served its historical purpose, is convulsively passing, to be replaced by a higher social order, Socialism'—Hardy began what would be four years of clandestine investigation into John Wren's life and his connections in Melbourne politics, gambling, sport, society and the Catholic Church.

In his author's note to *Power Without Glory* Hardy sets out his (unrealised) plan to write a series of novels on Australian life in the manner of Balzac's *La Comédie Humaine*. He also poses a question that would be asked across Australia—and later in a criminal court—within months of the novel's publication in 1950. The question was: 'Will the characters be real or invented?' Hardy's answer was: 'Characters—that is, people—cannot be invented; they must be based on persons drawn from real life. And I will not shrink from basing characters on rich and powerful persons where it is necessary.' In *Power Without Glory* Hardy used so many thinly disguised real people, including rich and powerful ones, that it became the sport of Melbourne to guess his characters' real identities. Lists were circulated providing the key to the characters: for example, Hardy's eloquent Frank Ashton was based on Labor politician Frank Anstey; Archbishop Malone on Archbishop Mannix; David Garside on criminal lawyer D Gaunson—and John West on John Wren.

Hardy published *Power Without Glory* himself and it was sold through underground channels—in bars, in factories, at political meetings, at Spencer Street Station. But news of the novel spread rapidly to the upper echelons of Melbourne society and within months the thirty-three-year-old author found himself charged with criminal libel by John Wren's wife, for having portrayed 'her' in *Power Without Glory* as an adulterer. The ensuing case became one of the most spectacular in Australia's legal and literary history. Hardy and the Communist Party meant his novel to be a political act, a revolutionary work. They could not have anticipated that it would become one of the biggest news stories in Australia, to be voted in 1999 as the most influential work of fiction published in Australia in the twentieth century. *Power Without Glory* became an international bestseller and catapulted Hardy into the spotlight of Australian literature and politics. He was found not guilty of libel.

The drama of the publication of *Power Without Glory* and trial of its author was heightened by the political manoeuvring being undertaken in the Victorian and Commonwealth parliaments at the time. As Hardy wrote with some disgust in his author's note, Marx's *Historical Materialism* is 'a philosophy that is, as I write, under threat of being "declared" illegal'. He was referring to the Royal Commission into Communism held by the Victorian government in 1949 and the federal government's controversial Communist Party Dissolution Act, which was passed in October 1950 (and overturned on appeal by the High Court in March 1951).

Hardy was born to a large Catholic family in 1917 in Southern Cross, Victoria, and grew up in Bacchus Marsh. He left school at thirteen and moved to Melbourne in 1937, where he married in 1940. During the Second World War Hardy was stationed with the army in the Northern Territory and became involved with his unit's newspaper, which he edited for two years. He returned to Melbourne after the war and wrote his first book, *Power Without Glory*. During his writing life Hardy produced short stories, plays, and nine other books, including *The Hard Way* (1961) about the

Christos Tsiolkas's favourite
Australian books

Okay, let's be brutal. Is there an essential Australian writing, a new world reconfiguration of the English language equivalent to what Mark Twain did with *The Adventures of Huckleberry Finn* or Richard Wright with *Native Son*; or what Gabriel García Márquez and Jorge Luis Borges did with the Spanish language? I don't think there is. This is not cultural cringe. There *is* an essential Australian music, there are essential Australian films. It's a dig at our writers—myself included—for not being able to produce a work of place as imperative as a 'From Her to Eternity' [Nick Cave] or 'Born Sandy Devotional' [The Triffids]; a *Mad Max* or *The Devil's Playground*. I fear the squattocracy got its clutches on Australian lit. early and never really let go. It is all gentility and safeness: Australian literature still—*still ?!?*—suckles from the toxic milk of the Mother Country's spent titties. But it doesn't have to be that way. The following selection, all in different ways, are the voices that most beguiled me, astonished me and excited me as an Australian reader over the last thirty years.

Oh Lucky Country by Rosa R Cappiello
Homesickness by Murray Bail
Conferenceville and *Grand Days* by Frank Moorhouse
Tourmaline by Randolph Stow
Capital Volume One by Anthony Macris
Lilian's Story by Kate Grenville
Jack by Jim McNeil
Mayakovsky in Bondi by Sasha Soldatow
24 Hours: The day the language stood still by π O
The Twyborn Affair by Patrick White
Poems of Life and Death by Jas H Duke

Kangaroo by DH Lawrence
The Children's Bach by Helen Garner

Christos Tsiolkas is the author of the acclaimed novels *Loaded* (1995), *The Jesus Man* (1999) and the award-winning *Dead Europe* (2005). *Loaded* was adapted for the cinema as *Head On* (1998).

30

'NO MORE BOOMERANG'

Oodgeroo Noonuccal (1920–1993)

In 1962 Oodgeroo Noonuccal, then known as Kath Walker, wrote a poem to read in Adelaide at a meeting of the Federal Council for the Advancement of Aborigines and Torres Strait Islanders (FCAATSI), of which she was the Queensland State Secretary. The poem was called 'Aboriginal Charter of Rights', alluding to the 1948 United Nations' Universal Declaration of Human Rights. Its opening lines are a passionate, rhythmic cry for hope, brotherhood and equality. After Oodgeroo had read her rousing forty-four lines of verse, there was silence. Then, as she later recalled, 'every black man and woman was on their feet saying "I want a copy", and I was frightened. "What have I done?" I thought.' She had captured in verse for the first time a vision of equal rights for her people. Oodgeroo continued to write poems and in 1964, through the Realist Writers' Group—associated with the Communist Party of Australia of which she was a member— her first collection was published by the Jacaranda Press. Called *We Are Going* by Kath Walker, its opening poem was 'Aboriginal

Charter of Rights'. *We Are Going* was the first book of verse ever published by an Aboriginal writer. For the first time Aboriginal Australians had a written voice, 'a book they could call their own'. *We Are Going* sold out in three days and by 1965 it had been published in the United States and Canada. In 1966 Oodgeroo won the Dame Mary Gilmore Medal for poetry.

During the 1960s, a period of intense political activism for Oodgeroo, she published two more collections of poetry—*The Dawn is at Hand* in 1966 and *My People: A Kath Walker Collection* in 1970, which included the poems from her previous two collections as well as nine new poems. Oodgeroo had deliberately chosen to voice her vision in poetry because she felt it was a natural extension of the traditional Aboriginal oral culture, of its storytelling and song-making. As she said in 1977: 'You could say a poet is born, but you're not born a poet. You have to work on it . . . I felt poetry would be the breakthrough for the Aboriginal people because they were storytellers and song-makers, and I thought poetry would appeal to them more than anything else. It was more of a book of their voices that I was trying to bring out, and I think I succeeded in doing this.'

Like most of Oodgeroo's poems, 'No More Boomerang' (see page 199) is concerned with her people's loss of culture and land at the hands of white Australia. In thirteen neat verses the poem's regular rhymes and rhythms beat out a litany of these losses, juxtaposing the old ways with the new imposed European economy and culture, supposedly more 'civilised', such as the exchange of boomerangs and spears for coloured bars and beer described in the first stanza. As the poem (with much humour) works through the range of inferior substitutes granted by Western culture, including the 'revolutionary' abstract art of Modernism in place of Aboriginal rock art, it shows that these new ways are not only meaningless and damaging to Aboriginal people, but they are potentially destructive to all humanity, in the form of the atom bomb. With its powerful message, plain speaking and simple rhythms, 'No More Boomerang' is one of Oodgeroo's most popular poems. It has been set to music many times, including by the Northern Territory band Coloured Stone.

Oodgeroo spent the 1960s travelling across Australia, energetically campaigning for Aboriginal rights, speaking at meetings, rallies and to politicians, including Prime Minister Harold Holt, and writing poetry. The massive campaigns of these years led to the 1967 Referendum which allowed the repeal of two sections of the Australian Constitution that discriminated against Aboriginal Australians. The Referendum received an overwhelming 'Yes' vote (90.77% of the vote) and enabled Indigenous Australians to be counted in the census and gave the Commonwealth government power to make laws for them. Oodgeroo continued to be a passionate advocate for her people and her land throughout her life, and became internationally known for her teaching on racism and the environment. In 1969 Oodgeroo travelled to London as the Australian delegate to the World Council of Churches Conference on Racism. She visited China in 1984 with a group that included Manning Clark, and in 1988 she published a collection of poetry, *Kath Walker in China*, with a foreword by Clark. She also travelled to Moscow, at the invitation of Mikhail Gorbachev, for the International Forum for a Nuclear Free World.

Oodgeroo was born of the Noonuccal people in 1920 on Minjerriba, or North Stradbroke Island, east of Brisbane. Her father taught her to be proud of her Aboriginality and her entertaining poem 'Ballad of the Totems' is a tribute to his traditional ways, with its tale of his reverence for a ten-foot carpet snake, his totem, which he insisted live alongside his family, much to his Peewee-clan wife's dismay. Oodgeroo left school in 1933, aged thirteen, and became a domestic worker in Brisbane. During the Second World War she joined the Australian Women's Army Service when it was formed in 1942. The same year she married Bruce Walker and in 1946 their son Denis was born. She later wrote the beautiful poem 'Son of Mine' for Denis, with its famous last verse envisaging black and white living side by side in brotherhood. When her marriage broke up, Oodgeroo returned to domestic work. During the 1950s she worked for the Brisbane doctors Sir Raphael and Lady Cilento, and had a second son, Vivian, who became an artist and later changed his name to Kabul.

Following the campaigns of the 1960s, Oodgeroo returned to live in Minjerriba in 1970. The same year she was made a Member of the Order of the British Empire (MBE) for her services to Aboriginal people. She lived on her land 'Moongalba'—or 'sitting-down place'—and established the Noonuccal-Nughie Education and Cultural Centre as a place of Aboriginal teaching. Over twenty years, she received 30,000 visitors, black and white, most of them children, who would camp, share stories and learn about Aboriginal ways. On Minjerriba Oodgeroo wrote mostly non-fiction and children's books, such as *Father Sky and Mother Earth* (1981) and *Australian Legends and Landscapes* (1990). In 1987, frustrated by the lack of progress on Aboriginal rights, especially land rights, Oodgeroo went to Canberra to return her MBE. And the following year, on the bicentenary of the British settlement of Australia, she gave up her European name, Kath Walker, and took the Aboriginal name Oodgeroo Noonuccal, Custodian of the Minjerriba. As with her writing, poetry and prose, her re-naming was a political act.

In 1989 in the Brisbane Concert Hall, the composer Malcolm Williamson premiered his choral symphony *The Dawn is at Hand*. It was based on a selection of Oodgeroo's poetry, chosen and arranged by Oodgeroo. Having been inspired by her poetry, Williamson had visited Oodgeroo at Moongalba and decided to set her work to symphonic music. Oodgeroo died in 1993.

Note: The estate of Oodgeroo Noonuccal does not permit the quoting of extracts from her poems, so the whole of 'No More Boomerang' is reproduced below.

NO MORE BOOMERANG

No more boomerang
No more spear;
Now all civilized—
Colour bar and beer.

No more corroboree,
Gay dance and din.
Now we got movies,
And pay to go in.

No more sharing
What the hunter brings.
Now we work for money,
Then pay it back for things.

Now we track bosses
To catch a few bob,
Now we go walkabout
On bus to the job.

One time naked,
Who never knew shame;
Now we put clothes on
To hide whatsaname.

No more gunya,
Now bungalow,
Paid by higher purchase
In twenty year or so.

Lay down the stone axe,
Take up the steel,
And work like a nigger
For a white man meal.

No more firesticks
That made the whites scoff.
Now all electric,
And no better off.

Bunyip he finish,
Now got instead
White fella Bunyip,
Call him Red.

Abstract picture now—
What they coming at?
Cripes, in our caves we
Did better than that.

Black hunted wallaby,
White hunt dollar;
White fella witch-doctor
Wear dog-collar.

No more message-stick;
Lubras and lads
Got television now,
Mostly ads.

Lay down the woomera,
Lay down the waddy.
Now we got atom-bomb,
End *every*body.

*Oodgeroo of the
tribe Noonuccal*

ROBERT GRAY'S FAVOURITE
AUSTRALIAN BOOKS

Short Stories by Henry Lawson
Voss by Patrick White
Selected Poems by Kenneth Slessor
Selected Poems by John Shaw Neilson
Maurice Guest by Henry Handel Richardson
Robbery Under Arms by Rolf Boldrewood
Child's Play or *Harland's Half Acre* by David Malouf
Collected Poems by Peter Porter, particularly the book *The Cost of Seriousness*
True Stories or *The Children's Bach* by Helen Garner
New Collected Poems by Les Murray
Things Happen by Philip Hodgins

Robert Gray is a poet and writer. His first book of poems
was *Introspect, Retrospect* (1970); his second, *Creekwater Journal*, was
published in 1973. He has since published eight volumes of
poetry, including *After Images* (2002), which won the *Age* Book of
the Year Award and the Victorian Premier's Prize for Poetry in
2002. Gray received the Patrick White Award in 1990.

31

STORM BOY

Colin Thiele (1920–2006)

First published in 1963, *Storm Boy* is set in the Coorong, South
Australia's region of ocean, estuary and sand, where Storm Boy
lives on 'the long, long snout of sandhill and scrub that curves away
south-eastwards from the Murray Mouth. A wild strip it is, windswept and tussocky, with the flat shallow water of the Coorong on
one side and the endless slam of the Southern Ocean on the other.'
After his mother's death, Storm Boy and his father Hideaway
Tom move to the Coorong from Adelaide. They live in a rough
hut of wood and flattened sheets of iron. Their closest neighbour
is Fingerbone Bill, who lives a mile up the beach and knows the
secrets of the natural world: 'He knew all the signs of wind and
weather in the clouds and the sea. And he could read all the strange
writing on the sandhills and beaches—the scribbly stories made
by beetles and mice and bandicoots and ant-eaters and crabs and
birds' toes and mysterious sliding bellies in the night.'

Storm Boy is named for his love of wild weather and the
windswept beach and ocean—'For he couldn't bear to be inside.

He loved the whip of the wind too much, and the salty sting of the spray on his cheek like a slap across the face, and the endless hiss of the dying ripples at his feet.' He does not go to school. All day he roams the shores and learns from Fingerbone Bill 'enough to fill a hundred books'. Thiele evokes the wild beauty of this landscape and its creatures with vivid intensity. Storm Boy and his idyllic world of beach, ocean, sky and birds are conjured to life, as are his two human companions, Hideaway Tom and Fingerbone Bill. *Storm Boy* is also a heart-breaking story about growing up. In the nearby sanctuary the birds are protected; hunters, trappers and dogs are forbidden. But during open season, hunters—'who call themselves *sportsmen*'—chase wounded ducks up the Coorong lagoon and disturb the birds, trampling their nests, smashing their eggs, using them for target practice. One day Storm Boy finds three baby pelicans, one almost dead, in a ruined nest and takes them home to nurse to health. The ensuing relationship between Storm Boy and one of the pelicans, whom he names Mr Percival, lies at the heart of Thiele's story.

Storm Boy is one of the most enduring Australian children's stories and has been in print ever since it was first published. In 1976 it was adapted for the cinema and the following year the film of *Storm Boy* won Best Children's Film at the Moscow Film Festival, and Jury and Best Film Awards at the Australian Film Institute Awards. David Gulpilil was nominated for Best Actor for his role as Fingerbone Bill. *Storm Boy* was the first feature film of director Henri Safran, who would later direct the miniseries of Albert Facey's *A Fortunate Life*. *Storm Boy* has also been adapted to the stage by the Bell Shakespeare Company, performed in 1996 and 1999 featuring puppets and music.

Made famous by *Storm Boy*, the Coorong is a long shallow lagoon cut off from the Southern Ocean by a peninsula of sand dunes. In 1966 a 50,000-hectare section of this unique region was declared a national park, to conserve the fragile ecology of its coastal dunes, lagoons, wetlands and numerous species of birds, fish and other animals. In 1975 the Coorong was included on the list of 'Wetlands of International Importance, especially as a Waterfowl Habitat' by the International Union for the Conservation of Nature and Natural Resources. Owing to the drying up of the Murray River, the Coorong is now in a critical condition.

Thiele was born in 1920 in a rich wheat, sheep and dairy farming district near Eununda, north of the Barossa Valley in South Australia. His grandfathers had arrived in Port Adelaide from Brandenburg and Hamburg in the 1850s, and German was the family's primary language. Thiele learnt English when he started school, aged four. With his brother and sisters, he helped on the family farm: 'We had absorbed the country through our boot soles, not only in our attitudes and our love of the place but in our rapport with what we called "real" Australians: the shearers, lumpers, carters, fettlers and road workers we liked to watch and talk to whenever we had the chance.' When Thiele finished at the local school, he was sent to live with his two uncles in Eununda to continue his education.

At his new school Thiele discovered Henry Lawson's *While the Billy Boils*, which he called 'a revelation. Here were people—Australian people—I could recognise from real life.' In Eununda he was also introduced to Shakespeare—and to a terrifying range of 'true' ghost stories told round the fire by his uncles. 'It seemed that the entire countryside had once been inhabited by wayward spirits: ghosts, ghoulies, wraiths, apparitions in white, demons with forked tails, invisible spirits and poltergeists, most of whom were victims of murders or purveyors of evil. No matter what denomination of ghost came up for discussion, Uncle Fred had encountered them all.' And when he started high school at

Kapunda and had to spend two hours a day on a train, Thiele read Thomas Hardy, Charles Dickens and Joseph Conrad. His bilingual childhood spent in rolling farm country with ghost stories, Lawson, Shakespeare and other great writers of English, instilled in him a love of the land, a knowledge of its animals and a lifelong passion for words and storytelling.

Aged sixteen, Thiele enrolled in the University of Adelaide in 1936. Two major movements in Australian literature were initiated in Adelaide around this time: the Jindyworobaks and the Angry Penguins. The Jindyworobaks were a group of poets founded by Rex Ingamells in 1938 to create a distinctive Australian art free from European influences which would express the uniqueness of the Australian landscape and experience. For this authentic Australia they drew on Aboriginal traditions, culture, language and legends. At the other end of the spectrum, the Angry Penguins wanted to charge Australian art with European Modernism. Formed by University of Adelaide students and poets Max Harris, Geoffrey Dutton, Sam Kerr and Paul Pfeiffer—under the guidance of poet and Professor of English Charles Rischbieth Jury—the Angry Penguins were inspired by the Surrealists and French Symbolists, by Stéphane Mallarmé, Marcel Proust, Franz Kafka and William Faulkner. The name 'Angry Penguins' was taken from the magazine *Angry Penguins* edited by Max Harris and first published in 1940. The painters Sidney Nolan, Arthur Boyd, Albert Tucker and Joy Hester also became Angry Penguins, influenced by Surrealism and German Expressionism. The Angry Penguins are perhaps most famous today for the Ern Malley hoax perpetrated at their expense by conservative poets James McAuley and Harold Stewart (see box on page 206).

In 1942 Thiele joined the Royal Australian Air Force and served in the Northern Territory and New Guinea. His poem 'Progress to denial', published in 1945 by Jindyworobak, was based on his war-time experience. (Thiele's friend, the poet and Angry Penguin Paul Pfeiffer, and fellow poet and Penguin Sam Kerr, were both killed during the Second World War.)

Thiele married in 1945 and worked as a school teacher before becoming an English lecturer at a teachers' college in 1957. He and his wife had two daughters. His first major book, *Sun on the Stubble*, was published to acclaim in 1961 and was made into a six-part television series in 1996. During the course of Thiele's writing life, hundreds of children wrote to him about his books. One letter told of a librarian's attempt to read *Storm Boy* to her class: when she 'got to page 91 she started to cry and couldn't go on. So she tried again but couldn't get it. In the end she tried five times and on the sixth try she got it.'

For his powerful and emotionally gripping storytelling, and his contribution to education, Thiele was made a Companion of the Order of Australia in 1977. He moved to Queensland for his health in 2000 and died in Brisbane in 2006. During his long life Thiele published over one hundred books, including children's stories, histories, biographies and poetry.

Ern Malley

The traditionalist Sydney poets James McAuley and Harold Stewart were vehemently opposed to the modernism of the Angry Penguins. In order to test if its proponents could distinguish 'a collection of garish images without coherent meaning and structure' from a real Modernist poem, McAuley and Stewart conducted a 'literary experiment'. They invented a poet named Ern Malley and wrote poetry in his name by randomly opening books, choosing words and phrases, and assembling them loosely together. As the fictional Ern had recently died, they invented his sister Ethel Malley, who sent her brother's poetry to *Angry Penguins* editor Max Harris for his literary opinion. Harris gave his seal of approval by publishing sixteen of Malley's poems in the autumn 1944 edition of *Angry Penguins*, with the cover title 'The Darkening Ecliptic' and a cover image by Sidney Nolan.

McAuley and Stewart's ruse was uncovered in June 1944—and Ern Malley and the drama that subsequently unfolded became international news. Twenty-three-year-old Harris was charged for distributing 'indecent advertisements' (Malley's poetry) and had to return to Adelaide from Melbourne to appear in court. The ensuing trial caused a sensation. Harris was forced to explain Malley's poetry line by line to the court, he was attacked by the media and spat at in the street. Harris defended the poetry, arguing that it was no more indecent than

Shakespeare or Chaucer. He was fined five pounds. McAuley later made up with Harris, and acknowledged that Harris owned the copyright in the ghostly Ern Malley's poems.

32

THE LUCKY COUNTRY:

Australia in the Sixties

Donald Horne (1921–2005)

In late December 1963 Donald Horne sat down with a pad of paper and a felt pen and, as he put it, 'began writing a book about Australia'. Horne had spent the 1950s working as a journalist, in London and Sydney, and had travelled through Asia. He had returned to Australia in 1954 to set up a weekly magazine for Frank Packer and had then launched the *Observer*, a fortnightly intellectual periodical, in 1958. Here he had run groundbreaking articles on Australia's place in Asia, on Aboriginal culture, racism and migrant Australia. When the *Observer* was merged with the 'bushman's Bible', the *Bulletin*, after Packer had bought it in 1960, the first thing Horne did was remove the words 'Australia For The White Man' from under the *Bulletin* banner. For this he was attacked vehemently by many of the *Bulletin*'s readers. By 1963, Robert Menzies' long era of conservative prime ministership (first 1939–41, then 1949–66) was drawing to an end. Increasingly frustrated by the unimaginative, derivative, philistine, Anglo-centric leadership of Australia by politicians, businessmen and intellectuals, Horne took up many of the themes of his years at the *Observer* and the *Bulletin* and attempted to capture in a book the new, changing, multifaceted scene of early 1960s Australia.

Horne wrote his book about Australia in three months. It was only after he had sent the manuscript to his publishers, Penguin, that his editor Geoffrey Dutton suggested a title, taken from the first sentence of the book's last chapter: 'Australia is a lucky country run mainly by second-rate people who share its luck. It lives on other people's ideas, and, although its ordinary people are adaptable, most of its leaders (in all fields) so lack curiosity about the events that surround them that they are often taken by surprise . . . A nation more concerned with styles of life than with achievement has managed to achieve what may be the most evenly prosperous society in the world. It has done this in a social climate largely inimical to originality and ambition (except in sport) and in which there is less and less acclamation of hard work. According to the rules Australia has not deserved its good fortune . . . On the face of it Australia has had gamblers' luck.'

This is the essence of Horne's *The Lucky Country*. The early chapters—including 'The Australian Dream' and 'What is an Australian?'—provide impressionistic sketches of suburban life and the broad commonalities and differences of Australians. It is when Horne moves his attention to foreign policy and the nature of business, unions and government in Australia that his book really comes into focus. Horne was keen to demonstrate that Australia's reverence for England under Menzies' leadership was outmoded and irrelevant in the modern world in every respect—historically, strategically, politically, economically and geographically—as was Australia's failure to break from Britain to become a republic. As Horne argues, 'strategically Australia became an Asian power in 1941'; it was America and not Britain that had saved Australia during the Second World War; Australia's nearest neighbours are

New Guinea, New Zealand and Indonesia; the Asia–Pacific was Australia's largest market; and almost half Australia's diplomatic service was deployed in Asia. Horne is careful to stress the multiplicity of 'Asia', to delineate the many different Asian nations. *The Lucky Country* is critical of Menzies, citing his elevation to the British Order of the Thistle as emblematic of his ludicrous regime; of the divided Labor Party's failure to put forward a decent opposition; of business run by the old school tie and club membership; and of academics and education. It also attacked racism and Australia's treatment of Indigenous Australians, and revived the idea of an Australian republic which had languished for fifty years.

Horne writes in a straightforward, lucid manner, making his observations and setting out his views, with few figures and little research. As he said, he was writing a book not of facts but of 'imagination and ideas'. Although Penguin Australia (which had just launched a new Australian imprint) received his manuscript enthusiastically, the head office in England did not think *The Lucky Country* was the sort of book that Australians would want: 'What Australians want is facts,' they said. But it turned out that *The Lucky Country* was exactly what many thousands of Australians wanted. On 1 December 1964 the serialisation of *The Lucky Country* was announced in the *Australian*. When Horne anxiously rang his publisher to ask if any books had been sold yet, he was told: 'Yes—all 18,000 of them—in nine days.'

Although some reviews of *The Lucky Country* were dismissive and one declared 'I have no doubt that Horne's little outburst will have been forgotten by the end of the summer', the book continued to sell and to be talked about long after the end of the summer of '65, and was defended by prominent Australian historian Manning Clark. Over the next twelve months it sold more than 40,000 copies and went on to become one of Australia's bestselling books, selling more than a quarter of a million copies. Its title has entered into the language and it has spawned shelves of books, from Rosa Cappiello's account of migrant experience in 1970s Australia, *Oh Lucky Country*, to Horne's own *The Death of the Lucky Country* and *On How I Came to Write 'The Lucky Country'*.

Horne attributed the success of *The Lucky Country* to timing, seeing it as part of the 'discovery' in the 1960s that 'the old images of Australia no longer worked'. Or, as Geoffrey Dutton's wife, writer Ninette Dutton, said: *The Lucky Country* was 'quite extraordinarily good' at 'putting into words a number of half-formed ideas that people have but that are not generally expressed'.

Donald Horne was born in 1921 in Muswellbrook in the Hunter Valley. His father, a schoolteacher, had a nervous breakdown when Horne was in secondary school and the family moved to Sydney. Horne studied arts at the University of Sydney but did not complete his degree. Instead he served in the army, in Darwin, during the Second World War. He then began his career as a journalist and moved to England in 1949, where he lived in a country village and considered a career as a Conservative Party member of parliament. Horne returned to Australia to launch a new magazine for Frank Packer in 1954, later editing the *Observer* and the *Bulletin* before working briefly in advertising. He returned to the *Bulletin* in 1967 and in 1972 took up an academic position lecturing in politics at the University of New South Wales, giving his first academic paper aged fifty-two, in 1973. Horne became a professor and later the Chancellor of the University of Canberra. He continued to be active in public life and debate, especially in the Australian republican movement, and chaired the Australia Council for six years during the 1980s. Horne wrote more than twenty books, including *Time of Hope*, *Money Made Us*, *The Intelligent Tourist*, *The Next Australia* and a three-volume autobiography. He died in 2005.

Manning Clark and
A History of Australia

In 1962 Manning Clark published *A History of Australia: From the Earliest Times to the Age of Macquarie*, the first volume of his groundbreaking and celebrated six-volume work, *A History of Australia*. Over the next fifteen years he would publish the remaining five volumes: *Vol. II: New South Wales and Van Diemen's Land*; *Vol. III: 1824–1851*; *Vol. IV: 1851–1888*; *Vol. V: 1888–1915* and *Vol. VI: 1916–1935*. *Volume I* was the first major history of Australia from the region's earliest exploration by Hindus, Chinese and Muslims, to the arrival of Christian Europeans (all of them searching for spices, gold and fragrant woods, many also seeking 'souls for the true religion'), to Australia's colonisation by Britain.

Over the six volumes Clark writes an epic tale, after first dismissing Australia's original inhabitants with: 'Of the way of life of these three peoples [the Negritos, the Murrayians and the Carpentarians] before the coming of European civilization, little need, or indeed can, be said.' He brings to his work the scholarship of the historian and the passion, energy and imagination of a great novelist, animating the characters and events that shaped European Australia. For example, when Clark writes in *Volume I* of Governor Hunter's conflict with John Macarthur, he tells history from the point of view of Hunter as if he is a character in one of the great Russian novels Clark so revered: 'All through 1797 he brooded over the paradox of this man Macarthur

who was drawing part of his income from the traffic in spirits, who was a member of the officers' ring and therefore in part responsible for such moral filth as existed in the colony, yet who dared to accuse him of encouraging wickedness.'

Clark said: 'I want to show that a knowledge of the history of Australia can help a person to find the answers to the great problems of life. I want to show how the discovery of Australia, threw light on all the things that had puzzled and bewildered me in life'—including his own complex heritage.

Clark was born in Sydney in 1915. His father was from the London working class and his mother from an old landed Australian family: 'My father was an immigrant, or, if you like to put it in Australian English, he was a "bloody pommy". My mother belonged to a family which had come to Australia in 1794. In my veins there was a conflict between immigrants and native-born . . . Between being an exile at heart and a dinkum Aussie.'

After winning scholarships to Melbourne Grammar and the University of Melbourne, Clark studied at Balliol College, Oxford University, from 1938 to 1940. He taught history at schools in England and Australia before joining the University of Melbourne. In 1946 Clark was asked to establish the first course in Australian history. Three years later he became the first Professor of History at what would later become the Australian National University (ANU) and in 1972 he became the first Professor of Australian History. Clark was made a Companion of the Order of Australia in 1975, in recognition of *A History of Australia*. He died in 1991. Among other things, Clark's wife Dymphna Clark lectured in German at the ANU and worked with Nugget Coombs and Judith Wright on the Aboriginal Treaty Committee.

Clark's *A History of Australia* has been acclaimed as one of the twentieth-century's great works of historical writing. It has also been criticised for inaccuracies and bias, and its controversial author has continued to stir debate long after his death, most recently in March 2007 when it was reported that his famous story of having witnessed the horror of the aftermath of Kristallnacht in Bonn in November 1938 was a fabrication. Clark was nevertheless a man of numerous talents, all of which he brought to bear on his work, as Geoffrey Blainey made clear when he spoke of Clark as 'a novelist, a painter, a theologian and prophet, and from these callings he brings some of the qualities of imagination, the sense of wonder, and the will to create order from chaos, which is as vital to the historian as those other more common and essential skills.' And as the author of the abridged version of *A History of Australia*, Michael Cathcart, said in 2003: 'There's little argument that Manning Clark gave many white Australians the sense that they had a genuinely rich history of their own, one that wasn't British or Colonial in its orientation.'

In 1988 *A History of Australia* was made into a musical as part of the bicentenary of British colonisation of Australia. *A History of Australia: The Musical* premiered in Melbourne on 16 January 1988, directed by John Bell. The script was written by Don Watson, Tim Robertson and John Romeril; the music by Martin Armiger, George Dreyfus and David King. The musical was not a success and just completed its six-week season.

Nicholas Jose's favourite Australian books

Settlers and Convicts by Alexander Harris
The Middle Parts of Fortune: Somme and Ancre 1916 by Frederic Manning
Tomorrow and Tomorrow and Tomorrow by M Barnard Eldershaw
Poems by John Shaw Neilson
The Far Road by George Johnston
The Cry for the Dead by Judith Wright
Visitants by Randolph Stow
Harland's Half Acre by David Malouf
Alone by Beverley Farmer
Ian Fairweather by Murray Bail

Nicholas Jose is the author of seven novels, including *Original Face* (2005), *The Red Thread* (2000) and *The Rose Crossing* (1994), short stories, essays and the memoir *Black Sheep: Journey to Borroloola* (2002). He holds the chair of Creative Writing at the University of Adelaide and is General Editor of the Macquarie PEN Anthology of Australian Literature.

33

MILK AND HONEY
Elizabeth Jolley (1923–2007)

Elizabeth Jolley's fifth novel, *Milk and Honey*, opens with a brief, fable-like prologue that tells of a wind blowing through Europe, which sweeps all the debris and dirt, 'the horse manure, the brickdust and the thistledown', up into the sky and transports it into another hemisphere where it sinks to earth. The novel is concerned with this European debris, with exiles in Australia. *Milk and Honey* seems set to tell the small-town story of a sales-man, Jacob, who aches with exhaustion, loneliness and failure. His opening lines evoke the ordinary: 'This was the street where Madge, suddenly worried that she had forgotten her tampax, drove slowly, unconcernedly, taking up the whole road while she fumbled mysteriously to find out.' But there is mystery here. Jacob's thoughts soon plunge backwards, to his childhood: 'As on other Sundays I stopped looking at my immediate surround-ings and looked back, I turned my thoughts back to the old house. Anyone passing that house could never, at the time when I was living there, have known or understood anything of what was happening there.' Jacob's story is about this house, and the people who live there. And it is about his discovery of music and Madge—and his loss of both.

The novel's title and one of its two epigraphs announce its preoccupation with exile. They are God's words, from Exodus, spoken from the burning bush to Moses: '. . . and to bring them up out of that land unto a good land and a large, unto a land flowing with milk and honey'. God tells Moses he will deliver the Israelites out of Egypt and lead them to the promised land of milk and honey. What he does not say is that they will endure forty years in the wilderness, where their faith will be tested. Jolley's haunting novel plays on all the notes of promise, exile, testing and plenty (milk and honey) that her title evokes, with its story not of Israelites but of a Viennese family, the Heimbachs, who have fled Europe during Hitler's regime and found themselves in Western Australia.

The Heimbachs are sealed off from the new world around them. They have transplanted their world of Mozart and Beethoven, high-buttoned collars, long skirts and quaint ways into the Australian wilderness, resisting change. As Eloise Heimbach says: 'It is not easy with one's needs and refinements to adapt to a new country. It was all so strange, language, customs, climate everything.' But change comes. The biblical imagery is extended when this exiled family takes in another exile, Jacob, from his home among the vines of his father's land. Jacob's father sends him to the Heimbachs to receive an education and to learn the cello, for which he is said to have a gift, and like the biblical Jacob who usurps the birthright of his older brother Esau to become God's chosen one, so Jacob becomes the chosen one in the Heimbach household. And yet he feels their reverence as a bind: 'I felt tied into the house, joined to the people by invisible cords. It was by their acts of kindness they imprisoned me.'

Jacob's introduction to the Heimbachs—father Leopold, his sisters Eloise and Tante Rosa, his beautiful dark-haired daughter Louise, and large imbecilic son Waldemar—is like a process of enchantment. Their ornate, shadowed house with its hidden boxes, packed-away treasures, church incantations, melancholy German music and secrets is like a house from Nathaniel Hawthorne's New England: dark, brooding and gothic—'The house was old, standing among other old houses. The sun was already behind the gabled roof and the front of the house was in shadow, screened from the road by Moreton Bay fig trees.' But the Heimbach house is situated in post-war Australia and it cannot contain Jacob in its European thrall for long. Jacob is seduced by the world beyond, by its plenty and its flesh. He becomes a go-between, a man torn between the pale and exotic Louise Heimbach and Madge's voluminous body and exuberant chat.

In his review of *Milk and Honey* in the *New York Times*, Peter Ackroyd compared Jolley to another writer of the American gothic: 'If Elizabeth Jolley was once close to Barbara Pym, on this occasion she is even closer to Edgar Allan Poe.' And yet from this bizarre, surreal and menacing world, Jolley miraculously manages to extract some continuity and life.

First published in 1984, *Milk and Honey* is a macabre fairytale, with its strange jarring of the myths and stories of Europe in an Australian context and its exploration of the many ambiguities of love, as foretold by the lines from William Blake's *Songs of Experience* which make up the novel's other epigraph. *Milk and Honey* is a remarkable achievement, as Peter Ackroyd implies: 'This is the first time that she has abandoned the omniscient third-person narrative, so valuable as a protective lace curtain, and has chosen instead to employ the resources of monologue; and it is as if the fall into the consciousness of another person has broken open her style, rendering it more haunting and ultimately more profound.'

Elizabeth Jolley was born in Birmingham in 1923, into a strict Quaker household. Her mother was Viennese and Jolley described her childhood home as 'half English and three quarters Viennese'. During the 1930s her parents took in refugees from Europe, which gave the young Jolley a vivid early experience of flight and exile: 'Looking back at a lifetime's writing, I have been pre-occupied with the territorial needs of people, migration and the refugee experience, the sense of exile.' After years of home schooling with governesses, Jolley was sent to a Quaker boarding school in 1934. She left school in 1940 and trained as a nurse. She met Leonard Jolley, a college librarian, in a hospital during the war and in 1950 she had her first child with him. They were later married and had two more children. In 1959 Leonard was offered the position of head librarian at the University of Western Australia and the Jolleys moved to Perth.

While caring for her family, Jolley worked as a door-to-door saleswoman, a cleaner and a nurse. Although she had been writing most of her life, it was only in 1965 that her first story, 'The Talking Bricks', was published. Jolley started teaching creative writing at the Fremantle Arts Centre in 1974 and two years later the Fremantle Arts Centre Press published her first book, *Five Acre Virgin and Other Stories* (1976). In 1978 Jolley took a position teaching creative writing at what would later become Curtin University, where her students included Tim Winton and Deborah Robertson, and where she became an Emeritus Professor in the School of Communication and Cultural Studies. Jolley became a prolific writer, publishing thirteen books from 1976 to 1986, many of which won awards, including *Milk and Honey* and *The Well*, which won the Miles Franklin Award in 1986 and was adapted for the screen by director Samantha Lang. *The Well* screened at the Cannes Film Festival in 1997. In 1988

Jolley became an Officer of the Order of Australia (OA). She died in 2007.

Milk and Honey won the New South Wales Premier's Award for fiction in 1984. It was adapted for the theatre by playwright Ingle Knight and premiered at the Perth Theatre Company in 1998. The play later won the 1998 Western Australian Premier's Screenwest Script Award for best script.

Jolley once wrote that many of her passages 'spring from the feelings of being uncherished and excluded. They spring too from the cruelties in human life. Bitter knowledge, grief and unwanted realisation, often in greater proportion, go side by side with acceptance, love and hope.' Her words perfectly capture the breadth of her achievement in *Milk and Honey*.

EMILY MAGUIRE'S FAVOURITE
AUSTRALIAN BOOKS

The Acolyte by Thea Astley
The Long Prospect by Elizabeth Harrower
Candy by Luke Davies
Coonardoo by Katharine Susannah Prichard
Lilian's Story by Kate Grenville
Loaded by Christos Tsiolkas
Praise by Andrew McGahan
My Brilliant Career by Miles Franklin
Akhenaten by Dorothy Porter
Patrick White: A Life by David Marr

Emily Maguire is a novelist, journalist and essayist. She is the author of *Taming the Beast* (2004) and *The Gospel According to Luke* (2007).

34

THE ACOLYTE
Thea Astley (1925–2004)

'Writing is incredibly hard work and I'm naturally lazy,' wrote Thea Astley in *Southerly* magazine in 1970. 'Perhaps that's why, if given a choice of talents, I would plump for a musical one, an ability to play jazz piano.' Astley's passion for music and her inability to master the piano left her with 'the deepest adulating envy of performers like Richter and Vince Guaraldi'. Two years after writing this, in 1972 Astley published *The Acolyte*, her novel about musical genius and its shadow side, adulation, and the devastating side effects of their inextricable bond. Jack Holberg is the musical genius, a virtuoso pianist and avant-garde composer, and Paul Vesper is the adulator, a self-confessed 'bum' without talent who is inexorably drawn to the magnetic pull of Holberg's accomplishment. It is Vesper who narrates the story—he is the acolyte of the title.

Vesper is a jaded, self-deprecating, satirical narrator, who relentlessly pursues the reader with his story told in great jazzy bursts of high colour like some bar room yarn. And colour is one of the novel's recurring motifs—because the rampant colour of subtropical Queensland with its sweeps of beach and ocean and vivid bird and plant life, and the pale blonde beauty of Holberg's lovers Ilse and Hilda, cannot be seen by Holberg. When Vesper wonders why the pianist does not take off his dark glasses, he discovers that Holberg is blind.

Set in the Gold Coast hinterland of southern Queensland from the 1930s to the 1960s, *The Acolyte* examines the effects of genius on those who come under its sway. As Vesper says, addressing the reader in his truculent way: 'Don't, listen, don't for one eyeball-searing second imagine this is going to be an analysis of the artist in *angst*. We're the ones—Bonnie, Faith, Vesper, Ilse, Hilda—who are the interesting cases, the fringe-dwellers in the suburbs of the great man's genius—any great man.'

As a boarding-school boy, Vesper is too middle-class comfortable to belong with the 'sub-male vitalism' he is attracted to: 'Since I didn't altogether fit in with the beady-eyed milk-bar boys, I was soaked in a kind of envy, fighting every inch of the cussing way for recognition'. And this becomes the pattern of his life. He is an outsider, lonely and quietly desperate, who drifts along, first directed by his 'rotary dad and CWA mum', then by women and then by Jack Holberg. Vesper first meets Holberg at an engagement party in Grogbusters, 'a border town of rangy street sprawl in the southern part of the State'. Loving music and finding no talent in himself, Vesper spends the whole evening by the piano, watching Holberg's hands 'turn melody inside out'.

Packed off to university to study engineering by his parents on the outbreak of war, Vesper instead immerses himself in music—and it is through music that he has his one moment of illumination. Towards the end of his dull engineering degree, he finds himself weeping while listening to the music of twentieth-century Swedish composer Dag Wiren: 'I asked myself why here?

Why doing this? . . . Not the birth of musicianship in novelettish manner. Birth of bum, if you like, no-hoper, bludger, drop-out, failure, slap in the face to parental care . . .' From that moment Vesper is lost to the world of achievement and career and heads aimlessly towards his sacrifice at the altar of music and Jack Holberg. After several half-hearted attempts to make his own life, Vesper abandons himself to Holberg, who has become an internationally acclaimed composer, writing 'beer-stein' quartets and Gold Coast symphonies while continuing to address everyone as 'matey'. Vesper becomes Holberg's eyes. 'Sometimes I have thought in azurous moments of divination that perhaps I am Holberg's other self, his seeing self'.

For Holberg in his blindness and need for musical inspiration requires Vesper as much as Vesper needs him—and Astley brilliantly portrays the psychology of their mutual dependence. The nature of Holberg's need for Vesper is evoked in the novel's epigraph, taken from Harry Graham's *Ruthless Rhymes*: '"There's been an accident!" they said, / "Your servant's cut in half; he's dead!" / "Indeed!" said Mr. Jones, "and please / Send me the half that's got my keys."' Like *The Vivisector*, Patrick White's 1970 portrait of a painter, *The Acolyte* is a study of the irresistible allure of the parasitic, monster artist, except that Astley's novel is told from the point of view not of the artist but of the one who is allured: '"There's something toxically attractive about the lineaments of talent," I insisted. "No one wants to be drawn in, but is."'

Thea Astley was born in Brisbane in 1925, and Queensland's steamy subtropics, beer-town humour and enervated emotional landscape became her inspiration. After spending twelve years at a convent school, Astley went to the University of Queensland to study arts. When she was eighteen, the editor and writer Clem Christesen of *Meanjin* (one of her journalist father's colleagues) introduced Astley to a group of young writers in Brisbane: 'It was then that I gave up struggling with the twenty-fourth Chopin prelude . . . and out of the emotional wallow of listening, I levered myself with phrases that tried to describe what I felt and heard.' She began to write short stories and later novels. When Astley graduated from university in 1947 she became a teacher, in the small Queensland towns that would appear in her fiction, and later in New South Wales. She was interested in life on the margins—'The outsider interests me enormously—not self-conscious phoney arty outsiders, but bums and old ladies and people who are lonely, seedy and unsuccessful'—and she was particularly drawn to the tall-tale eccentricities of northern Queensland: 'You do hear remarkable stories up there. And I think one reason is because people are so far away from the centre of government, they can act out their own peculiarities.'

In 1948 Astley married Jack Gregson, with whom she had a son, and moved to Sydney. Her first novel, *Girl with a Monkey*, was published in 1958. In 1962 her third novel, *The Well Dressed Explorer*, won the Miles Franklin Award. It would be the first of four Miles Franklin Awards for Astley's novels: *The Slow Natives* won in 1965; *The Acolyte* in 1972; and in 2000 she won her fourth Miles Franklin Award with *Drylands*. In 1968 Astley became a senior tutor at Sydney's Macquarie University and was appointed a Fellow in Literature and Creative Writing in 1978. She retired from the university in 1980 and moved to Cairns in far north Queensland. Astley and her husband later returned to New South Wales where they lived on the south coast near Nowra. In 1989 Astley received the Patrick White Award for her services to Australian literature. After declaring in 1994 that *Coda* would be her last novel, Astley was awarded an Australian Artists Creative Fellowship for literature by Paul Keating, with which she wrote two more novels: *The Multiple Effects of Rainshadow* (1996) and

MARIAN MACGOWAN'S FAVOURITE AUSTRALIAN BOOKS

The Acolyte by Thea Astley
The Man Who Loved Children by Christina Stead
The Eye of the Storm by Patrick White
Lilian's Story by Kate Grenville
An Imaginary Life by David Malouf

Marian Macgowan is a film producer whose films include the acclaimed *Lilian's Story* (1995), *Two Hands* (1999) starring Heath Ledger and Bryan Brown, and the forthcoming film about Harry Houdini, *Death Defying Acts*, starring Guy Pearce and Catherine Zeta-Jones.

35

THE GLASS CANOE

David Ireland (1927–)

First published in 1976, David Ireland's comic masterpiece *The Glass Canoe* is a story of Australian pub life told in Ireland's characteristic fragmented style and evocative, luminous vernacular. The glass canoe of the title is that sacred vessel of Australian pub culture, the beer glass: 'On hot days we jumped fully clothed into our bottomless beer glasses and pushed off from shore without a backward look. Heading for the deep, where it was calm and cool.' The brief chapters, each with its own distinctive, telling title—'The Silver Dew', 'The Great Lover', 'Forty-three Minutes And Blood'—are recounted by the nature-loving golf-course keeper Meat Man, so named for the magnitude of his endowment in 'the meat department'. Meat Man is writing the story of his local suburban Sydney pub, the Southern Cross, and all its seedy seamy life: 'These things in the past few pages are general things I put down first when I got the idea of making a book about the Southern Cross and our life here. I think now I'll tell you about some of the people of our tribe.'

Meat Man's story is a pub dreaming. He uses the language of Aboriginal tribal behaviour for his own beer-drinking tribe: 'While your tribe's waterhole flowed, you never went walkabout to another tribe's waterhole.' Initiation into manhood in Meat Man's tribe comes not when you turn eighteen, but when you can pass for eighteen and buy the beers. Beer is their golden god: 'we swallowed him. To give him power over us, that was why. No voice of his own, he was compelled to speak through us.' And the Southern Cross tribe does not have a leader, just men of influence: 'As in the aboriginal tribes we'd pushed out, there was no chief in our tribe. Just a fairly loose system of elders, who laid down laws and dispensed wisdom from the shoulder.' The pub locals range from Alky Jack, who is the resident wise man and like a father to Meat Man, to the Great Lover ('Sex dozed from every pore') and tough boys Mick, the King and Serge. And then there are the occasional blow-ins like Ernie, who takes up the sport of each new boss in the hope of promotion. His latest boss is a weekend fisherman, so Ernie struggles determinedly to catch a fish. When his great catch turns out to be only a stingray, he thinks: 'Never mind that, it lived in the water and he'd caught it. It was a fish.'

The Glass Canoe is a funny, poignant novel. Like *Such is Life*, Tom Collins's turn-of-the-century bush novel, *The Glass Canoe* is a series of yarns about the adventures of a distinct group of drifting Australians, mostly men—beer drinkers rather than bullockies—in their natural habitat. Tom Collins's itinerant bush culture has entered the city. And like Collins, Meat Man is often unable or unwilling to connect and interpret the events around him, and engages in philosophical speculation with Alky Jack, who is given to pronouncements like: 'The Australian just wants to be left alone, he doesn't want to hear nasty things or be bothered by politics, he's not ambitious, he doesn't want too much fun. Look at the bar.' Only Meat Man listens to Jack. The others care more about the races, footy or the latest murder.

Meat Man names his share-house on the hill 'Fortress Australia'. The world of the Southern Cross simmers with violence and the men need it as they need their beer; they itch for an outbreak, it is part of their ritual communion and it provides them with their sense of identity: 'Maybe if we didn't push each other away with fists we might get so close we'd end up being a warm jelly mass, no guy able to tell where he ended and others began.' There is sex but few women in this world, apart from the barmaid Sharon, who fills the beer glasses that wait 'on the nearer shore of this day's Styx', like the boatman Charon from classical Greek mythology who ferries the souls of the dead across the River Styx to Hades' realm. And beyond the pub is 'My Darling', Meat Man's radiant, exuberant girlfriend: 'And people looked at her because of the light shining out of her.' Meat Man finds beauty on the dewy golf greens ('Grass-spider cobwebs were weighted down in the middle with diamonds'), in beer, in a football tackle, in his Darling. As well as drawing on the language of Aboriginal culture, *The Glass Canoe* evokes the bucolic myths of the ancient world and of early bush Australia.

Although the narrative is told in small anecdotes, the pieces build into a story about a group of people whose idiosyncratic lifestyle is threatened because it does not fit in with the dominant culture. Ireland brilliantly plays on this idea by introducing the character Sibley, who went to school with Meat Man but has gone on to university and is now taking a PhD in psychology. Sibley has returned to study the behaviour of this endangered subculture, the drinkers, for his PhD: 'That's my aim, the aim of the thesis. To investigate means of assimilating the drinker into the main body of society.' Sibley classifies, analyses, probes and interrogates the drinkers at the Southern Cross, taking notes and sipping his beer so slowly it goes warm: 'My effect will be to take you away from gambling, from wasted time, wasted lives, from poverty, to constructive pursuits, educational interests, work that is for the benefit of all'. But although Meat Man's tribe and their way of life appear to be vanishing, in the novel's closing pages they are firmly and wildly reasserted.

Ireland was born on a kitchen table in Lakemba, Sydney, in 1927. His father was an insurance salesman during the Depression and later became an invalid, having been gassed during the First World War. Ireland was then forced to leave high school after only three years to go out to work, an experience which determined him to become a writer: 'I thought: Now what can you do, where your experience, you yourself, not your formal education, makes the difference? The answer was writing.' After first writing for the theatre, Ireland turned to novels, publishing ten from 1968 to 1997. Ireland married in 1955, living with his wife in Winston Hills, north-west Sydney. They had four children. For most of the 1960s Ireland did shift work at the Shell oil refinery in southern Sydney, and he wrote his first novel, *The Chantic Bird* (1968), during this time. His work at the refinery shaped his second novel, *The Unknown Industrial Prisoner* (1971), which won the Miles Franklin Award.

In 1973 Ireland took up writing full-time and moved from his family home to Elizabeth Street, in the centre of Sydney (he was divorced in 1976). He finished the first draft of *The Glass Canoe* in 1974. On the advice of critic and editor Douglas Stewart, Ireland substantially reworked and cut the manuscript and the novel was published in 1976. (Ireland used many of the deleted chapters from *The Glass Canoe* as the basis of his 1981 novel *City of Women*, changing the male characters to women.) *The Glass Canoe* won the Miles Franklin Award in 1976 and was later barred from use in schools because of its explicit sex scenes. Douglas Stewart wrote of *The Glass Canoe*: 'In a flash of inspired vision

David Ireland has perceived that the real centre of Australian life, and the last shaky refuge from industrialism is the pub . . . which the novelist demonstrates and enlarges upon with great verve and menace and macabre humour.'

Ireland won his third Miles Franklin Award in 1979 with *A Woman of the Future*. He was awarded the Order of Australia in 1981 and the Gold Medal of the Australian Literature Society in 1985. His most recent novel is *The Chosen*, published in 1997. Ireland has been influenced by two masters of fragmented, disrupted fiction: the Brazilian novelist Joaquim Maria Machado de Assis (1839–1908), regarded as Brazil's greatest novelist and called 'the greatest author ever produced in Latin America' by Susan Sontag; and Laurence Sterne (1713–1768), whose *The Life and Opinions of Tristram Shandy, Gentleman* also influenced Machado.

Ireland has been an elusive figure on the Australian literary scene. After interviewing him in 1991, literary critic Rosemary Sorensen wrote: 'he has a quiet tentativeness about him, as though he wants to be left alone to move through the world observing but not participating', adding 'I do like to think that there's something a bit wizard-like about David Ireland.'

Caroline Baum's favourite Australian books

These are the books that helped me make sense of where I had come to.

Tracks by Robyn Davidson
Lucinda Brayford by Martin Boyd
Voss by Patrick White
Cloudstreet by Tim Winton
My Brother Jack by George Johnston
The Fatal Shore by Robert Hughes
True History of the Kelly Gang by Peter Carey
My Brilliant Career by Miles Franklin
The Savage Crows by Robert Drewe
Tirra Lirra by the River by Jessica Anderson

(And my supplementary books might be *Dancing on Coral* by Glenda Adams or Murray Bail's *Eucalyptus*. It is very hard to leave out Helen Garner in general and Kate Grenville's *The Secret River*.)

Caroline Baum moved to Australia from the United Kingdom in 1984. She was the founding editor of *Good Reading* magazine and the presenter of the ABC's *Between the Lines* and Foxtel's *Talking Books*. She is now a writer and documentary producer.

36

THE TYRANNY OF DISTANCE:

How Distance Shaped Australia's History

Geoffrey Blainey (1930–)

In 1966 historian Geoffrey Blainey published a book whose title
would resonate into the twenty-first century—*The Tyranny of
Distance*. It would encapsulate like no four words before it the
challenges inherent in Australian civilisation, especially after
1788, when a fragment of Britain was planted on soil half a world
away. The idea that distance influences the Australian experience
was hardly original, as Blainey makes clear. It is, after all, a feature of its geography: 'Distance is as characteristic of Australia as
mountains are of Switzerland. By sealanes or airlanes most parts
of Australia are at least 12,000 miles from western Europe, the
source of most of their people, equipment, institutions and ideas.
The coastline of Australia also stretches for 12,000 miles . . . The
distance of one part of the Australian coast from another, or
the distance of the dry interior from the coast, was a problem as
obstinate as Australia's isolation from Europe.'

But what was to make Blainey's book a landmark work, one
of the most influential in the study of Australian history, was

his use of distance as a tool for analysing Australian history: 'Australians have always recognized that distance or isolation was one of the moulds which shaped their history, but it is fair to suggest the factor of distance has been surprisingly unsuccessful as an explanation of important Australian events or situations or characteristics.' In *The Tyranny of Distance* Blainey set out to explain these important Australian events and characteristics through the lens of Australia's distance, not just from the world of which for many decades it was a part, Great Britain and Europe, but the distances within its own boundaries. The idea was so compelling, the concept so apt, that the book's title has become ingrained in the language and continues to be invoked to describe aspects of Australian experience—despite the fact that many of the conditions of Australian life at the end of the long Menzies era when Blainey was writing his book, most notably Australia's singular focus on Britain, have now drifted into history.

When setting out to write this book on Australia, Blainey had intended to write about the 'taming of distance' in Australia with the arrival of new transport and communication technologies like the railway, steamship, telegraph and car (or 'Horseless Road Carriage'). But as he wrote he realised that this was only one part of a greater story that had preceded it, and that was the story of distance itself, in the days of the sailing ship and bullocky. When Blainey 'ceased to see the book upside down, I found I had ended up with a kind of history of Australia'—because, it seemed, 'distance was a central factor in Australia's history'. Given that distance is a relative concept, there has to be an entity which Australia is distant from. In Blainey's telling, that entity was primarily Great Britain, the founding mother of a penal colony at Botany Bay in 1788. As he says, the usefulness of distance as a historical tool for the colonial experience is that it keeps in mind the motherland: 'It may be that distance and transport are revealing mirrors through which to see the rise of every satellite land in the new world, because they keep that land's vital relationship with the old world in the forefront.'

Seen through Blainey's lens of distance, the European history of Australia suddenly takes on a new unity and complexion—which prompts new questions of interpretation of the events of Australia's past. And as Blainey says, 'Distance itself may not explain why they happened, but it forces a search for new explanations.' It is these new questions that Blainey proceeds to explore in *The Tyranny of Distance*. And in his first and perhaps most provocative question—the one most taken up for debate on the book's publication—Blainey asks just why the British had chosen to transport their convicts to a place so far away, on the other side of the world. Taking his characteristic economic or material approach to history, he remarks: 'The settling of eastern Australia was a startlingly costly solution to the crowded British prisons.' He then takes up an idea presented by an amateur historian (KM Dallas) in Hobart in 1952, who proposed that England needed a new sea base to strengthen 'her commercial empire in the East', and argues that there were commercial and strategic reasons for the settlement of Botany Bay, as well as penal.

But this is just the first of many questions that distance raises and can illuminate in Blainey's hands. It can shed light on why the new colony nearly collapsed; on the placement of military camps around the coast; and on the development of Australia's key export industries, such as whaling, wool and gold. In Blainey's telling, distance can even help to explain why Australia is relatively egalitarian and peaceful, and offers new perspectives on 'the flow of investment and technology, the rise of cities and regions, changes in social life, and some of the fascinating episodes of Australian transport'. But despite the advent of new transport technologies and the shrinking of the world through air travel and electronic communications, distance continues to be a factor that shapes Australian life. As Blainey remarks about his own era of twentieth-century Australia: 'We still live in one of the billabongs of the world, away from the mainstream.'

Blainey's prose is famously lucid, elegant and accessible. His history comes to life with entertaining anecdotes, such as his story of the 'strange event' reported by the president of the Victorian Institute of Engineers on 11 March 1896: 'He reported that in Chicago a contraption had won a road race by attaining a speed of 16 miles an hour. Lest some of his audience should have been wondering what this monster of lightning speed actually was, he added: "I refer to the Horseless Road Carriage, which is now beyond the experimental stage, and will soon be as useful in its own way as the bicycle." Peering again into the future, he predicted that the new vehicles would not necessarily require more expensive roads because they "will not destroy the macadam as much as do the feet of draught animals."'

Blainey was born in Melbourne in 1930, the son of a Methodist clergyman. He studied history at the University of Melbourne and was a brilliant student. After graduating with first-class honours, the twenty-year-old Blainey was recommended by his professor to the Mount Lyell Mining and Railway Company in Tasmania to research and write its history. He would be paid for a year by both the university and the company while he wrote the book. So instead of continuing in academia as might have been expected, Blainey travelled to the isolated, rocky west coast of Tasmania to research the history of Mount Lyell. So thorough were Blainey's researches, that he drew not only on the company's masses of official documents, but visited every mine associated with the company, often travelling on foot through rugged terrain with a tin of fruit and a couple of eggs for lunch; he played football with the company's employees, and listened to their stories about the early days.

When the year was up and Blainey had still not finished his book, he found a job as a geologist's assistant to support himself while he continued to write. Two and a half years later, he had completed his rounded corporate history, filled with character portraits as well as business dealings: *The Peaks of Lyell*, which was published in 1954 to critical acclaim. Blainey returned to Melbourne and married in 1957. He continued to write corporate histories for six years, including *Gold and Paper: A history of the National Bank of Australia Limited* (1958) and *Mines in the Spinifex: The story of Mount Isa Mines* (1960). In the dealings of all these Australian businesses—one an outpost on the most inhospitable coast of Tasmania (Mount Lyell); one a bank far from the centres of capital and many of its customers (the National Bank); and one a mining town in arid western Queensland (Mount Isa)—distance was a prevailing factor.

In 1962 Blainey was appointed to the Department of Economic History at the University of Melbourne. The following year the first of his popular histories of Australia was published, his bestselling *The Rush That Never Ended: A History of Australian Mining* (1963). His next book, *The Tyranny of Distance* (1966), has been in print since it was first published. In 1968 Blainey became Professor of Economic History and in 1977 he took the Ernest Scott Chair of History, which he held until 1988. Blainey was Chair of the Australia Council from 1977 to 1981, and in 1982 the Australian Broadcasting Commission made a television documentary on his approach to history. Called *The Blainey View*, it explored Blainey's vision of history as 'primarily the history of ordinary people: their hopes, their failures, their triumphs'. Blainey was appointed foundation Chancellor of the University of Ballarat in 1993. During the course of his career Blainey has published over thirty books, including *Triumph of the Nomads: A History of Ancient Australia* (1975; the subtitle was later changed to *A History of Aboriginal Australia*), *Game of Our Own: Origins of Australian Football* (1990), *A Shorter History of Australia* (1994) and *A Short History of the World* (2002). Blainey was made Companion in the Order of Australia in 2000.

Always provocative, Blainey caused outrage in 1984 with his comments to a Rotary meeting in Warrnambool on Asian immigration when he argued that the rise in Asian immigration was detrimental to Australia's social harmony, a view that he expounded in *All For Australia* (1984). He was also critical of the *Mabo* and *Wik* High Court judgements in the 1990s and supported the 'No' vote in the 1999 Republic Referendum. So controversial have been Blainey's views that a seminar was held to reassess his contribution to Australian history and politics. A book drawn from the conference—*The* Fuss *That Never Ended: The Life and Work of Geoffrey Blainey*—was published in 2003. In his review of *The Tyranny of Distance* taken from the conference, historian Geoffrey Bolton acknowledges its enduring impact: 'How few of us possess the imagination to coin a phrase which embraces so rich a complex of implications that it passes into the common currency of the language and attains the venerable status of a cliché! It is a fine thing to enter the anthology of quotations, and Geoffrey Blainey has achieved it.'

37

THE TRANSIT OF VENUS

Shirley Hazzard (1931–)

Shirley Hazzard spent the first fifteen years of her life in Sydney's harbourside suburb of Mosman, during the 1930s and 40s. Her early years were marked by the suffering of the Great Depression and the aftermath of the First World War. Her Welsh father had fought in the trenches of the Western Front and never spoke of it, but veterans parading with missing limbs and amputees begging in the streets of Sydney brought home to her the war's unspoken horror. When war was declared in the Pacific in 1941 and a Japanese invasion of Sydney was feared, Hazzard's school, Queenwood, was briefly evacuated to Penrith, west of Sydney. She has said of this time away from the city: 'Anywhere in the country then was desolate. There was a feeling you might be forgotten there, and at night the silence was the silence of a convent.' One evening as the sun fell, she went to milk the cows: 'Oh, to be more sad than this would hardly be possible. It was like a scene out of Thomas Hardy. It felt hopeless.'

The Australia in which Hazzard grew up was not only one of

economic depression and two world wars; it was also philistine, devoid of interest in books and art, and isolated, a six-month boat trip away from Europe. For a schoolgirl devoted to poetry, Hazzard's Australian years were boring and unhappy: 'I was born into the British Empire. In those days, there was only one way out for a bookish girl with aspirations, and that was a one-way ticket to Europe.' Fortunately for Hazzard, in 1947 her father was posted to Hong Kong as Australian Trade Commissioner and she left school and Australia for good.

These early Australian experiences and Hazzard's delivery from them into a new world of international adventure are at the heart of her critically acclaimed novel *The Transit of Venus*. First published in 1980, *The Transit of Venus* centres on two orphaned Australian sisters, Caroline and Grace Bell, who have managed to escape 1940s Sydney for post-war London. As its title suggests, with its reference to the Roman goddess of love and beauty, *The Transit of Venus* is concerned with love. But always beyond it, informing the characters' lives and the state of their nations, is the ruin wreaked by two world wars. The novel opens with a storm in the English countryside: 'It was simply that the sky, on a shadeless day, suddenly lowered itself like an awning. Purple silence petrified the limbs of trees and stood crops upright in the fields like hair on end.' The storm—'By nightfall the headlines would be reporting devastation'—sets the scene for the tempests of passion and illicit emotion that run through the story, as well as the violent upheavals of the twentieth century that form the novel's background, from the lingering effects of the First World War to the assassinations of John F Kennedy and Martin Luther King.

Told in four parts—The Old World, The Contacts, The New World and The Culmination—*The Transit of Venus* opens in England, the 'Old World', then cuts back to Australia to the sisters' childhood, and moves eventually to New York, the 'New World'.

Hazzard captures in rich detail not only the two sisters, but also their stepsister Dora and the central men in their lives, astrophysicist Ted Tice, senior government official Christian Thrale, and charismatic playwright Paul Ivory ('Paul Ivory was a star: any firmament would do'), as well as several other key characters. But it is Caroline, or Caro, with her passion for love, literature and beauty, who is the novel's Venus: 'Again they looked at Caro, established as a child of Venus.' Hazzard's skilful interweaving of so many lives in a narrative that resonates with literary allusion and twentieth-century history makes *The Transit of Venus* a novel of unusual depth and complexity.

Ever the child of Australia ('Australia was the first fifteen years of my life and you are already Australian for life by doing that'), Hazzard extends the reference of 'Venus' beyond its evocation of the Roman goddess to its serendipitous role as the planet Venus in Britain's earliest acquaintance with the east coast of Australia. In August 1768, Captain James Cook sailed from England to the recently charted Tahiti to watch a rare transit of Venus across the face of the sun on 3 June 1769, as part of Britain's quest to measure longitude. Cook then sailed west and 'discovered' the east coast of Australia. And so the astronomer Professor Thrale can say to Caro: 'You owe your existence to astronomy, young woman.' And in her defence Ted Tice can say: 'The calculations were hopelessly out . . . Calculations about Venus often are.'

The Transit of Venus is an elegantly composed, artfully structured novel, foreboding and foretelling characters' fates. The opening scene contains the entire tragedy of the story, hidden in a few cryptic clues, so that as the novel draws to its ordained conclusion it gathers the momentum of a thriller. And Hazzard's mesmeric prose is powerful, precise and certain. It is not surprising that when she sent her first stories to the fiction editor William Maxwell at *The New Yorker* they were accepted immediately, with barely an alteration. Nor that *The Transit of Venus* received the National Book Critics Circle Award for best novel in the United States in 1980.

Hazzard can portray in concise, witty sketches whole psychologies and social phenomena, such as: 'Christian knew the type. She was one of those persons who will squeeze into the same partition of a revolving door with you, on the pretext of causing less trouble'; and 'Like Christian Thrale before her, she found [the Australian sisters] insufficiently conscious of their disadvantage, and would have liked to bring it home to them.' Hazzard juxtaposes the cultural poverty of Australia—'Sydney could never take for granted, as did the very meanest town in Europe, that a poet might be born there or a great painter walk beneath its windows'—with the remarkable ability of the sisters, especially Caro, to transcend it. The novel is also rich with literary allusion and poetry, Hazzard's great love. She can quote extensively from poets Robert Browning, William Wordsworth, Thomas Hardy and WH Auden. The novelist Joseph Conrad is also a great influence, as is Leo Tolstoy's *War and Peace*.

Hazzard was born in Sydney in 1931 to a Welsh father and a Scottish mother who had met in the 1920s when they were working for the British engineering firm that built the Sydney Harbour Bridge. She began reading poetry as a child, especially Robert Browning. Following the Second World War, her father joined the foreign service and was posted to Hong Kong in 1947. Hazzard left Sydney with her parents, stopping first at the port of Hiroshima where she saw the aftermath of the atomic bomb, a vision that affected her deeply and recurs in her fiction: 'A catastrophe of which no one would ever say, the Will of God.' In Hong Kong the sixteen-year-old Hazzard found work at the British intelligence office and was exposed to an alluring world of international politics and literature. When her father was posted to New Zealand two years later, Hazzard found the experience of its quiet, conservative society shattering after the exotic life of Hong Kong and later said of her time in Wellington, 'I died spiritually there.'

In 1950 Hazzard's father was appointed Trade Commissioner in New York. When her parents separated the following year and subsequently left New York, Hazzard stayed behind and found a job as a typist at the United Nations (UN): 'I went, like many other people then, to apply to the United Nations in a spirit of idealism, little dreaming indeed that idealism was the last thing that was wanted there.' Hazzard remained at the UN until 1962, when she was able to support herself with her writing. She later attacked the UN for its failure to live up to those early ideals in her book *The Defeat of an Ideal: A Study of the Self-Destruction of the United Nations*, published in 1973. It was in 1956 with the UN that Hazzard first visited Italy, a country that changed her life, where she spent a year working with an international peace-keeping mission during the Suez crisis. In Italy Hazzard found everything that her Australia had lacked—mystery, poetry and passion, 'the impassioned life that is animated by awareness of eventual death'.

In 1961 Hazzard's first story was published in *The New Yorker*. She had sent it to the literary editor William Maxwell: 'I hadn't ever written a story before. I sent it to *The New Yorker* absolutely cold, not even bothering to keep a copy.' Maxwell accepted it without revision and continued to publish her stories with such frequency that the following year Hazzard was able to resign from her position at the UN. In 1963 her first book was published, the short story collection *Cliffs of Fall*. The same year she met Francis Steegmuller, translator of Gustave Flaubert's letters and biographer of Jean Cocteau and Guillaume Apollinaire, at a party given by Muriel Spark and they were married that December.

Together they divided their time between apartments in Manhattan's Upper East Side and Naples and Capri, where they befriended Graham Greene in the late 1960s. Steegmuller, twenty-four years older than Hazzard, died in 1994. Hazzard was made an honorary citizen of Capri in 2000.

Hazzard has written four novels, including her first, *The Evening of the Holiday* (1966); *The Bay of Noon* (1970); and *The Great Fire* (2003), which took her twenty years to write. *The Great Fire* won the 2004 Miles Franklin Award and the 2003 National Book Award for fiction in the United States. Her non-fiction works include *Countenance of Truth: The United Nations and the Waldheim Case* (1990) and *Greene on Capri: A Memoir* (2000). Hazzard is working on her fifth novel.

ALISON CROGGAN'S FAVOURITE
AUSTRALIAN BOOKS

In no particular order . . .

An Imaginary Life by David Malouf
The Magic Pudding by Norman Lindsay
Gould's Book of Fish: A Novel in 12 Fish by Richard Flanagan
The Arrival by Shaun Tan
The Chapel Perilous by Dorothy Hewett
Tourmaline by Randolph Stow
The Fatal Shore by Robert Hughes
Voss by Patrick White
Translations from the Natural World by Les Murray
Collected Poems by Judith Wright

Alison Croggan is a poet and author of seven volumes of
poetry, including *This is the Stone* (1991), *Attempts at Being* (2002)
and *Ash* (2007). She is also a theatre critic and the author of
the *Pellinor* series of young adult fantasy novels.

38

An Imaginary Life
David Malouf (1934–)

When David Malouf's novel *An Imaginary Life* appeared in 1978, he had already contributed to one and published three volumes of poetry—and he brought to this extraordinary novel a poet's concern for language and gift for making the very simplest of things, such as a scarlet poppy, resonate with whole worlds of beauty and meaning; with loss, love, joy, promise, sorrow. Malouf had also published one novel, *Johnno* (1975), an autobiographical story of a boy growing up in wartime Brisbane, and so tested his narrative powers.

Set on the furthest north-eastern edge of the Roman Empire in the first two decades AD, *An Imaginary Life* is told by the Roman poet Publius Ovidius Naso, known as Ovid, who has been exiled from his beloved Rome and his beloved language Latin, into a world of semi-barbarism. Because of the exotic, fantastic and rudimentary nature of the world Ovid enters into, and Malouf's ability to strip back experience to its essentials and convey it in words, the novel reads like a fable. And with the timeless power of a fable, it echoes down the ages from the frontier of first-century Rome to the twenty-first century and Australia, formerly one of the southernmost frontiers of the British Empire.

The novel opens with an italicised fragment, conjuring early memories of a wild boy who lives among wolves and stories of wolf men, '*changing themselves painfully at the moon's bidding*'. The narrator then takes up his story from the end of his first and most traumatic year of exile, when he is utterly alone, unable to communicate, locked into his Roman being and Latin language among strangers: 'We are at the ends of the earth. Even the higher orders of the vegetable kingdom have not yet arrived among us . . . My days in this place, my nights, are terrible beyond description.' He introduces himself as Ovid, 'born on the cusp between two houses of the zodiac, where the Fishes, tugging in their opposite directions, plunge below the horizon, and the Ram ascends; between two cycles of time'. Sharing his birthday with Malouf and born on 20 March 43 BC, Ovid was indeed between two cycles of time: living not only in the years that Republican Rome was transformed by Augustus into the Roman Empire (in 27 BC), but at the moment of the birth of a child—Jesus of Nazareth—who would be symbolised by a fish, inspire one of the world's most powerful religions and lead to the destruction of the old gods of Rome. *An Imaginary Life* is much preoccupied with meditations on 'the Child' and with the creation of gods from men: 'if the gods are there, it is because you have discovered them there, drawn them up out of your soul's need for them and dreamed them into the landscape to make it shine'.

Gradually Ovid learns the foreign tongue of the people among whom he lives, in Tomis on the Black Sea, and becomes involved in village life, planting a garden and befriending the man who watches over him and whose house he shares. The drama of this meditative novel is announced when Ovid is invited to hunt for deer one autumn with the men of the tribe and sights human footprints among the deer prints: 'And among them, astonishingly, though the others seem unsurprised, the prints of a human foot, bare, small, the prints perhaps of a child.' The poet becomes obsessed with this child—'I know it is not an ordinary boy. It is the Child'—and knows he must one day take him from the woods and bring him into the village. It is only when the boy is brought in from the wilds that Ovid, famed for his masterpiece *Metamorphoses*, begins the ultimate transformation, from life into death: 'Slowly I begin the final metamorphosis. I must drive out my old self and let the universe in.' Just as the wild child must take his self from out of the universe: 'He has not yet captured his soul out of the universe about him.'

The historical Ovid on whom Malouf based his novel was banished to Tomis (now Constanta, the largest sea port in Romania) in AD 8, aged 51, by the Emperor Augustus. It is not known why Augustus banished him, although Ovid said cryptically that it was for 'a poem and a mistake'. Ovid would never see Rome again, dying in exile in AD 17 or 18. By the time of his banishment, Ovid was the most popular poet in the Roman Empire—there are graffiti lines from Ovid on the walls of Pompeii—and had published several volumes on love, including *Amores*, a collection of love poems; *Heroides*, verse letters written by mythological heroines to their lovers; and *Ars Amatoria*, a handbook on love. He had also published *Metamorphoses*, his epic work on transformation and the history of the world from the flood and the creation of the gods to the assassination and deification of Julius Caesar. *Metamorphoses* was one of the most influential texts of the ancient world, and was later used as a source and inspiration by many great writers of Europe, including Geoffrey Chaucer, Dante Alighieri, Edmund Spenser, William Shakespeare and John Milton.

As well as being the moving story of an ageing poet and a child on the border of the known world, *An Imaginary Life* is a lyrical meditation on change, on metamorphosis. The power of language and its ability to shape the world is one of Malouf's abiding concerns, and it lies at the centre of this novel. As Malouf's Ovid says: 'We have only to conceive of the possibility and somehow the spirit works in us to make it actual. This is the true meaning of transformation. This is the real metamorphosis.' Malouf has spoken of the fact that in Australia we use a language that has been imported from elsewhere, a language that does not fit our landscape, just as Ovid's Latin does not fit the 'enormous landscape' in which he finds himself. As Malouf has said: 'everything about the English language derives from a particular place, a particular landscape . . . That's not true here. We've brought this language here, and we've made it apply to a world which is very different. It makes us more self-conscious about language and the uses of language, and the way language fits, than a speaker in England might need to be, and ought to make us more conscious of language as something which is partly willed rather than simply natural.' This is the way in which Ovid's experience connects with Australia's. Ovid eventually comes close to understanding a new language, the Child's language: 'When I think of the tongue that has been taken away from me, it is some earlier and more universal language than our Latin, subtle as it undoubtedly is. Latin is a language for distinctions, every ending defines and divides. The language I am speaking of now . . . is a language whose every syllable is a gesture of reconciliation.'

Malouf was born in 1934 in Brisbane, Queensland, of English and Lebanese ancestry. He went to Brisbane Grammar School and the University of Queensland, where he taught for two years before travelling to Britain when he was twenty-four. Malouf lived in England from 1959 until 1968, working as a teacher. When he returned to Australia he moved to Sydney and took up a position in the Department of English at the University of Sydney. His first publication was his contribution of twelve poems to the collection *Four Poets: David Malouf, Don Maynard, Judith Green, Rodney Hall*, published in 1962. His first solo volume was *Bicycle and Other Poems* (1970). In 1975 he published his first novel, *Johnno*. Although many critics seemed surprised that a poet had published a novel, Malouf says he had been 'writing prose from the beginning. It was just that until 1972, when on the seventh or eighth attempt I got *Johnno* into publishable form, I had written nothing I wanted to see in print'.

Malouf left the University of Sydney in 1977 to devote himself to writing full-time. *An Imaginary Life* was published in New York the next year and won the 1979 New South Wales Premier's Literary Award. Malouf is a prolific author who writes in many forms. He has published poetry; six novels, including *The Great World* (which won the 1991 Miles Franklin Award), *Remembering Babylon* (which was shortlisted for the 1993 Booker Prize and won the 1996 IMPAC Dublin Literary Award) and *The Conversations at Curlow Creek* (1996); short story collections; non-fiction and autobiography; a play, *Blood Relations* (1988); and the librettos for four operas, including the opera based on Patrick White's *Voss* and one on Charlotte Brontë's *Jane Eyre*. Malouf's most recent works are the short story collection *Every Move You Make*, published to acclaim in 2006, and *Typewriter Music* (2007), his first collection of poetry in twenty-six years.

JAMES BRADLEY'S FAVOURITE
AUSTRALIAN BOOKS

The Fortunes of Richard Mahony by Henry Handel Richardson
The Tree of Man by Patrick White
Illywhacker by Peter Carey
Bodysurfers by Robert Drewe
An Imaginary Life by David Malouf

James Bradley is the author of *Wrack* (1997), *The Deep Field* (1999)
and *The Resurrectionist* (2006).

39

THE CHANT OF JIMMIE BLACKSMITH

Thomas Keneally (1935–)

As a schoolboy Thomas Keneally dreamt of playing five-eighth for the Australian rugby side and winning the Nobel Prize for Literature. But after leaving his Christian Brothers high school, Keneally entered St Patrick's Seminary in the Sydney beachside suburb of Manly in 1952 to train for the priesthood. Eight years later, suffering severe depression, he left the seminary before his ordination and devoted himself to one of his schoolboy callings: writing. Keneally published his first story, 'The Sky Burning Up Above the Man', in the *Bulletin* in 1962 under the name 'Bernard Coyle'. Two years later his first novel appeared, *The Place at Whitton* (1964). And so Keneally began his successful, disciplined and extraordinarily productive career as a writer of international acclaim. By the time *The Chant of Jimmie Blacksmith* came out in 1972, Keneally had already published six novels, including *Bring Larks and Heroes*, which won the Miles Franklin Award in 1967.

The Chant of Jimmie Blacksmith is based on the life of Jimmy Governor, hanged in Darlinghurst Gaol on 18 January 1901 just before the federation of Australia. In Keneally's powerful telling, Governor's life becomes the story of Jimmie Blacksmith, born in the Brentwood Aboriginal camp to Aboriginal woman Dulcie Blacksmith and 'some white man'. Bright and keen to please—'eager, sober, polite Jimmie Blacksmith'—Blacksmith is the favoured pupil of the Reverend HJ Neville, who has taught him to read and write and to aspire to the ways of the European world. Neville has encouraged Blacksmith to believe that if he abides by the values of white society he will reap its simple rewards—a job, a house, a white wife—like a white man. The novel opens with Jimmie's uncle Tabidgi Jackie Smolders, who has just heard the news that Jimmie has married a white girl in a Methodist church. Smolders is travelling to confront his nephew, carrying Jimmie's initiation tooth as a protest: the tooth will 'lay a tribal claim on Jimmie'. Already from the opening page, the two great worlds that Jimmie straddles, Aboriginal tribal law and his adopted Christianity, are in conflict over his soul.

During the course of the novel, at every turn Jimmie will discover the unbridgeable gap that lies between the life he has been encouraged to dream of and the inevitable reality of his place at the bottom of society as an Australian with Aboriginal blood in the nineteenth century. As the Reverend Neville queries: 'one wonders if society is yet ready to accept the ambitious aborigine.' Having endured prejudice, injustice, insult and humiliation, determined to rise above white expectations of him, Jimmie's patience and hopes are finally exhausted when his boss Mr Newby refuses him and his wife their rightful food rations—and Jimmie's murderous rampage ensues. As with Jimmy Governor, Blacksmith's retribution takes place as Australians debate the uniting of the colonies to form the Commonwealth of Australia in 1901, the much lauded Federation: 'Joseph Chamberlain had declared the new Australian constitution a highly advanced model of parliamentary and monarchic democracy.' In his enraged, deeply moving story, Keneally reveals how Australia's birth as a nation was shadowed by the desecration of Aboriginal Australia through European hypocrisy and ignorance. As McCreadie, the schoolteacher taken hostage, muses: 'if the Taree footballers had not fallen to celebrating their skill on the consecrated stones of another race, there would have been no killing at the Newbys'.'

First published in 1972, *The Chant of Jimmie Blacksmith* became a bestseller and was shortlisted for the Booker Prize. The novel appeared five years after the 1967 Referendum permitted the repeal of two sections of the Australian Constitution that discriminated against Aboriginal Australians, which became symbolic of a new era in black and white relations. Keneally has said of that time: 'by the early 1970s, I and others were excited by a new awareness that Australia had an ancient map—as Bruce Chatwin would later say, a spaghetti of *Iliads* and *Odysseys* expressed in geological terms. To me, that Aboriginal planet Australia explained the meaning of Australia, the nature of the gods of its landscape.' Keneally wanted to celebrate this in his novel. He now feels that writing from an Aboriginal point of view was 'an act of presumption and impoliteness'. In 2001, as the centenary of Federation was being celebrated, Keneally said that if he were writing *The Chant of Jimmie Blacksmith* today, he would write from the point of view of a white character and not from that of Jimmie Blacksmith: 'It would be insensitive to write from that point of view now.' Although the novel is told in the third person by an omniscient narrator who cuts between several characters, including Jimmie in the bush and the butcher and hangman Wallace Hyberry in Balmain, it does mostly look at the world from Jimmie's point of view.

Keneally wrote *The Chant of Jimmie Blacksmith* towards the end of 'a period of darkness', which lasted until about 1973, when he was struggling to find his place in the world. At the time he was writing about Jimmie Blacksmith, Keneally was haunted by the idea that on earth there were 'a few saved souls in a mass of stupidity and philistinism'. Only later did he discover his true nature as 'a hedonist and a partygoer and a storyteller', which subsequently altered the course of his writing. It is perhaps this suffering in his own life that so fiercely charged *The Chant of Jimmie Blacksmith* with the passion of an outsider helpless in an alien world and made it one of Keneally's most enduring and popular novels. The film adaptation by Fred Schepisi was released in 1978 to wide acclaim. It starred Tommy Lewis as Jimmie Blacksmith, Bryan Brown, Robyn Nevin and Ruth Cracknell.

Born in Sydney in 1935, Keneally grew up on the north coast of New South Wales. In 1942 his family moved to Homebush, in Sydney's west, while his father was in the Middle East with the Australian Air Force. After school Keneally began his studies for the Catholic priesthood, abandoning them in 1960. He then worked as a labourer, clerk and schoolteacher to support himself while he wrote. In 1965 he married Judy Martin, a nurse and ex-nun, and they had two daughters. Keneally became a prolific author, publishing over thirty-five books to date. He is particularly known for his historical novels, such as *Bring Larks and Heroes* (1967); *Blood Red, Sister Rose* (1974) about Joan of Arc; *Confederates* (1979) about the American Civil War; and the bestselling *Schindler's Ark*, which won the 1982 Booker Prize and was adapted to screen by Steven Spielberg in the 1993 Academy Award-winning film *Schindler's List*.

Keneally is a prominent figure in the Australian landscape. In the 1980s he was a member of the Literature Board of the Australia Council and President of the National Book Council; he has also been a staunch supporter of an Australian republic.

JOHN HUGHES'S FAVOURITE
AUSTRALIAN BOOKS

Such lists are always somewhat provisional (I'm sure that if you were to ask me in six months' time there would be at least one new inclusion, or the recollection of a terrible omission) but I've spent a few days now thinking about my reading and these are the books that I return to most often, or those that have exerted the strongest influence on my own writing or thinking and have thus assumed a special significance in my memory.

12 Edmonstone Street by David Malouf
Visitants by Randolph Stow
Midnite: The Story of a Wild Colonial Boy by Randolph Stow
Maurice Guest by Henry Handel Richardson
Collected Poems: 1969–1999 by John Forbes
The Watcher on the Cast-Iron Balcony by Hal Porter
Collected Poems: 1942–1985 by Judith Wright
The Tree of Man by Patrick White
Collected Poems by Kenneth Slessor
The Turning by Tim Winton

John Hughes is the author of *Someone Else* (2007) and the award-winning autobiographical essays *The Idea of Home* (2004). He is Senior Master in English at Sydney Grammar School.

40

VISITANTS
Randolph Stow (1935–)

Having published four acclaimed books, at the age of twenty-four literary prodigy Randolph Stow decided to give up writing to become an anthropologist in Papua New Guinea. In 1959 he took up a post as cadet patrol officer and assistant to the government anthropologist in the Trobriand Islands, but it was to be a short-lived career. During the course of his work he contracted malaria, had a severe psychological breakdown, and was forced to return to his home town of Geraldton, north of Perth, to recuperate. Stow drew on this traumatic experience—and on the widely reported sighting in 1959 of a disc-shaped craft containing four human-like figures hovering over the Papuan island of Boianai—for his extraordinary sixth novel *Visitants*. Told in five sections—Prologue, Sinabada, Visitants, Cargo, Troppo—the novel opens with the following words: 'On June 26th, 1959, at Boianai in Papua, visitants appeared to the Reverend William Booth Gill, himself a visitant of thirteen years standing, and to thirty-seven witnesses of another colour.' The prologue recounts the well-documented historical sighting by the Reverend Gill, an Anglican missionary, and his companions of a flying saucer hovering over their island.

First published in 1979, *Visitants* is a powerful story about visitation—the invasion of bodies, minds, islands and planets— and about the complex interweaving and generation of systems of belief, myths and legends. The visitants in Stow's novel travel to Kailuana Island, off the south-east coast of Papua. They include two of the Australian government officials who manage the territory, Alistair Cawdor and his assistant, cadet patrol officer Tim Dalwood; a local planter, MacDonnell, who arrived on the island in 1908 and announced to the local people that he owned it; Metusela, a disturbing newcomer to the local village with the large, changeless saucer eyes of a zombi; possible extraterrestrial visitants whose rumoured sightings start a cargo cult; and the elusive visitant that seems to have possessed Cawdor himself, as he retreats further and further from human society into alcohol and malarial madness: 'And he screamed: The house is bleeding. There is nobody inside, he said.'

Visitants is told in fragments, in the voices of five witnesses to an inquiry into an outbreak of violence over the succession to an ageing village chief on Kailuana Island. The inquiry is held in November 1959 before Mr JG Browne, the Assistant District Officer, who also contributes his voice to the story. The five witnesses are: Dalwood; the planter MacDonnell; one of his servants, the young girl Saliba; the Government Interpreter Osana; and Benoni, the heir to the local chief. But although the inquiry is sparked by the violent destruction of a village on the island, the focus of the testimony is the young patrol officer Alistair Cawdor, 'sprawled there in his underpants like a zoo animal that had given up', and his failing health and mental instability. Cawdor's own contribution to the story consists of fragments of italicised notes on the lore and history of the island: '*When asked why they should connect the stones with the space-ship, all the men implicated said that they had heard of the connection through BENONI, who had heard it from me.*'

Stow's fluid prose beautifully evokes the islands and their inhabitants, from a cockatoo—'As I watched there was a sudden commotion in the air, and a white cockatoo came out of nowhere and skidded to a halt on the crown of the hat'—to a sunset: 'That evening, between Kaga and Kailuana, the sea died to a smooth curve of bottomless blue, and the blue of the sky faded and changed to green; an apple-green peacock-green sky pouring down a pink and golden light.' Stow vividly conveys the constant flux and disintegration of the tropics, from Cawdor's health and the power structures of the local village to the very materials of MacDonnell's house itself: 'Time has not smoothed or mellowed the fabric of the house. Grey splinters fur the walls of the central room, where maps and ships' pennants fade to a neutral dun. A smell of mildew circulates, from chests and cupboards where clothes, bedding, papers, moulder in the hot damp.' . . . 'Rain was written on everything, fifty years of rain.'

Visitants is a rich and resonant novel told with lyrical precision, and steeped in the simmering suspicion and menace that haunt the novels of Joseph Conrad, a writer Stow admires. TS Eliot has also been an influence. On his final decline, Cawdor scribbles a note for Dalwood in the local language, which Osama translates into English—but cannot capture the rhythmic beauty of the original: it is a mistranslation of lines from Eliot's *Four Quartets*.

The true story of the sighting of flying objects over Boianai in 1959 by the Reverend William Booth Gill and his companions was widely reported in the media, whose coverage was based on the extensive notes and drawings made by Gill. A copy of Gill's report was circulated to every member of the House of Representatives in Australia's federal parliament. In December 1959, Gill was interviewed by the Royal Australian Air Force, but his sighting was dismissed, despite the large number of witnesses. The air force concluded that at least some of the lights that had been observed in the sky in June 1959 were the planets Jupiter, Saturn and Mars. In the ensuing years, a number of explanations for the phenomenon have been suggested, including one that postulated the experience had been the result of the deluded visions of those in thrall to a cargo cult.

Stow was born in Geraldton in 1935. By his early twenties he had published three novels, his first—*A Haunted Land* (1956)—was written when he was only eighteen. Stow studied law at the University of Western Australia, before changing to French and English and graduating in 1956. The following year saw the publication in London of his second novel, *The Bystander*, and his first collection of poetry, *Act One*, which received the Australian Literature Society's Gold Medal. Stow worked in various universities in Australia, including the universities of Adelaide, Sydney and Western Australia. In 1957 he spent several months on an Anglican mission near Wyndham, a coastal town in far north Western Australia, which inspired his third novel, *To the Islands*, about an ageing missionary who runs an Aboriginal mission station. Published in 1958, *To the Islands* won the Miles Franklin Award. Stow was twenty-three.

In 1959 Stow travelled to Papua New Guinea, an experience that proved so traumatic that although he had completed by early 1970 the first three sections of his novel based on this time, he could not write the final section of *Visitants*, 'Troppo', for nine more years, until 1979. In the meantime, Stow published *Tourmaline* (1963) and *The Merry-Go-Round in the Sea* (1965), the autobiographical novel for which he is best known. In 1967

Margaret Fink's favourite Australian books

Early autobiographies can have a freshness and unpretentiousness which later earnest works lack. For instance Miles Franklin's *My Brilliant Career*, which is not surprising as one of my choices.

In this vein I'd add *The Education of Young Donald* by Donald Horne, Clive James's *Unreliable Memoirs* and Hal Porter's *The Watcher on the Cast-Iron Balcony*.

One of the most important novels of the twentieth century and up there with the greats is Christina Stead's *The Man Who Loved Children*.

I'd also include:

Nine Parts of Desire: The Hidden World of Islamic Women by Geraldine Brooks
The Twyborn Affair by Patrick White
The Children's Bach by Helen Garner
Tirra Lirra by the River by Jessica Anderson
Lucinda Brayford by Martin Boyd
Here's Luck by Lennie Lower

(An aside: Barry Humphries once amusingly referred to Xavier Herbert's *Poor Fellow, My Reader* and on *The Chaser* show in its CNNN incarnation, they once mentioned Marcus Clarke's *For the Term of His Natural Lifestyle*.)

Margaret Fink is a film producer whose award-winning films include the acclaimed *My Brilliant Career* (1979), *For Love Alone* (1986) and *Candy* (2006).

41

GRAND DAYS

Frank Moorhouse (1938–)

Grand Days is Frank Moorhouse's exuberant, richly detailed account of an Australian woman, Edith Campbell Berry, who travels to Geneva in the 1920s to take part in an exhilarating new venture in international politics—the League of Nations, the first organisation established to safeguard the world. The League was founded during the Paris Peace Conference of 1919–20 in the wake of the First World War, with the intention of preventing any further such horrors. Schooled in an Australian-style straight-talking diplomacy by her mentor, the historical John Latham, Berry soon finds herself in a more subtle and arcane realm of international relations, which reaches from the bedroom to the boardroom. Although she finds Latham's maxim 'When you understand the workings of a committee . . . you understand the workings of an Empire' continues to hold true, in Europe Berry is opened to whole new orders of politics and life she had never known in Australia. In Geneva she plunges willingly into a fluid world where the borders between male and female, between individuals and states, are in constant flux. It is a world of cross-dressing, bisexuality, betrayal, international spies and counterfeit. In one of the strange twists of chance that Moorhouse so delights in, on her train trip to Geneva Berry meets the man who will be her guide to sex, love and politics continental-style: Major Ambrose Westwood, English doctor, League colleague and First World War veteran.

Moorhouse had been fascinated by the League of Nations since his school days. He had long wanted to write about it, to delve into its 'haunted, bitter and embarrassing stories' as well as to celebrate it as 'a human experiment of immense grandeur'. In the 1980s, when he first started to plan the book, Moorhouse thought of it as 'the hitherto untold story of the League of Nations and what I called the major diplomatic tragedy of the twentieth century, the failure to stop the Holocaust and the failure to stop World War II'. Through Berry, Moorhouse brings to his novel all the passion and hope the League inspired during its early days, when it seemed to promise a new world and a new humanity: 'She was helping to make the future of the world,' Berry thinks. The optimism that surrounded the possibilities of the League is echoed in Berry's dying mother's words, urging her daughter not to return home to Jasper's Brush on the south coast of New South Wales: 'I would rather think of you going on with your fine work in this one chance that the world has to set things aright than to have you moping at my bedside'. Moorhouse also artfully reveals the League's shaky foundations, its fraught internal politics, its financial struggles and its multitude of conflicting responsibilities.

Edith Campbell Berry is a brilliant creation. She travels through the bizarre life she finds in Geneva, open to 'the fluttering of the unruly and unseen things going on in mysterious dangerous ways about her', from which she methodically draws life lessons. She is paradoxically a supreme individual and the consummate committee woman: 'Back in Australia, she'd liked astonishing people by saying that she revelled in a good committee meeting.' Employing the techniques of committee procedure, Berry extracts life wisdom from the smallest of details to distil into her many 'Ways of Going', such as the 'Way of All Doors', 'Way of the Silent Void' and the 'Way of Compulsive Revelation'. She brings her Ways and pragmatic wisdom to the League, responding to its daily challenges with an audacity, ingenuity and presence of mind that rapidly transports her into the inner sanctum of the League's bureaucracy.

On 25 January 1919, the Paris Peace Conference formally accepted the proposal to found a League of Nations to maintain peace and resolve international disputes. The League's head-quarters were established in Geneva on 1 November 1920. This first attempt to institutionalise international relations and found a peaceful community of nations lasted officially for twenty-six years. Following the League's failure to prevent the Second World War, it was decided at the Yalta Conference in 1945 to found a new international body to take up the role of international peacekeeper and mediator, which became the United Nations. In April 1946, the League was formally dissolved and its assets were transferred to the United Nations.

With the assistance of an Australia Council Creative Arts Fellowship, Moorhouse was able to spend two years researching *Grand Days* at the League of Nations archive in Geneva, investi-gating many previously unexamined records. The result is a remark-able fusion of history and fiction, with real people and imagined people living side by side and working through the events of the 1920s, from the building of a new League headquarters, the crisis over Germany's entry into the League and the annexing of the Ruhr by France, to small details like the existence of a novel about the League that Moorhouse's researches uncovered. The novel was Alison Ritchie's *The Peacemakers*, published in 1928 in

London by the Hogarth Press. Moorhouse seamlessly weaves this into *Grand Days* through his character Caroline Bailey, who is writing a novel on the League which is published by Virginia Woolf's husband Leonard Woolf at the Hogarth Press. Moorhouse includes a long list of his characters both real and fictional at the end of *Grand Days*, as well as the Covenant of the League of Nations.

Grand Days was published in 1993 to international acclaim. In London the *Independent on Sunday* called it 'a big, luminous, affectionate and beautifully managed novel. It shows Frank Moorhouse passing from days of wine and rage to his own grand days.' The following year the judges of the 1994 Miles Franklin Award ruled *Grand Days* (along with two other novels) ineligible for the award under the conditions stipulated by Miles Franklin's bequest: that the prize be awarded to a literary work that presents 'Australian life in any of its phases'. Their decision prompted outrage and controversy, and Moorhouse considered legal action. The outrage at the novel's exclusion from the award was vindicated seven years later when its companion novel *Dark Palace* (2000) won the 2001 Miles Franklin Award.

Moorhouse was born in 1938 in Nowra, on the south coast of New South Wales. He moved to Sydney in the mid 1950s and became a cadet reporter for the *Daily Telegraph* in 1956. His first short story was published in *Southerly* magazine in 1957. As a journalist, Moorhouse worked on various newspapers in regional New South Wales, such as the *Wagga Wagga Daily Advertiser* and *The Boorowa News*, and edited the *Australian Worker* in Sydney. He was the founding editor of small independent magazines *City Voices* and *Tabloid Story*, which published the new writers of the late 1960s and 1970s. Moorhouse also worked as an administrator and tutor for the Workers Educational Association (WEA), which was connected with the 'Sydney Push'. In the 1970s he became a full-time fiction writer, writing short stories about drugs, sex and relationships around the inner-city Sydney suburb of Balmain, the heart of Sydney's bohemia which included Michael Wilding, David Williamson, Murray Bail and Peter Carey. Moorhouse's first collection of interlinked short stories, *Futility and Other Animals*, was published in 1969. Preoccupied by 'the accidental, the unintended consequence, the non-rational factors of human conduct and behaviour', Moorhouse developed a writing style that captured this unpredictable interrelatedness of life which he came to call a 'discontinuous narrative'—clusters of interrelated stories in which characters appear and reappear. For example, an older Edith Campbell Berry first appeared in *Forty-Seventeen*, Moorhouse's first novel.

Forty-Seventeen was published in 1988 and won the *Age* Book of the Year Award. After receiving a three-year Australia Council Creative Arts Fellowship in 1990, Moorhouse was able to embark on his League of Nations project and spent most of the 1990s in Europe and the United States researching it, primarily in Geneva. The result of his labours were *Grand Days* and *Dark Palace*.

Moorhouse is the author of acclaimed short story collections; non-fiction, including *Martini: A Memoir* (2005); and screen-plays. He has edited several anthologies, including his celebrated 1970s collection, *Days of Wine and Rage* (1980), and *The Best Australian Stories*. Moorhouse is a prominent figure in Australian public life and was awarded the Order of Australia (AM) in 1985 for his services to literature. He is currently working on a third volume to *Grand Days* and *Dark Palace*.

Margaret Harris's favourite Australian books

I have been shamelessly self-indulgent in this selection, choosing books that I regard as classics in their genre, and that have particular significance for me.

Rolf Boldrewood's bushranging romance, *Robbery Under Arms* (1888), has remained a favourite since I first read it at about age nine. While its excitements are now tempered by my immersion in many other Victorian novels, it retains the magic of the melodramatic.

Seven Little Australians (1894) has some of the same primal narrative charge: the death of Judy still brings tears to my eyes. Ethel Turner's account of the mischief of the Woolcot children revels in the opportunity to develop an Australian ambience.

I read and re-read the works of Ion Idriess in my childhood, for their access to exotic worlds of pearling, gold-mining in New Guinea, the Red Centre, and the ubiquity of potassium permanganate in first-aid procedures in remote places. As representative both of Idriess's work and of a rich non-fiction tradition, I single out *Headhunters of the Coral Sea* (1940).

Voss was the first novel I read by Australia's only Nobel Laureate to date, Patrick White. It explores physical terrain also traversed by Idriess, opening metaphysical resonances of an entirely different order from Idriess's descriptions. I somehow got hold of it soon after its 1957 publication, and was transfixed by the way White presents the epic obsession of man with nature, together with the obsessions of love. While I now think *The Twyborn Affair* to be White's best novel, *Voss* remains for me the Great Australian Novel.

Another confronting but exhilarating reading experience is Miles Franklin's *My Brilliant Career* (1901), which tilts headlong at the social (and literary) conventions governing the behaviour of young women. It 'beats *Jane Eyre* or the *African Farm*' declared Henry Lawson, as he pressed its claims with the publisher Blackwood.

Christina Stead's *The Man Who Loved Children* (1940) also challenges many orthodoxies. A passionate portrait of the artist as a young woman, in which the author transposes her girlhood at Watson's Bay on Sydney Harbour to Baltimore and the Chesapeake River, its revival in the mid-1960s introduced Stead to a new generation of readers.

Drusilla Modjeska's *Stravinsky's Lunch* (2001) extended the testing of generic boundaries that she had begun in *Poppy* in 1990, where biography and novel merge. From one perspective, *Stravinsky's Lunch* is a reappraisal of the careers of two Australian painters, Stella Bowen and Grace Cossington-Smith; from another, it is a moving and illuminating set of reflections on how women's lives are to be understood and written.

I confess that poetry is under-represented in my selection, and in opting for an icon in Banjo Paterson's *The Man From Snowy River* I have turned away from more subtle possibilities in favour of robust and rousing verse depicting the stuff of Australian legend in the precipitous ride by 'a stripling on a small and weedy beast'. Hear the rhythm?

It's perhaps tokenistic to include just one play, but I come down on Ray Lawler's *Summer of the Seventeenth Doll*, first produced in 1955. The naturalism of the drama of the cane-cutters coming south to Melbourne in the off-season was what first impressed me, and still does—but along with the pains and pleasures of romantic love I now find the poignancy of ageing and the ambiguities of mateship.

I learned to cook from *The Commonsense Cookery Book*, compiled by the NSW Public School Cookery Teachers' Association. It is foolproof: no step is omitted, though the instruction 'Serve on a doily on a cakestand' is one I have never obeyed. Margaret

Fulton and Stephanie Alexander are to the 1980s and 1990s what this book was to earlier generations: my 1969 reprint ('half a million copies sold') is now a museum piece, documenting the determinedly Anglo-Celtic cuisine of a bygone era.

Finally, I nominate a picture book of amazing beauty and artistry, Graeme Base's *Animalia* (1986). Notionally for children, this 'take' on the medieval bestiary is one of the most original books ever to come out of Australia.

Margaret Harris is Challis Professor of English Literature at the University of Sydney.

42

'THE BULADELAH-TAREE HOLIDAY SONG CYCLE'

Les Murray (1938–)

Les Murray and his poetry are deeply rooted in Australia and the Bunyah Valley, his sacred place in the coastal hinterland north of Sydney. Murray spent his early years roaming his parents' Bunyah Valley dairy farm and the neighbouring farms of his relatives. An only child, Murray did not go to school until he was nine and so, like John Shaw Neilson before him, he kept company with the land and its creatures. When he was four, Murray taught himself to read and from then on he read compulsively whatever he could find, from newspapers and Bugs Bunny comics to the Bible.

Murray is obsessed with words, with their rhythms and meanings. He has a prodigious memory and a gift for languages (he knows at least twenty). This genius for words runs in the Murray family—his nineteenth-century Scottish ancestor, Sir James Augustus Murray, was a lexicographer and the first editor of *The Oxford English Dictionary*.

Murray brings to his poetry his freakish fluency with words and his uncanny affinity with the landscape and all it holds—from machinery and plants to horses and birds and stars—as well as an abiding curiosity about the world. His poetic achievement is vast, ranging over fourteen collections—including *Lunch and Counter Lunch* (1974), *Translations from the Natural World* (1992) and *Subhuman Redneck Poems* (1996)—and two verse novels, *The Boys Who Stole the Funeral* (1980) and *Fredy Neptune* (1998). Although he remains essentially a bush poet, there are many sides to the poet Murray. It seems he can turn poetry from whatever catches his eye, seizing it effortlessly with words, such as this precise picture of ibis landing: 'leaning out of their wings, they step down'. And then there are the cool, staccato lyrics of the child crushed by the senseless loss of his mother in 'The Steel', an abrupt poem about his mother's death from a miscarriage: 'Thirty-five years on earth: / that's short. That's short, mother, / as the lives cut off by war // and the lives of spilt children are short.' In his poetry Murray also addresses the broad life of Australia and, inspired by history and his international travels, of the world. His second verse novel *Fredy Neptune* covers the first half of the twentieth century, from the First World War to the atomic bomb, narrated by German-Australian Fredy Boettcher: international adventurer, strongman and sailor.

With its humour, wide-ranging metaphors and easy rhythms, 'The Buladelah-Taree Holiday Song Cycle' is classic bush poet Murray; the stretch of Pacific Highway from Buladelah to Taree lies near his home territory. From his 1977 collection *Ethnic Radio*, the thirteen poems that make up this song cycle tell of the Christmas holiday season on the north coast of New South Wales. Families return home, the cars of holiday-makers crawl north up the highway, campers cook in the open air, children play by water, farm work continues and the stars turn in the sky, 'for this is the season when children return with their children / to the place of Bingham's Ghost, of the Old Timber Wharf, of the Big Flood That Time'. From this special yet remarkably mundane and ragged time, Murray creates poetry. He evokes with dazzling precision not only the world around him of the holiday-makers, the pastures of cows, the cousin on horseback, 'the tractor crankcase furred with chaff', the birds and trees, the heavens, but also his own connection to the valley through his ancestors buried nearby and the ancient Aboriginal ties to the land.

Centuries of verse and song both Celtic and Aboriginal resonate through the poem's rhythms and expression: 'It is the season of the Long Narrow City; it has crossed the Myall, it has entered the North Coast, / that big stunning snake; it is looped through the hills, burning all night there.' Through the alchemy of poetry, Murray has transformed a line of holiday traffic into a serpent, fusing Aboriginal, rural and urban Australia. Murray has described his deep connection to the land as 'Aboriginal' and defers to Aboriginal culture as Australia's 'senior culture'. At a conference in Rotterdam in 1998 Murray said: 'The continent on which I live was ruled by poetry for tens of thousands of years, and I mean it was ruled openly and overtly by poetry. Only since European settlement in 1788 has it been substantially ruled by prose. The sacred law which still governs the lives of traditional Aborigines is carried by a vast map of song-poetry attached to innumerable mythic sites.'

Born in 1938 in the Bunyah Valley, Murray roamed wild until he turned nine and was sent to school. When he was twelve his life was shattered by his mother's death and the subsequent collapse of his father. He became obsessed with war and wanted to leave school to train as an army officer, but his father had promised his wife that their son would receive an education, so Murray went to Taree High. Here the large boy suffered profoundly from the taunts of the other children, which he has since described in his poem 'Burning Want' as 'erocide: destruction of sexual morale'. The experience left him with a lifelong abhorrence of mobs. But it was at Taree High that Murray discovered poetry, especially Gerard Manley Hopkins and TS Eliot's 'The Waste Land'. And his teacher also introduced him to the poetry of John Shaw Neilson, David Campbell, Bruce Dawe, Kenneth Slessor and Mary Gilmore. It was a revelation. Through these poets Murray learnt that Australians could write poetry about their own country.

After leaving school, Murray wrote his first ten poems on Christmas Day aged eighteen. The following year he went to Sydney University on a Commonwealth Scholarship. Here, at last, he found himself among kindred spirits, including Bob Ellis and poet Geoffrey Lehmann; Clive James published his poem 'Property' in the university magazine. But Murray soon became unsettled in the city and began to sleep on the streets. He went walkabout through Victoria and South Australia in 1961—the year his first poem was published in the *Bulletin*: 'The Burning Truck', which he had revised in a truckies' café near Gundagai during his wanderings. When Murray eventually returned to university he met Valerie Morelli. They married in 1962 and have five children. In 1964 Murray converted to Catholicism, his wife's religion, which he found more imaginatively rich than the Calvinist church of his childhood. For Murray, poetry and religion are almost synonymous—'I once said that any real religion is a big slow poem, while a poem is a small fast religion'—and he dedicates his poetry 'to the glory of God'.

In 1963 the Murrays moved to Canberra, where Murray used his talent for languages working as a translator at the Australian National University. His first book of poetry, *Ilex Tree* (co-authored with Geoffrey Lehmann), was published in 1965. After travelling to Europe, in 1968 the Murrays moved to Sydney. Here Murray became friends with the poet Kenneth

Slessor, whom he calls his 'model and master'. Two years after the publication of his second collection, *The Weatherboard Cathedral* (1969), Murray left his job, determined never to have another one. In 1974 he was able to buy 'The Forty Acres', part of the farm on which he grew up and where the Murrays have lived since 1986. Soon after his return to the Bunyah Valley, when he turned fifty Murray fell into a severe depression he calls 'the Black Dog'. Eight years later in 1996, after being in a coma for twenty days with an abscess on his liver, Murray finally left the Black Dog behind. When he regained consciousness, his depression had gone.

Despite his passion for his native ground, Murray travels widely to literary festivals around the world. As he has said: 'There is also still some room for poetry at literary festivals, where we are apt to be wheeled in like trolleys of dim sum between portentous slabs of prose conference.' Internationally acclaimed, Murray won the prestigious German Petrarch Prize in 1995; the TS Eliot Award in 1996 for *Subhuman Redneck Poems*; and, on the recommendation of the poet Ted Hughes, was awarded the Queen's Medal for Poetry in 1999. Clive James has called Murray's *Collected Poems* 'a book precious beyond all prizes: one of the great books of our contemporary world.'

Murray is a bush bard of enormous complexity and contradiction. The poet Peter Porter has commented on Australia's continual bafflement with Murray, the apparent paradox that 'someone who espouses country rituals' should be 'the most sophisticated and accomplished poet Australia has yet produced'. Murray best captured the essence of his own paradox when he called himself 'the Subhuman Redneck who writes poems'.

Samantha Trenoweth's favourite Australian book

Damned Whores and God's Police: The Colonization of Women in Australia
by Anne Summers.
1975: International Women's Year; The Dismissal; 2JJ and
colour TV invaded our airwaves; Anne Summers published
Damned Whores and God's Police. Summers's reassessment of women's
place in Australian history came as revelation in a year when
there was no shortage of them. It transformed this mild-
mannered Aussie schoolgirl into a placard-wielding, pinko
feminist, and it significantly influenced changes in attitude and
legislation that have transformed women's lives since.

Samantha Trenoweth still waves the occasional placard. Between
demonstrations, she has written *The Future of God* (1995), *A Big
Life: Jenny Kee* (2006) and co-authored with Toby Creswell *1001
Australians* (2006), and edited *Screwed: Stories About Love and Sex*
(1998) with Ruth Hessey.

43

THE FATAL SHORE:

A History of the Transportation of Convicts to Australia 1787–1868

Robert Hughes (1938–)

In 1974, wandering through the haunted ruins of one of Britain's most notorious penal settlements—Tasmania's Port Arthur—art critic Robert Hughes was struck by how little he knew about his country's convict past. This was not surprising. According to Hughes, 'the idea that the convicts might *have* a history worth telling was foreign to Australians in the 1950s and 1960s'. Even by 1974, this history was not taught in schools and there was only one general book on the subject in print. As Hughes puts it: 'Behind the bright diorama of Australia Felix lurked the convicts, some 160,000 of them, clanking their fetters in the penumbral darkness. But on the feelings and experiences of these men and women, little was written.' Hughes decided to write their story.

The subject—Australia's bizarre and brutal eighty-year convict history—was not only perfectly suited to Hughes's baroque, icono-clastic imagination, but it allowed him to strip bare the shrouded past of Australia, the land with which he has such an 'intense love-hate relationship'. Rising to the occasion, Hughes embarked on a work he believed would be a straightforward undertaking. But instead it became a massive endeavour that consumed ten years of his life. The result of his long labours was *The Fatal Shore*, published in 1987, Hughes's vital telling of the horrors and achievements of the first eighty years of modern Australia, the penal colony that would become a nation.

The Fatal Shore is a vast narrative that reaches into the dim recesses of colonial Australia's birth on the east coast of an 'utterly enigmatic continent'; a coast that would, as Hughes puts it so graphically, 'witness a new colonial experiment, never tried before, not repeated since': an entire continent would become a gaol, its new inhabitants would be criminals and their gaolers. *The Fatal Shore* is classic Hughes; it is a dextrous interweaving of the fruit of his wide-ranging researches—letters, diaries, reports, statistics— with portraits of people well-known from history like Captain Arthur Phillip, John Macarthur, Governor Lachlan Macquarie, WC Wentworth, Sir George Arthur, as well as those previously lost to it, and digressions on politics, society and economics, all told in Hughes's trademark erudite, evocative and energetic prose.

With his encyclopaedic embrace, Hughes begins his story with the arrival of Captain Cook in Botany Bay and a brief history of the region's original inhabitants, including the Aboriginal tribes who lived around Port Jackson. He then turns to the unwieldy state of Georgian Britain, with its rapidly increasing crime rate, overcrowded prisons, numerous hanging offences, the loss of its American colonies (which had for decades been a repository for Britain's convicts)—all its social and economic upheaval, which inevitably led to vexing problems of crime and punishment.

The idea of a colony in far-flung New South Wales was first suggested in 1783. The following year, a new transportation act was passed in Britain to allow the transport of convicts to unnamed places 'beyond the seas'. When the coast of south-west

Africa was found to be unsuitable for a convict settlement, the choice fell to Botany Bay. According to the author of the scheme, this new colony would be the cure for 'the evils' of the rampant and alarming rise in the number of British felons. And so, in 1787, a retired naval captain, Arthur Phillip, set sail with the First Fleet, eleven ships containing the bad seeds of Britain destined to be planted in the utterly unknown soil of a land on the far side of the globe.

Hughes brilliantly portrays this almost accidental choice of New South Wales for a penal colony and the tenuous, improvised nature of the new nation's emergence. The members of the First Fleet struggled to survive. Unable to farm the land, they were forced to subsist on ever-diminishing rations. For the first five years, hunger was constant. 'Every person who came out with a design of remaining in this country were [sic] now most earnestly wishing to get away from it,' wrote Lieutenant-Governor Ross in despair.

And yet from these unlikely beginnings as a penal colony, a strange new world began to emerge. *The Fatal Shore* gives a close-up portrait of the gradual, faltering transition of this penal colony into a land of free citizens, its developing polity and social strata, its emerging economy with its dependence on wool, the spreading settlement, as well as the formation of what many still consider to be the Australian character. Hughes brings to life the men and women transported to New South Wales for crimes committed on the other side of the world, and their gaolers, some compassionate, a couple visionary, and many sadistic thugs who flogged men to the bone and prostituted the women. One Norfolk Island convict, his back mangled by two hundred lashes, wrote that he was 'literally alive with Maggots and Vermin . . . to such a wretched and truly miserable state was I reduced, that I even hated the look and appearance of myself'. On Norfolk Island under Major Foveaux, 'all the women would join in the dances of the Mermaids, each one being naked with numbers painted on their backs so as to be recognized by their admirers'.

The Fatal Shore is riveting. As Susan Sontag wrote: 'Hughes has a story to tell as vivid, large-scale and appalling as anything by Dickens or Solzhenitsyn, but one that's virtually unknown—until the writing of this splendid book.' Hughes is a compelling story-teller and his vivid prose marshals his extensive knowledge of European culture and betrays his first love, painting. Here is the 'forbidding grandeur' of the Southern Ocean through Hughes's eye: 'tottering hills of indigo and malachite glass, veined in their transparencies with braids of opaque white water, their spumy crests running level with the ship's cross-trees'. He sees Norfolk Island through the canvas of European art: 'The mornings are by Turner, the evenings, by Caspar David Friedrich, calm and beneficent, the light sifting angelically down towards the solemn horizon.'

Born in Sydney in 1938, Hughes went to the University of Sydney intending to study arts/law, while secretly dreaming of becoming an artist in Paris. In 1957 he enrolled in the Faculty of Architecture, where painter Lloyd Rees taught art. While at university, Hughes wrote for the university newspaper *Honi Soit* and drew cartoons, among which was a comic on the university's Libertine Society, a group that spawned the famed 'Sydney Push' (see box on page 285). Hughes also contributed cartoons to the Sydney journal the *Observer*, and in 1958 its editor Donald Horne hired him as art critic. So began Hughes's illustrious career as an art critic, which fortuitously coincided with a new fervour in Australian paint-ing. In 1962 Penguin commissioned Hughes to write a book on Australian art, *The Art of Australia*, which was published in 1965, the same year as his book *Donald Friend*.

By this time Hughes was living in Italy with his mentor, the writer Alan Moorehead (to whom *The Fatal Shore* is dedicated), having left Australia to immerse himself in European art. Hughes then returned to London determined to survive as a writer, where he contributed art criticism to the *Sunday Times*, *Sunday Telegraph* and *Spectator*, and became the regular art critic of the *London Magazine*. But it was a book—his third book, *Heaven and Hell in Western Art* (1968)—that precipitated his rise to the international stage. *Heaven and Hell* so impressed the managing editor of *Time* magazine that he invited Hughes to become *Time*'s art critic. In 1970 Hughes moved to New York and has lived there ever since. Ten years later, Hughes published *The Shock of the New* (1980), his landmark work on modern art, which became a television series and brought him global acclaim.

In 1999, while making his most recent television series, *Beyond the Fatal Shore* (2000), Hughes had an almost fatal car crash near Broome, Western Australia. This near-death experience, which broke him body and soul and left him in a coma for several weeks, opens the first volume of his memoirs, *Things I Didn't Know*, published to acclaim in 2006. The crash and its bitter, litigious aftermath destroyed 'the rather innocent and nostalgic love of Australia' that Hughes had felt since permanently leaving its shores forty years before.

Towards the end of *The Fatal Shore*, Hughes asks whether Australians would have done things differently if Australia had not started its colonial life as 'the jail of infinite space'. He replies emphatically in the affirmative: 'Certainly they would. They would have remembered more of their own history. The obsessive cultural enterprise of Australians a hundred years ago was to forget it entirely, to sublimate it, to drive it down into unconsulted recesses. This affected all Australian culture, from political rhetoric to the perception of space, of landscape itself.'

The 'Sydney Push'

The 'Sydney Push' was the name given to a group of bohemian intellectuals, artists, writers, lecturers and students who met at Sydney University and in various city pubs during the 1950s and 60s. They were an amorphous group united by their radical politics and social values, and their interest in talking, drinking, horse-racing and sex.

The name 'Push' was taken from a group of street criminals who lurked in the Rocks in 1890s Sydney. Their wild ways were immortalised in 'The Bastard from the Bush', a poem attributed to Henry Lawson:

> As the night was falling slowly over city, town and bush,
> From a slum in Jones's Alley came the Captain of the Push,
> And his whistle loud and piercing woke the echoes of the
> Rocks,
> And a dozen ghouls came slouching round the corners of
> the blocks.

The post-Second World War Push grew from the Libertarian Society, a political group founded at the University of Sydney in 1950 and connected to the university's Freethought Society, which was started by the influential John Anderson, Professor of Philosophy at Sydney University from 1927 to 1958. In the university's 1958 Orientation Handbook, the Libertarian Society put its position as follows: 'The libertarian standpoint is that of opposition, in every field of human activity, to authoritarian forces and to their social and political demands ... libertarians are found to be atheists, supporters of sexual freedom and opponents of repressive institutions, particularly that great destroyer of independence and initiative, the political State.'

This way of thinking characterised the Push, whose members shared a belief in a 'life of inquiry'. Original Push members included politically committed libertarians like Darcy Waters, Jim Baker and Harry Hooton. Among later members were many who came to national and international prominence, such as Germaine Greer, Clive James, John Olsen, Frank Moorhouse, Richard Neville, Wendy Bacon and Eva Cox. Robert Hughes drank at the favourite Push haunt, the Royal George Hotel in Sussex Street, and he painted a mural in its back bar.

Hughes has paid tribute to his association with the Push: 'I certainly heard the basic message of Sydney libertarianism loud and clear—that you should never believe anything someone says merely because he/she is saying it. This has been of fundamental value to me as a writer. It was not, of course, invented in Sydney in the late 1940s, but in Athens about 2300 years before that. Nevertheless I first encountered it in Sydney through the medium of the Push.'

Germaine Greer, who came to the Push from Melbourne in 1959, has also acknowledged its influence: 'When I first encountered the dingy back room of the Royal George, I was a clever, undisciplined, pedantic show-off . . . In Sydney, I found myself driven back, again and again, to basic premises, demonstrable facts. The scrupulosity that I had missed in my irreligious life was now a part of my everyday behaviour.' This radical thinking marked Greer's seminal work, *The Female Eunuch*, published in 1970.

TIM WINTON'S FAVOURITE
AUSTRALIAN BOOKS

The People's Otherworld by Les Murray
To the Islands by Randolph Stow
*Yorro Yorro: Aboriginal Creation and the Renewal of Nature; Rock Paintings and
    Stories from the Australian Kimberley* by David Mowaljarlai and Jutta
    Malnic
Story About Feeling by Bill Neidjie
On Purpose by Charles Birch
Taming the Great South Land: A History of the Conquest of Nature in Australia by
    William J Lines
Confederates by Thomas Keneally
Tourmaline by Randolph Stow
Cosmo Cosmolino by Helen Garner
Wartime Trilogy by Ray Parkin

Tim Winton is the acclaimed, award-winning author of eight
novels, including *Cloudstreet* (1991), *The Riders* (1994) and
Dirt Music (2001), and the bestselling short story collection
The Turning (2004).

44

THE PLAINS

Gerald Murnane (1939–)

In 2006 Gerald Murnane was invited to open the Monash University Library Rare Books exhibition 'Sports'. Using a treasured multicoloured glass marble as his starting point, Murnane recounted a tale of sport and life. The history of the marble turned out to contain the story of Murnane's obsessions with horse-racing, foot-racing and Australian Rules Football (AFL). For over the course of Murnane's childhood, the marble had had three incarnations: first as a racehorse named 'Idaho', part of the seven-year-old Murnane's stable of racehorse marbles which he raced in his Bendigo living room; then it became the foot-racer SJ Tupper; and then in the 1950s, after his mother had banned racing games with marbles in the hope of preventing her son from becoming a gambler like his father, the marble became the AFL player Bob McKenzie. Through this story Murnane demonstrated the power of sport to shape life—or, as Murnane would have it, the potential of horse-racing to encapsulate everything: 'Someone has written that all art aspires to the condition of music. My experience is that all art, including all music, aspires to the condition of horse-racing.'

Murnane brings to his fiction this obsessive, private, interior quality (horse-races in the living room) and this ability to spin complex and suggestive tales from small premises (a tale of life from a marble). His third novel, extracted from a much larger work which was not completed, takes a region of western Victoria that Murnane calls 'the plains' and weaves from it an elaborate fiction about its inhabitants—the plainsmen and -women—and the artists they recruit to celebrate their families and their land, the golden brown plains that sweep featureless towards the blue-green horizon. From this unlikely landscape and its people, Murnane conjures an evocative novel that becomes a meditation on art, on patronage, on the geography, politics and history of Australia, on human experience and identity: *The Plains*.

First published in 1982, *The Plains* has the timeless simplicity of a parable and a parable's multitude of possible interpretations. The narrator announces his preoccupation with meaning in the opening paragraph: 'Twenty years ago, when I first arrived on the plains, I kept my eyes open. I looked for anything in the landscape that seemed to hint at some elaborate meaning behind appearances.' The ostensible reason the narrator must observe so closely in order to divine meaning is that he is a filmmaker and has come to the unnamed town in the hope of being chosen by one of the wealthy landowners as a client. And the erudite, cultured landowners judge the worth of their prospective clients by their ability to extract meaning from things large and small. The landowners gather in the bar in town and drink until they are sober again, while periodically calling in one or more of the waiting writers, painters, architects, designers of emblems, founders of religions, for an interview. If an artist is successful, he will travel to the landowner's estate and there devote his life to extracting the esoteric meaning of the landowner's life, the history of his family, the meaning of his land, and celebrating it all in his chosen form.

As the narrator says: 'I followed the custom of sending in my name with one of the townsmen who happened to be called early. Then I learned what I could about the men in the remote lounge and wondered which of them would surrender a portion of his fortune and perhaps his own daughter in return for seeing his estates as the setting for the film that would reveal the plains to the world.' The plainsmen's lifelong task is to shape 'from uneventful days in a flat landscape the substance of myth'. The history of the region has been influenced by two competing groups of plainsmen—the Horizonites and the Haremen—and their various arcane practices and associated symbols and colours (cloudy blue-green and subdued yellow), which are reflected in everything from children's games ('Hairies and Horrors') to the colours of their respective polo teams: 'The dual colours of the horsemen hinted every moment at some pattern about to appear out of the dusty field.'

During his many years on the plains, labouring over his film, writing scripts in a darkened room about the world beyond, the narrator finds himself unable to capture in film the many mysteries of the plains his mind suggests: 'It was still a place out of sight in a scene arranged by someone who was himself out of sight. But anyone might have decided that I recognised the meaning of what I saw.'

The Plains is as beautifully written—measured, spare and commanding—as it is provocative and evocative. It reverberates with a wry humour as well as a great seriousness. Murnane is widely admired in Sweden, where critic Svenska Dagbladet perfectly expressed the allure of *The Plains*: 'Murnane may be a demanding and utterly thought-provoking writer, but he is not difficult to read. Of course one can read the story just as it is, full of feeling, poetic and evasive, a description of an enigmatic parallel world quite close to our own. Murnane's style is breathtakingly beautiful. The language is both crystal clear and dreamlike.'

Murnane was born in 1939 in Melbourne. His childhood was spent moving from house to house, in Melbourne, Bendigo and Warrnambool, as his father struggled to support his gambling. A brilliant student, after finishing school in 1957 Murnane moved to Sydney to train for the priesthood. After three months he abandoned the priesthood and returned to Melbourne, where he trained as a primary school teacher. He taught in primary schools from 1960 to 1969. In 1966 he married, and he and his wife have three sons. Murnane was made an editor in the Publications Branch of the Victorian Education Department in 1969, but left in 1973 to write and care for his sons. The following year his first novel was published: *Tamarisk Row* (1974), about a Catholic boy, his gambling father and horse-racing. His second novel, *A Lifetime on Clouds*, was published in 1976. Although it was not as widely praised as *Tamarisk Row*, the poet Les Murray wrote of *A Lifetime on Clouds*: 'I was particularly admiring of the author's unfailing ability to say just enough and no more, and of the book's quiet, dryly affectionate tone.'

In 1980 Murnane became a creative writing teacher at Melbourne's Prahran College of Advanced Education, which later became a campus of Deakin University. From the late 1970s until the early 1980s, he worked on a massive novel which was never completed. But it contained a section that would become Murnane's most celebrated novel: *The Plains*, published in 1982. Murnane's next books were *Landscape with Landscape* (1985), six interconnected stories; and *Inland* (1988), his most complex and demanding novel. Two collections of short stories followed,

Velvet Waters (1990) and *Emerald Blue* (1995). Murnane retired from teaching in 1995. His most recent book is a collection of essays published from 1983 to 2003: *Invisible Yet Enduring Lilacs* (2005). The title essay is about Marcel Proust and the collection includes essays on horse-loving poet Adam Lindsay Gordon and Jack Kerouac, Murnane's literary hero (and another writer who, unbeknownst to the young Murnane, used glass marbles as racehorses, ten years before Murnane was born). In 1999 Murnane received the Patrick White Literary Award and in 2006 the British bookmaker Ladbrokes had him at 33–1 to win the 2006 Nobel Prize for Literature (which was won by Turkish writer Orhan Pamuk, the writer Ladbrokes had as favourite).

PETER CRAVEN'S FAVOURITE
AUSTRALIAN BOOKS

I like all of Patrick White from *The Aunt's Story* to *The Twyborn Affair*, except for the strange warped book *The Solid Mandala* which I may be wrong about. I'm therefore a bit like Orson Welles when he said, 'I studied the great American movies. That is to say John Ford and John Ford and John Ford.' I'm a bit inclined to say 'Patrick White and Patrick White and Patrick White.'

On the other hand, Christina Stead's *The Man Who Loved Children* is as great as anything White wrote and I also like *For Love Alone*.

What else? Martin Boyd and *The Cardboard Crown*.

Amy Witting, especially *I for Isobel*.

The poetry of Kenneth Slessor, Judith Wright, AD Hope. John Forbes, of course. Les Murray is as great as his reputation and Peter Porter is a poet of great power.

Alan Wearne's *The Nightmarkets*.

David Malouf in *Johnno* and the short stories.

All of Helen Garner, especially *The Children's Bach* and the essays.

Elizabeth Jolley.

All of Gerald Murnane.

Various detective stories by Peter Temple, Peter Corris and Carmel Bird.

Blinky Bill by Dorothy Wall.

The Magic Pudding by Norman Lindsay.

Robert Hughes, always, especially *The Fatal Shore*, an extraordinary masterpiece.

Peter Craven is an influential literary critic, journalist and editor. In 1981 he co-founded the literary magazine *Scripsi* with Michael Heyward (now publisher at Text Publishing). It ran until 1994.

45

MONKEY GRIP

Helen Garner (1942–)

In 1972 Helen Garner lost her job as a high school teacher for her frank discussions of sex. It was the same year that Gough Whitlam led the Australian Labor Party to victory in the federal elections, ending twenty-three years of conservative government in Australia. In inner-city Melbourne, Garner was living a bohemian life outside the nine-to-five routine. Informed by feminism and new political ideals, Garner and her friends lived in shared households and threw themselves into casual relationships, sex, drugs and creative expression. After she lost her job as a teacher, Garner devoted herself to writing. During 1975 she spent her days in the State Library of Victoria working on a novel based on her diaries and her life as a single mother with a young daughter, living with friends in rambling houses in the inner suburbs of Melbourne.

When she had finished her manuscript, Garner gave it to Hilary McPhee, one of the founders of the new publishing group McPhee Gribble. Established in 1975 in Melbourne by McPhee and Diana Gribble, McPhee Gribble was committed to publishing Australian writing in beautifully designed books with the intention of introducing more Australian voices to a market dominated by imported literature. One of McPhee Gribble's first successes was its publication in 1977 of Garner's autobiographical novel: *Monkey Grip*. The novel became a bestseller and went on to win the National Book Council Award for fiction in 1978. Apart from its vivid portrait of 1970s counterculture and its powerful exploration of addiction—especially to love and heroin—and of motherhood outside marriage, *Monkey Grip* is striking for the crystalline purity, immediacy and energy of Garner's prose.

Monkey Grip introduced a powerful new voice into Australian literature, one that was intensely personal, probing, fearless in its frank engagement with sex, drugs, shifting relationships and the emotions they engender. The novel, told in a series of fragments that capture the flux of this new uncertain life, opens joyfully: 'In the old brown house on the corner, a mile from the middle of the city, we ate bacon for breakfast every morning of our lives . . . It never occurred to us to teach the children to eat with a knife and fork. It was hunger and all sheer function: the noise, and clashing of plates, and people chewing with their mouths open, and talking, and laughing. Oh, I was happy then.' The narrator, Nora, navigates the uncharted waters of spontaneous sex, love, motherhood, creative work, drugs, making it all up as she goes along with her friends, lovers and young daughter. Nora is sleeping with Martin but falling for their friend Javo, 'the bludger, just back from getting off dope in Hobart: I looked at his burnt skin and scarred nose and violently blue eyes.'

The scene cuts to the Fitzroy baths. While Martin and Javo sit on the warm concrete, Nora plays around in the water, at the deep end 'where the sign read ACQUA PROFONDA'. Nora is in deep water—she is falling in love with Javo: 'afterwards, it is possible to see the beginning of things, the point at which you had already plunged in, while at the time you thought you were only testing the water.' The novel's loosely arranged fragments are held together by the recurring image of water—and by the spiral of Nora's addictive love for Javo, who is in the throes of his own addiction to heroin, and by the wise and abiding presence of Gracie, Nora's four-year-old daughter. Nora wheels through the suburbs of Melbourne with Gracie clinging to her back: 'We rode home, speeding along, Gracie on the back of my bike like a quiet monkey. The moon hung in the deep, deep blue sky; the air was dotty with stars. We sailed serenely through floods of warm autumn air.'

Nora's story is focused on her addiction to Javo and his addiction to heroin ('Smack habit, love habit—what's the difference? They can both kill you'); on everyone's struggles with jealousy and other powerful emotions as they try to live in open relationships where casual sex is cool; on the tension between her love for her daughter, the overwhelming weight of her responsibility for another human being, and her need for freedom; and on her constant preoccupation with love and sex: 'I thought about the patterns I made in my life: loving, loving the wrong person, loving not enough and too much and too long.'

Monkey Grip was made into a critically acclaimed film of the same name. Released in 1982, the film starred Noni Hazlehurst as Nora (for which she won an AFI Award for best actress); Colin Friels as Javo; Alice Garner as Gracie; and Chrissie Amphlett as Angela, one of Nora's friends. The film was directed by Ken Cameron, who later directed the miniseries of *My Brother Jack* (2001).

Garner was born in 1942 in Geelong, on the Victorian coast south-west of Melbourne. The eldest of six children, Garner finished her schooling at a private girls' school where in her final year she was dux and head prefect. She won a scholarship to the

University of Melbourne and studied English and French. After graduating in 1965, Garner became a high school teacher. In 1967 she travelled to Europe and spent time working as a teacher in London, where she met up with actor and playwright Bill Garner. They returned to Melbourne and were married in 1968. The following year their daughter Alice was born (the marriage ended in 1971). Garner continued to work as a teacher until she was dismissed from Fitzroy High School in 1972 for her frank discussions with the students and her alleged use of four-letter words in the classroom. Already active as a writer with the alternative magazine *Digger*, which appears in *Monkey Grip*, and in the Women's Theatre Group with its feminist production *Betty Can Jump* (1972), Garner turned to writing full-time.

Following the publication and success of *Monkey Grip* in 1977, Garner travelled to France and spent two years in Paris. There she wrote *Honour and Other People's Children* (1980) and met the French journalist Jean-Jacques Portail, whom she married in 1980. They moved to Melbourne, where Garner continued to write. In 1983 she published her second novel, *Moving Out*. Her widely acclaimed third novel, *The Children's Bach* (1984), was published the following year. *The Children's Bach* won the South Australian Premier's Literary Award in 1986 and her short story collection, *Postcards from Surfers* (1985), won the New South Wales Premier's Award the same year. In 1988 Garner moved to Sydney (her marriage to Portail had ended in 1985) where she met the writer Murray Bail. They moved to Melbourne in 1991, married in 1992 and returned to Sydney three years later. Garner's next work of fiction appeared in 1992: *Cosmo Cosmolino*, two stories and a novella which all feature angels. Garner was becoming increasingly interested in spiritual matters and around this time she began to read the Bible, as she recalls in her essay 'Sighs Too Deep for Words: On being bad at reading the Bible'.

In 1992 Garner became engrossed by the story of a charge of sexual misconduct brought by two students against the Master of Ormond College at the University of Melbourne. Three years later she published her controversial book on the case, *The First Stone: Some Questions about Sex and Power* (1995), in which she explored these allegations of sexual harassment. Her personally engaged, sympathetic portrayal of the accused man, who had lost his job, and her questioning of the motivations of the women involved in the case, provoked outrage among many readers and two books by young feminists were published in reply: Virginia Trioli's *Generation F: Sex, Power and the Young Feminist* (1996) and *bodyjamming* (1997), edited by Jenna Mead. In the wake of the controversy, *The First Stone* became a bestseller.

After her marriage to Bail ended in 1998, Garner began to research a court case in Canberra, drawn by the story of two young women who had been accused of killing the boyfriend of one of them—the engineer Joe Cinque—with a drug overdose in 1997. Garner returned to live in Melbourne in 2000 and four years later published her book on the death of Joe Cinque and the extraordinary events that surrounded it: *Joe Cinque's Consolation: A True Story of Death, Grief and the Law* (2004). As with her earlier foray into personal non-fiction, *Joe Cinque's Consolation* became a bestseller.

Garner has worked extensively as a freelance journalist, reviewer and essayist, and won a Walkley Award for journalism in 1993. Her journalism and essays have been published in *True Stories: Selected Non-fiction* (1996) and *The Feel of Steel* (2001). Garner has also written two screenplays, *The Last Days of Chez Nous* and *Two Friends*. Garner was awarded the prestigious Melbourne Prize for Literature in 2006.

Tegan Bennett Daylight's favourite Australian books

Up the Duff: The real guide to pregnancy by Kaz Cooke
Cosmo Cosmolino by Helen Garner
Honour and Other People's Children by Helen Garner
Snugglepot and Cuddlepie by May Gibbs
Making Stories by Kate Grenville and Sue Woolfe
The Great World by David Malouf
The Drums Go Bang by Ruth Park and D'Arcy Niland
Miss Bobbie by Ethel Turner
The Tree of Man by Patrick White
The Turning by Tim Winton

Tegan Bennett Daylight is the author of the novels *Bombora* (1996), *What Falls Away* (2001) and *Safety* (2005). In 2002 she was named as one of the *Sydney Morning Herald*'s 'Best Young Novelists'.

46

OUR SUNSHINE

Robert Drewe (1943–)

'I can bend from the saddle at full gallop and snatch a lady's handkerchief from the ground. I can stand and lie on the saddle at full gallop. I can jump fences kneeling on the horse's back.' This is 'Our Sunshine', a swaggering, bearded boy of twenty-four years who finds himself with an inn-full of hostages in Glenrowan in north-east Victoria in 1880. He is holed up with his so-called 'Gang'—his brother Dan Kelly and friends Joe Byrne and Steve Hart—impatiently waiting on the arrival of a police train, which he expects to be derailed. While he waits, he muses over his life and how he came to be in the Glenrowan Inn, recalling the exploits that have led to his infamy throughout the colonies as the 'Devil incarnate of the Antipodes, Satan's right hand, our Mephisto, the Vulture of the Wombat Ranges, beast of prey, outback monster . . .' and so the names continue. But his father called him 'Sunshine': '*In my daze he called me Sunshine.*'

'Our Sunshine' is Ned Kelly, the most celebrated and once most reviled of bushrangers, transformed by time, filmmakers, artists and writers into one of Australia's most enduring icons. *Our Sunshine* captures Ned Kelly at the end of his life, as his legend is being born. As Robert Drewe says: 'This book is about a man whose story outgrew his life.'

First published in 1991, Drewe's *Our Sunshine* opens with a lion's moan. To enhance the carnivalesque atmosphere of his final stand, Ned Kelly has held up and stolen a circus—and from time to time Ned's story is broken by the roar of a caged beast. In first and third person narratives, *Our Sunshine* explores in Ned's boastful, mocking, outraged voice the vast gap that lies between the newspaper accounts of him, his brother and their two friends as 'the Monster and his Gang', and the truth of his life as he has experienced it, as one of a persecuted tribe of impoverished Irish selectors at the mercy of police misrepresentation and prejudice. Of all the bushrangers of Australia's nineteenth century, none understood so well the power of words as Ned Kelly did—his written testimony survives in the State Library of Victoria—and none was turned into such media fodder as Kelly was.

Ned Kelly's two surviving documents are his *Cameron Letter* and *Jerilderie Letter*, both of which inform *Our Sunshine*. The *Jerilderie Letter* is Kelly's most substantial testimony, dictated to his friend Joe Byrne. Around 8000 words, the *Jerilderie Letter* is an impassioned plea of innocence. It is also an appeal for understanding and fair treatment for his family and the other poor Irish selectors of his community. In it Kelly gives his own account of his escapades with the police and of the events at Stringybark Creek where he killed three policemen. When Kelly and his mates travelled to the New South Wales town of Jerilderie in February 1879 to hold up a bank, Kelly had his letter with him, hoping to give it to the editor of the *Jerilderie Gazette*. Instead, he left it with the bank's accountant with instructions that it be published. It was not (until many years after Kelly's death).

And so *Our Sunshine* is Ned's testimony. 'You don't know the half of it. That's the trouble when your story's seen through other eyes.' It is Drewe's imagined recreation of Kelly's version of the events of his life—and it is pitted against a media that was able to use new technology to keep the public rapidly informed of Kelly's activities via special edition newspapers: the telegraph. The Glenrowan siege was the first widely reported and photographed criminal story in Australian history (outdoor photography had only recently become possible). Drewe, who in his early years was a journalist, allows Kelly not only to tell his own story but also to probe the ludicrous exaggerations of his media portrayal: 'Massacre, now there's a word. Worse than killing, worse than murder, worse than slaughter. Massacre's what they said we did. *What I, the monster, did.* "The Massacre at Stringybark Creek." But is it a massacre if they're shot going for their guns? If they're police? . . . Anyway, massacre sounds like killing many more than three. (Maybe ten and over.)'

Like an impresario, Ned addresses his hostages in the Glenrowan Inn, and his readers: 'Ladies and gentlemen—thank you, thank you—I've been asked to relate how I got started in my outlaw ways . . . Well, they locked up my mother, didn't they?' From the outset, *Our Sunshine* stresses Kelly's youth—'Still a boy myself under the whiskers,' he tells the young girl he dances with as he awaits the inevitable showdown—and the provocations that have sparked his rampages. His mother has been imprisoned in Pentridge Gaol and Ned has been obliged to shoot three policemen in self-defence. *Our Sunshine* powerfully imagines the life of this feisty boy who became head of his large household at eleven-and-a-half on his father's death; the string of events that lead to his going beyond the law; and then the thrills of successful bank robbery and outwitting the law. 'But I guess we four were always flash. The best riders and shooters ended up together. And we had the steel of grudge; we were the Micks who hit back twice as hard.'

The Kellys moved to Glenrowan—now known as 'Kelly Country'—after the death of Ned's father, 'Red' Kelly. At the time Glenrowan was a small settlement, a coach staging point on the road between Benalla and Wangaratta in north-eastern Victoria, 230 kilometres from Melbourne. In 1880 it became the venue for Ned Kelly's last stand.

Born in 1855 near Melbourne, Ned Kelly was the son of an Irish convict father who had been transported to Van Diemen's Land in 1842, possibly for the theft of two pigs. Red Kelly moved to Victoria on his release in 1848 and married the daughter of farmer James Quinn, for whom he worked. They had eight children; Edward 'Ned' Kelly was their eldest son. Ned had several run-ins with the police and prison system, the first at fourteen when he was accused of assaulting a Chinese pig farmer.

The breaking point came in April 1878 when Ned, his brother Dan and mother Ellen were accused of attacking policeman Constable Alexander Fitzpatrick. Ellen was taken into custody with her baby daughter and was still in prison when Ned was executed in 1880. Ned and Dan went into hiding, where Joe Byrne and Steve Hart later joined them. Following Ned's killing—in October 1878 at Stringybark Creek—of three of the four policemen who had set out to capture him, rewards were set for the Kelly brothers' heads and they were declared outlaws. Two bank robberies (including one where the mocking outlaws dressed as policemen) and another murder followed. During the showdown at Glenrowan in 1880, Joe Byrne was fatally wounded and Dan Kelly and Steve Hart died, possibly by suicide. Ned survived to be captured, tried and sentenced to hang. Ned Kelly was hanged in Melbourne on 11 November 1880. Melbourne's *Age* and the *Herald Sun* reported Kelly's last words as 'Such is life.' Following Kelly's death the Victorian Royal Commission into the Victorian Police Force (1881–83) led to changes in police practices throughout the colony.

Robert Drewe was born in 1943 in Melbourne, the eldest child of three. When Drewe was six, his father became the Western Australian state manager of Dunlop and the family moved to Perth. A successful student, Drewe was school captain, sports captain and editor of the school magazine. After school he became a cadet journalist and married young. As a court reporter he was confronted daily with the brutal underworld of crime and corruption, which he later drew on in his fiction and memoirs. Drewe moved to Melbourne to take up a job with the Victorian newspaper the *Age* and the following year was sent to Sydney to head its office there. He then wrote a daily column for the *Australian*. Frustrated by the limits of journalism, Drewe left the *Australian* to write fiction and has since published six novels and two short story collections. His novels include *The Savage Crows*, his first novel, about racism and the fate of the Tasmanian Aborigines, which was published to acclaim in 1976; *A Cry in the Jungle Bar* (1979); and *The Drowner* (1997), which won the Vance Palmer Prize for fiction. In 1983 Drewe published his celebrated collection of short stories, *The Bodysurfers*. His acclaimed memoir, *The Shark Net*, was published in 2000 and adapted for television in 2003. Drewe has won two Walkley Awards for journalism, in 1976 and 1982. He married the writer and editor Candida Baker in 1987, with whom he has two children (and five from his previous marriages). He lives on the far north coast of New South Wales. His most recent novel is *Grace*, published in 2005.

In 2003 *Our Sunshine* was adapted to the screen in the acclaimed film *Ned Kelly*. Directed by Grigor Jordan, *Ned Kelly* starred Heath Ledger as Ned Kelly, Orlando Bloom as Joe Byrne, Geoffrey Rush and Naomi Watts.

HELEN BARNES'S FAVOURITE
AUSTRALIAN BOOKS

Praise by Andrew McGahan. A beautifully unsentimental but gentle story of something resembling love.

An Older Kind of Magic by Patricia Wrightson. This is a wonderful kids' story about the collision between a pompous planning minister, a whole host of indigenous spirits and a magical comet. Her book *The Nargun and The Stars* is lovely, too.

Illywhacker by Peter Carey. In fact, just about everything by Peter Carey.

A Private Man by Malcolm Knox. A succinct yet devastating peek into the dark side of Australian cricket and the dynamics of an ambitious family.

Our Sunshine by Robert Drewe. I stop people in the street and tell them to read this gorgeous book.

The Riders by Tim Winton. I loved this book and I loved the way it baffled and irritated a lot of people.

Helen Barnes is the author of novels *The Crypt Orchid* (1994), *The Weather Girl* (1996) and *Killing Aurora* (2000), and co-writer of the screenplay of the 2007 film *Lucky Miles*.

47

True History of the
Kelly Gang

Peter Carey (1943–)

Peter Carey's bestselling *True History of the Kelly Gang* was first published in 2000, the year Ned Kelly featured in the 'Tin Symphony' at the Opening Ceremony of the Sydney Olympic Games. The novel is Carey's comprehensive retelling of the life of this legendary outlaw. The most striking feature of *True History of the Kelly Gang* is Carey's extraordinary act of incarnation— working from Kelly's distinctive voice as it speaks publicly in the *Jerilderie Letter*, Carey forged a facsimile of Kelly's private voice as it is expressed vividly and evocatively through his fictional testimony to his baby daughter. And Carey sustains this for over 450 pages. The success of Carey's feat of recreating Kelly's life in his 'own' voice was acknowledged by the awards and international acclaim his novel received. *True History of the Kelly Gang* won the 2001 Man Booker Prize, the 2001 Commonwealth Writers' Prize and the Victorian Premier's Literary Award for fiction. Writing in the *New York Times*, Anthony Quinn said of Carey's novel: 'Whatever one's (slight) misgivings about its status as a "true history", the book's power as a narrative is nearly over-whelming. The twang of Ned's untutored but vibrant prose would be hypnotic in itself, yet Carey adapts it to a series of set pieces —Ned's rescue of the drowning boy, a boxing match, his first meeting with the woman who will become his wife, the ambush, even the small drama of felling a tree—that are as gripping as any you could wish to read . . . he has transformed sepia legend into brilliant, even violent, color, and turned a distant myth into warm flesh and blood.'

Carey was first gripped by Ned Kelly's story after reading the *Jerilderie Letter* in the early 1960s, when he was nineteen or twenty. He was so struck by the power of Kelly's voice that he typed up a copy of the letter for himself, planning to do something with it some day: 'This is not a fantastically well-educated man, but very smart and very angry and very funny.' When Carey reread Kelly's letter years later, he was reminded of Paul Keating's gift for dazzling verbal abuse, only 'in a way I think Ned takes that Irish invective to an even higher order'. Carey lost his copy of the letter, but Kelly's story returned to him in New York, Carey's home since 1989. In the mid-1990s Carey took various New York friends to see Sidney Nolan's first series of Ned Kelly paintings from the 1940s. His friends did not know the story of Ned Kelly, so Carey found himself telling and retelling Kelly's story. And as he told it he realised that he had to write a novel about Kelly's life—and that there was only one way he could tell it: by using the voice of the *Jerilderie Letter* to make Kelly 'speak from beyond the grave'.

True History of the Kelly Gang is presented as a series of histor-ical documents held by the Melbourne Public Library. In Carey's telling, following the shootout at Glenrowan in June 1880, a 'small round figure in a tweed hat' made off with 'thirteen parcels of stained and dog-eared papers, every one of them in Ned Kelly's distinctive hand' and transported them to Melbourne inside a metal trunk. These thirteen parcels contain the 'true' story of Kelly's life, written for his fictional baby daughter. Kelly's opening words to her are: 'I lost my own father at 12 yr. of age and know what it is to be raised on lies and silences my dear daughter you are presently too young to understand a word I write but this history is for you and will contain no single lie may I burn in Hell if I speak false.' Like *Our Sunshine*, *True History of the Kelly Gang* closely follows the events of Ned Kelly's life as documented by history but clothes them with Kelly's imagined, fully-formed consciousness.

Unlike *Our Sunshine*, Carey's novel opens with Ned as a child and enters deeply into the circumstances of his early life, its hardship—'The land were very good at Avenel but there were a drought and nothing flourished there but misery'; his family's persecution by the police; their inferior place as Irish Catholics and as selectors at the mercy of the squatters; and Ned's relationships with his father Red Kelly, his beloved mother Ellen and his many siblings. The famed incident of the young Ned's rescue of a boy from drowning and his reward of a green sash is portrayed in great detail, highlighting the Kellys' grinding poverty and Ned's own modesty, courage and goodness: 'I looked down at my person and seen not my bare feet my darned pullover my patched pants but a 7 ft. sash. It were peacock green embroidered with gold TO EDWARD KELLY IN GRATITUDE FOR HIS COURAGE FROM THE SHELTON FAMILY.'

It is this green sash that Kelly wears beneath his armour for the final stakeout. When Joe Byrne first tries on the helmet they have forged from plough metal Kelly says: 'The 3 of us stood back in silent veneration as the Soldier of Future Time turned his back to walk with steady tread there were a slight squeak from the cockplate swinging from its wires did ever such machine of war tread upon the earth before?' This remarkable voice, drawn from the

Jerilderie Letter, is also transfused by the rhythms and language of the Bible: 'And lo they did applaud us with their eyes bright their faces red', writes Ned of their captive audience's response to his gang's horseback antics after their successful bank robbery at Euroa in December 1878: 'Joe Byrne that begun the display of flashy riding prior to our departure we showed them what Wild Colonial Boys could do we demonstrated riding the like of which were never seen before . . .' Compared by critics to the work of William Shakespeare, Charles Dickens, Mark Twain and Sidney Nolan, *True History of the Kelly Gang* is an extraordinary, beautifully composed Australian novel.

The youngest of three children, Peter Carey was born in the town of Bacchus Marsh, west of Melbourne, where his parents ran the local General Motors dealership. He went to Geelong Grammar School and in 1961 began a science degree at Monash University, but left the following year to work as an advertising copywriter in Melbourne. In 1967 Carey moved to London, where he lived for three years and travelled through Europe, working on three novels that were never published and writing short stories. Carey returned to Melbourne in 1970, where he continued to work in advertising and to write. His first two published works were short story collections: *The Fat Man in History*, published in 1974, the year he moved to Sydney; and *War Crimes* (1979), which won the New South Wales Premier's Award for fiction. Carey wrote most of the stories in *War Crimes* while he was living in an alternative community near Yandina, southern Queensland, where he moved in 1977. *War Crimes* shows the influence of South American writers like Gabriel García Márquez and their magic realism. In 1981 Carey's first published novel, the award-winning *Bliss*, appeared to wide acclaim. Four years later the feature film of *Bliss* (1985), starring Barry Otto and directed by Ray Lawrence, won three AFI awards, including Best Film and Best Script, which Carey co-wrote.

Carey returned to Sydney in 1980 to set up his own advertising company. The following year he moved to northern New South Wales, where he wrote his second published novel, *Illywhacker* (1985), which was shortlisted for the 1985 Booker Prize. In 1984 Carey met theatre director Alison Summers and they were married the following year. They have two sons. Carey's third novel, *Oscar and Lucinda*, was published in 1988 and won the Booker Prize. In 1997 the acclaimed film of *Oscar and Lucinda* was released, directed by Gillian Armstrong and starring Ralph Fiennes and Cate Blanchett. Carey moved to Greenwich Village, New York, in 1989 and has lived in New York ever since. Six more acclaimed novels followed *Oscar and Lucinda*, including *The Tax Inspector* (1991); *Jack Maggs* (1997), his retelling of the story of Abel Magwitch from Charles Dickens's *Great Expectations*; and *My Life as a Fake* (2003). Carey's most recent novel is *Theft: A Love Story*, published in 2006, which won the Christina Stead Prize for fiction at the 2007 New South Wales Premier's Literary Awards.

Margaret Merten's favourite Australian books

Wake in Fright by Kenneth Cook (my absolute No. 1—Australian Gothic—so scary)

The Man Who Loved Children by Christina Stead

The Transit of Venus by Shirley Hazzard

The Merry-Go-Round in the Sea by Randolph Stow

An Open Swimmer by Tim Winton

My Place by Sally Morgan

Bliss by Peter Carey

Monkey Grip by Helen Garner

The Glass Canoe by David Ireland

The Harp in the South by Ruth Park (not so much for its writing but because it told the urban working-class story for the first time)

Journalist Margaret Merten is the associate editor of *Harper's Bazaar*. She was previously editor of *Vogue Entertaining + Travel* and features editor of *Vogue* magazine.

48

LILIAN'S STORY

Kate Grenville (1950–)

Lilian's Story opens with the birth of a girl on a night in which the order of the universe is upturned: 'It was a wild night in the year of Federation that the birth took place. Horses kicked down their stables. Pigs flew, figs grew thorns.' While the father, 'a man of moustaches and of shiny boots', had not expected a girl, he rallies within a day to announce: '*Lilian. She will be called Lilian Una.*' The mother, on the other hand, 'lay on her white bed at home, her palms turned up, staring at the moulding of the ceiling with the expression of surprise she wore for the next twenty years.' Their exuberant daughter Lilian narrates the story of her life growing up on Sydney Harbour with her younger brother as she struggles through school and university to find her way in a world for which she is too large, too loud, too clever—and the wrong sex: 'It was impossible to believe that nothing would come of all those hours I had spent dreaming out at rain on the harbour. I would have liked to be Wilberforce, anxious about slaves, or Dickens, bringing tears to everyone's eyes. I would have liked to be Socrates . . .'

Told in a series of outbursts and yet beautifully measured, Lilian's story is vivid with life and humour. Lilian's progression from the narrow confines of her family home where dark impulses fester to her freedom on the streets of Sydney is poignant, traumatic and triumphant.

When Kate Grenville began thinking about the novel in the 1980s, she had just completed two years in the University of Colorado's creative writing program and was about to return to Australia after spending seven years overseas. As her thoughts turned to Sydney, one of the images that emerged was of Bea Miles, the eccentric daughter of a wealthy businessman who had taken to living on the streets of Sydney. In the story of Miles, Grenville saw a woman who had defied convention to create her own freshly minted idiosyncratic, big, brazen life, which was exactly the sort of story Grenville wanted to tell. But although inspired in part by Miles, Grenville wrote several drafts of *Lilian's Story* before reading the details of Miles's life—so that the novel became Grenville's vital conjuring of a woman whose life bears the outline of Miles's but who is Grenville's original bold creation: the massive presence that is Lilian Una Singer, excessive in every respect. One of the challenges that Grenville faced in writing *Lilian's Story* was to work out how Lilian came to be living on the streets having started life as the well-educated daughter of an affluent family. Grenville's rationale for Lilian's transformation is the dark heart of *Lilian's Story*.

Patrick White, a great admirer of Grenville's work, said of *Lilian's Story* when it was first published in 1985: 'Kate Grenville has transformed an Australian myth into a dazzling fiction of universal appeal. It is a pleasure to be able to praise a true novelist.' *Lilian's Story* was adapted to the screen as a feature film of the same name in 1995. Produced by Marian Macgowan, *Lilian's Story* starred Ruth Cracknell, Barry Otto and Toni Collette, who won an AFI Award for Best Actress in a Supporting Role for her performance.

Bea Miles was born the daughter of a wealthy businessman in Sydney in 1902 and grew up on Sydney's affluent North Shore. She was a student of Abbotsleigh school and went to the University of Sydney, first to study medicine, later transferring to arts. Unable to fit into her parents' Wahroonga milieu, Miles left home in 1926 to begin her life of adventure. She became notorious for her manipulation of Sydney's taxi drivers, jumping into their cars at intersections and refusing to get out, and once requested a trip to Broken Hill via Melbourne on Christmas Day. She also travelled to Western Australia in a taxi to collect wildflowers. Miles paid her taxi fares with the allowance she received from her father. Known for her recitations of Shakespeare, Miles would stand on the steps of the Mitchell Library and recite Shakespearean sonnets for threepence and scenes from his plays for sixpence. Miles spent the last nine years of her life in the Little Sisters of the Poor home for the aged in Randwick, where she was known for her compassion and kindness. At her request, a jazz band played popular Australian songs such as 'Waltzing Matilda' at her funeral procession and her coffin was draped with a ribbon that said: 'One who loved Australia'.

Kate Grenville was born in Sydney in 1950. Her father was a barrister and her mother a high school teacher. After school Grenville enrolled at the University of Sydney where she studied English literature. After graduating in 1972, Grenville worked in the Australian film industry before leaving Sydney for London, where her first stories were published. She was inspired as a writer by Jane Austen, Virginia Woolf and Patrick White; and by the feminist works of Germaine Greer, whose *The Female Eunuch* was first published in London in 1970, and Anne Summers's *Damned*

Whores and God's Police: The Colonization of Women in Australia, which was published five years later. When Grenville was thirty, her first story was published in *Southerly*, the University of Sydney's literary magazine. In 1980 Grenville went to the United States to take an MA in the creative writing program at the University of Colorado. She returned to Sydney in 1983, where she completed her novel *Dreamhouse*; compiled her first published book, the short story collection *Bearded Ladies* (1984); and worked on *Lilian's Story*. In 1984 Grenville submitted the manuscript of *Lilian's Story* to the *Australian*/Vogel Literary Award and it won. It was published the following year, in 1985.

In 1986 Grenville married the cartoonist and writer Bruce Petty and together they have two children. Since *Lilian's Story* Grenville has published five novels, including *Dreamhouse* (1986); *Joan Makes History: A Novel* (1988), a feminist retelling of Australian history; and *The Idea of Perfection* (1999), which won the 2001 Orange Prize for Fiction. In 1994 the companion novel to *Lilian's Story* was published: *Dark Places* (published in the United States as *Albion's Story*), which is the story of Lilian's father, Albion Gidley Singer. Grenville has also published books about writing, including *The Writing Book* (1990) and *Making Stories: How ten Australian novels were written* (1993), co-authored with Sue Woolfe. Grenville's most recent novel, *The Secret River*, was published in 2005 and won the 2006 Commonwealth Writers' Prize and the New South Wales Premier's Award for fiction. *The Secret River* is the story of a young man who works on the Thames River in London and is transported as a convict to New South Wales. With his family he is later among the first to settle on the Hawkesbury River north of Sydney. Grenville's most recent book is *Searching for the Secret River* (2006), her account of writing *The Secret River*.

Gaby Naher's favourite
Australian books

It was not until *Lilian's Story*, by Kate Grenville, was published
in 1985 that any Australian novel truly resonated with me.
When I first read it I loved everything about this rich, gutsy and
profoundly human novel. Bea Miles—the real-life character
on whom Grenville based her own protagonist, Lilian Singer—
featured in some of my own family's Kings Cross stories.
Grenville wrote about Sydney more evocatively than anyone else
I'd read; it was with some dismay—when I set up my new study
here in Moscow a year ago—that I realised I had come to this
new life without Lilian.

My *other* Australian classic is May Gibbs's delightful *Snugglepot
and Cuddlepie*. All through my childhood I looked at the
Australian bush through the eyes of a girl who saw a gumnut
baby under every leaf.

Gaby Naher is the author of the novels *The Underwharf* (1995)
and *Bathing in Light* (1999); the memoir *The Truth About My Fathers*
(2002); and *Wrestling the Dragon: In Search of the Boy Lama Who Defied
China* (2004).

49

My Place
Sally Morgan (1951–)

My Place is the story of Sally Morgan's quest to find her place in the world. After learning from her younger sister that their ancestors are Aboriginal, the fifteen-year-old Morgan is compelled to uncover the truth of her family and its history. Puzzled and frustrated by her mother and grandmother's denials and silence on the subject—and baffled that all her life they have told her she is Indian—in 1979 Morgan decides to write a book on her family's history. Determined to learn the truth, Morgan persists in questioning anyone who can tell her anything about her grandmother's life, from Judy Drake-Brockman—the daughter of the pastoralist who owned the Pilbara station Corunna Downs, where her grandmother worked as a young woman—to her grandmother's brother Arthur Corunna.

And in a library in Perth Morgan discovers a shameful history, as she tells her mother: 'Well, when Nan was younger, Aborigines were considered sub-normal and not capable of being educated the way whites were. You know, the pastoral industry was built on the back of slave labour. Aboriginal people were forced to work, if they didn't, the station owners called the police in.' Eventually Morgan travels with her mother, husband and children to the Pilbara in far north Western Australia, the home of her Palyku people, to question the local people and see the country from which she is descended.

First published by the Fremantle Arts Centre Press in 1987, *My Place* is the deeply moving story Morgan began to piece together from fragments in 1979. Through her persistence, Morgan eventually drags to light some of the secrets of her grandmother Daisy Corunna's life, in the process unlocking Daisy's long-buried devastation over the loss of her two daughters. Her younger daughter, Gladys, is Morgan's mother; she was taken from Daisy when she was three: 'I ran down to the wild bamboo near the river and I hid and cried and cried and cried. How can a mother lose a child like that?' *My Place* contains Morgan's own story, which opens with her visit to her father in hospital, where he spent much of his time before he committed suicide when Morgan was nine. The Coroner's Report attributed his suicide to the after-effects of the First World War. *My Place* also contains the story of Arthur Corunna, a stockman, recorded and transcribed by Morgan. Arthur's testimony is filled with his longing for land and fired by his anger over its theft: 'Take the white people in Australia, they brought the religion here with them and the Commandment, Thou Shalt Not Steal, and yet they stole this country. They took it from the innocent.' Morgan's book also includes the recorded stories of her mother Gladys and grandmother Daisy, with their sagas of loss and reunion.

Morgan originally wrote *My Place* for her family and for her children, so that they would not grow up without knowing their history, as Morgan had. But the story of *My Place* has travelled well beyond Morgan's family. Since its publication in 1987, the year before the bicentenary of white settlement in Australia, *My Place* has sold over 550,000 copies and has been published in eleven countries. Following the bestselling success of *My Place* and the wide transmission of Morgan's story, the Drake-Brockman family has contested some of its details, such as the direct relationship between Howden Drake-Brockman and Morgan's mother and grandmother. In 2001 Howden's daughter, Judith Drake-Brockman, published her own account of her family and their relationship with their Aboriginal employees in her autobiography *Wongi Wongi*.

In the background of Daisy Corunna and her daughter Gladys's lives is the Western Australian Aborigines Act of 1905 (later amended to become the Native Administration Act in 1936), which decreed that children of mixed Aboriginal and European parentage could be taken from their families and placed in institutions or foster homes; and that all children of Aboriginal descent were under the legal guardianship of the Chief Protector of Aborigines until they were sixteen. This law remained in force until the early 1970s. In April 1997 the publication of the Australian Human Rights and Equal Opportunity Commission's harrowing report *Bringing Them Home: National Inquiry into the Separation of Aboriginal and Torres Strait Islander Children from Their Families* provided the first comprehensive record of the Aboriginal and Torres Strait Islander children who had been taken from their families, and includes the testimony of many of those children. The inquiry was established in 1995 in response to concern amongst Indigenous Australians that the public's ignorance of the forced removal of children was preventing the recognition of the needs of the stolen children and their families. Under the inquiry, an extensive program of hearings was conducted across Australia from December 1995 to October 1996. Seven hundred and seventy-seven submissions were made.

Born in Perth in 1951 to Gladys and William Milroy, Sally Morgan was often asked at school where she came from, because of her dark skin and hair. Her mother Gladys and grandmother Daisy told her their family was Indian, afraid that Sally and her four siblings could be taken from them if it were discovered that they were Aboriginal. When Morgan learned her true identity as a teenager, she began a quest to uncover her past. After successfully completing high school, the first in her family to do so, Morgan went to the University of Western Australia to do a Bachelor of Arts, majoring in psychology. While she was at university she met Paul Morgan, a school teacher who had grown up in the north-west of Western Australia, mostly in Derby, as the son of missionaries. In 1972 Paul and Sally were married and they have three children. Two years later, in 1974, Morgan graduated with a Bachelor of Arts. She then undertook further study in counselling psychology and computing and library studies.

Following the successful publication of *My Place* in 1987, Morgan published a book about her grandfather through Aboriginal kinship, *Wanamurraganya: The Story of Jack McPhee*, in 1989. She is also the author of several children's books, including *The Flying Emu and other Australian Stories* (1992), *Dan's Grandpa* (1996) and *In Your Dreams* (1997). Her play *Sistergirl* was first performed in Perth in 1992 and Morgan is also an acclaimed artist. In 1997 Morgan was appointed Director of the Centre of Indigenous History and the Arts at the University of Western Australia's School of Indigenous Studies. Through her work at the university, she is involved with Indigenous oral history and art projects. Morgan is currently working on a trilogy of three historical novels.

ANNA FUNDER'S FAVOURITE
AUSTRALIAN BOOKS

The Man Who Loved Children by Christina Stead
Terra Australis: Matthew Flinders' Great Adventures in the Circumnavigation of
 Australia by Matthew Flinders
Cloudstreet by Tim Winton
Fredy Neptune by Les Murray
Bringing Them Home by the Australian Human Rights and Equal
 Opportunity Commission
The Aunt's Story by Patrick White
Monkey Grip by Helen Garner
The Chant of Jimmie Blacksmith by Thomas Keneally
The Magic Pudding by Norman Lindsay
Romulus, My Father by Raimond Gaita

Anna Funder is the author of *Stasiland: Stories from Behind the Berlin Wall*, which won the 2004 BBC FOUR Samuel Johnson Prize for Non-Fiction.

Elizabeth Webby's favourite Australian books

Collected Poems by Charles Harpur
His Natural Life by Marcus Clarke
Robbery Under Arms by Rolf Boldrewood
Collected Stories by Henry Lawson
My Brilliant Career by Miles Franklin
Capricornia by Xavier Herbert
The Man Who Loved Children by Christina Stead
The Twyborn Affair by Patrick White
The Children's Bach by Helen Garner
My Father's Moon by Elizabeth Jolley

Elizabeth Webby is Professor of Australian Literature at the University of Sydney and editor of *The Cambridge Companion to Australian Literature* (2000).

you came to buy a *West Australian* and talk about the progress of the war with your neighbours'. Lamb Smallgoods becomes such an institution that it is known in the neighbourhood as 'Cloudstreet'.

And yet in the cavernous house the two families remain divided, driving each other mad. As Sam thinks: 'The house vibrated with hustle these days, groaning laborious as a ship with those Lambs going at it night and day, singing, working, laughing, shifting boxes and furniture morning and night and their blasted rooster going off like a burglar alarm at all hours . . . You'd think they were carrying the nation on their backs with all that scrubbing and sweeping . . .' And the indolent Pickles equally irritate the Lambs. *Cloudstreet* is Tim Winton's earthy, boisterous, funny story of the Lambs and the Pickles ('It's gunna sound like a counter lunch—lamb and pickles'), reaching from the Second World War to the 1960s, as they find themselves gradually making their home together on Cloud Street. Told in ten parts, each broken into small titled sections, *Cloudstreet* moves in a circular motion to end where it began, in an ecstatic moment of freedom and release.

Winton began writing *Cloudstreet* in 1986. During part of the four years he took to write it, he was living in Europe, missing Western Australia. *Cloudstreet*, with its vibrant vernacular and celebration of Australian ways, is Winton's hymn to his native land and to his own childhood spent in the embrace of a large family of storytellers in Western Australia. Winton writes in a fluent, rolling prose that is as easy with the small moments of intimacy between husband and wife, or brother and brother, as it is with the excesses of a family riot: 'From the pub verandah men saw the Lambs barrelling down the hill like mad bastards, and they heard them singing and shouting like they were ready for rape and revenge, and the sight of them rioting on the open tray of that Chev suddenly put people in the street.' Over the course of the novel's unfolding, its epigraph, a fragment of a nineteenth-century hymn—'Shall we gather at the river / Where bright angel-feet have trod . . .'—takes on an almost excruciating poignancy, for at the heart of this exuberant novel is the faltering enchanted world of Fish Lamb: 'But Quick held his brother's head in his hands and knew it wasn't quite right. Because not all of Fish Lamb had come back.'

First published in 1991, the bestselling, award-winning *Cloudstreet* is Winton's fifth novel. *Cloudstreet* won the 1991 Western Australian Fiction Award, the National Book Council Banjo Award for Fiction, the Deo Gloria Award (UK) in 1991, and the 1992 Miles Franklin Award. In 2003 *Cloudstreet* was voted by the members of the Australian Society of Authors as the most popular Australian novel of all time. Writing in the *Washington Post*, Elizabeth Ward said of Winton's novel: '*Cloudstreet* gets you inside the very skin of post-war working-class Australians the way Joyce makes you feel like a turn-of-the-century Dubliner . . . People get up from where they have fallen, they try, they keep on. Above all, they laugh, at themselves, sometimes bitterly, but much more often riotously.' *Cloudstreet* was adapted for the stage by Nick Enright and Justin Monjo. First performed to acclaim in Australia and Europe in 1999, the play of *Cloudstreet* toured again in 2001, to the United States and England.

Tim Winton was born in the Perth suburb of Mosman Park in 1960, the eldest of four children. His father was a policeman and the son of a policeman. Winton's childhood was rich with large family gatherings, family stories and beach holidays, often spent at Greenough River, north of Perth. His lifelong love of the sea and surfing pervades his writing. Always a compulsive reader, by the age of ten Winton knew he would be a writer—he had written a bush ballad at school and his teacher liked it so much that in response Winton declared he would be a writer. His family moved to Albany on the south coast of Western Australia when he was twelve and returned to Perth in 1973, where Winton finished school at Scarborough High. By the time he was in his final year of school, Winton had written dozens of stories and after completing school he enrolled in the Western Australian Institute of Technology (now Curtin University), where he majored in creative writing and was taught by Elizabeth Jolley. Aged nineteen and still at college, Winton began his first novel, *An Open Swimmer*. In 1981 he submitted it to the *Australian*/Vogel Literary Award and it was the joint winner (with *Al Jazzar* by Chris Matthews). *An Open Swimmer* was published in 1982 and Winton became a full-time writer. The same year he married Denise Fitch, with whom he has three children.

Following his first novel, Winton published almost a book a year for a decade. His second novel, *Shallows*, was published in 1984 and won the Miles Franklin Award. His third book was a short story collection, *Scission*, published the following year. His third novel, *That Eye, The Sky*, was published in 1986 and has since been adapted to stage and film. In 1987 Winton won the Marten Bequest travelling scholarship and left Australia for the first time. He travelled with his wife and family to Europe, where they lived in France, Ireland and Greece. When they returned to Perth at the end of 1988 they bought a shack in Lancelin, on the coast north of Perth.

Winton has since written five more novels for adults, including *In the Winter Dark* (1988), *The Riders* (1995) and *Dirt Music* (2001), which won the Miles Franklin Award, and three short story collections, including the bestselling *The Turning* (2004). Winton has also written books for children, including *Jesse* (1988) and his trilogy about Lockie Leonard, the first volume of which was *Lockie Leonard, Human Torpedo* (1990). In 1993 Winton published a memoir about his obsession with the beach and ocean called *Land's Edge*.

Winton is the patron of the Tim Winton Award for Young Writers sponsored by the City of Subiaco in Western Australia. He is an active environmentalist and in 2002 he donated the $25,000 Western Australian Premier's Award prize money he won for *Dirt Music* to save Ningaloo Reef, Western Australia's equivalent to the Great Barrier Reef. Winton remains a passionate surfer and reader, and most of the time lives in Fremantle, Western Australia.

GABRIELLE CAREY'S FAVOURITE
AUSTRALIAN BOOKS

Midnite: The Story of a Wild Colonial Boy by Randolph Stow
The Chantic Bird by David Ireland
It's Raining in Mango by Thea Astley

Gabrielle Carey is the author of *In My Father's House* (1992), *The Borrowed Girl* (1994) and the memoir *So Many Selves* (2006). She is the co-author with Kathy Lette of *Puberty Blues* (1979).

Index to boxes

The *Bulletin* — 30
Ern Malley — 206
Federation — 72
Gold — 13
Manning Clark and *A History of Australia* — 212
The Paterson–Lawson Duel — 65
Robin Boyd and *The Australian Ugliness* — 123
The 'Sydney Push' — 285
The Tichborne Case — 38
Vance and Nettie Palmer — 45

Favourite Australian books

Helen Barnes — 305
Caroline Baum — 233
Georgia Blain — 153
James Bradley — 253
Gabrielle Carey — 328
Peter Craven — 293
Alison Croggan — 247
Sophie Cunningham — 104
Tegan Bennett Daylight — 299
Delia Falconer — 187

Margaret Fink	265
Anna Funder	321
Helen Garner	23
Nikki Gemmell	98
Jamie Grant	117
Robert Gray	200
Gideon Haigh	136
Andrew Hansen	182
Margaret Harris	271
John Hughes	259
Gail Jones	111
Nicholas Jose	215
Leonie Kramer	240
Marian Macgowan	227
Emily Maguire	221
David Malouf	53
Margaret Merten	311
Jane Messer	159
Frank Moorhouse	165
Laura Moss	79
Les Murray	59
Gaby Naher	316
Garth Nix	171
Louis Nowra	92
Mandy Sayer	142
Jeffrey Smart	86
Meg Stewart	129
Samantha Trenoweth	279
Christos Tsiolkas	193
Elizabeth Webby	322
Tara June Winch	148
Tim Winton	287
Charlotte Wood	177

Bibliography

Adams, Paul & Lee, Christopher, *Frank Hardy and the Literature of Commitment*, The Vulgar Press, Carlton North, 2003.

Anderson, Jessica, *Tirra Lirra by the River*, Picador, Sydney, 1978.

Astley, Thea, *The Acolyte*, Penguin Books, Melbourne, 1972.

Barry, Elaine, *Fabricating the Self: The Fictions of Jessica Anderson*, University of Queensland Press, St Lucia, 1996.

Baynton, Barbara, *Bush Studies*, Angus & Robertson, Sydney, 1990.

Blainey, Geoffrey (ed), *Henry Lawson*, The Text Publishing Company, Melbourne, 2002.

Blainey, Geoffrey, *The Tyranny of Distance*, Sun Books, Melbourne, 1983.

Boldrewood, Rolf, *Robbery Under Arms*, Lloyd O'Neil, Hawthorn, 1970.

Boldrewood, Rolf, *Robbery Under Arms*, Eggert, Paul & Webby, Elizabeth (eds), University of Queensland Press, St Lucia, 2006.

Boyd, Martin, *Lucinda Brayford*, Penguin Books, Ringwood, 1985.

Boyd, Robin, *The Australian Ugliness*, Penguin Books, Melbourne, 1968.

Carey, Peter, *True History of the Kelly Gang*, Random House Australia, Sydney, 2005.

Chisholm, AR & Quinn, JJ (eds), *The Verse of Christopher Brennan*, Angus & Robertson, Sydney, 1960.

Clark, Manning, *A Short History of Australia*, Macmillan Company of Australia, Melbourne, 1981.

Clarke, Marcus, *His Natural Life*, University of Queensland Press, St Lucia, 2001.

Clarke, Patricia & McKinney, Meredith, *With Love and Fury: Selected Letters of Judith Wright*, National Library of Australia, Canberra, 2006.

Collins, Tom, *Such is Life*, The Hogarth Press, London, 1986.

Cusack, Dymphna, Inglis Moore, T, Ovenden, Barrie, *Mary Gilmore: A Tribute*, Australasian Book Society, Sydney, 1965.

Drewe, Robert, *Our Sunshine*, Picador, Sydney, 1991.

Facey, AB, *A Fortunate Life*, Penguin Books, Camberwell, 2005.

Franklin, Miles, in association with Kate Baker, *Joseph Furphy: The Legend of a Man and his Book*, Angus & Robertson, Sydney, 1944.

Franklin, Miles, *My Brilliant Career*, Angus & Robertson, Sydney, 2001.

Franklin, Miles, *My Brilliant Career*, and *My Career Goes Bung*, HarperCollins, Sydney, 2004.

Gare, Deborah, Bolton, Geoffrey, Macintyre, Stuart, Stannage, Tom (eds), *The Fuss That Never Ended: The Life and Work of Geoffrey Blainey*, Melbourne University Press, Carlton, 2003.

Garner, Helen, *Monkey Grip*, McPhee Gribble Publishers, Melbourne, 1977.

Gelder, Ken, *Atomic Fiction: The Novels of David Ireland*, University of Queensland Press, St Lucia, 1993.

Gilmore, Mary, *Fourteen Men*, Angus & Robertson, Sydney, 1954.

Gordon, Adam Lindsay, *Bush Ballads and Galloping Rhymes: Poetical Works of Adam Lindsay Gordon*, Lloyd O'Neil, Hawthorn, 1970.

Green, HM, *Christopher Brennan*, Angus & Robertson, Sydney, 1939.

Grenville, Kate, *Lilian's Story*, Allen & Unwin, Sydney, 1996.

Guha, Ramachandra (ed), *The Picador Book of Cricket*, Pan Macmillan, London, 2001.

Hall, Richard, *Banjo Paterson: His poetry and prose*, Allen & Unwin, Sydney, 1993.

Hardy, Frank, *Power Without Glory*, Lloyd O'Neil, Victoria, 1972.

Hazzard, Shirley, *The Transit of Venus*, Macmillan London, London, 1980.

Herbert, Xavier, *Capricornia*, Angus & Robertson, Sydney, 2002.

Hewitt, Helen Verity, *Patrick White, Painter Manqué: Paintings, painters and their influence on his writing*, The Miegunya Press, Melbourne, 2002.

Hope, AD, *Collected Poems*, Angus & Robertson, Sydney, 1975.

Hope, AD, *Selected Poems*, Angus & Robertson, Sydney, 1992.

Horne, Donald, *How I Came to Write 'The Lucky Country'*, Melbourne University Press, Melbourne, 2006.

Horne, Donald, *The Lucky Country*, Penguin Books, Ringwood, 1964.

Hughes, Robert, *The Art of Australia*, Penguin Books, Harmondsworth, Middlesex, 1970.

Hughes, Robert, *The Fatal Shore*, Pan Books, London, 1987.

Hughes, Robert, *Things I Didn't Know: A Memoir*, Knopf, Sydney, 2006.

Hutton, Geoffrey, *Adam Lindsay Gordon: The man and the myth*, Faber and Faber, London, 1978.

Ireland, David, *The Glass Canoe*, Sydney University Press, Sydney, 2003.

Johnston, George, *My Brother Jack*, Angus & Robertson, Sydney, 1990.

Jolley, Elizabeth, *Milk and Honey*, Fremantle Arts Centre Press, South Fremantle, 1996.

Keneally, Thomas, *The Chant of Jimmie Blacksmith*, HarperCollins Publishers, Sydney, 2001.

Krimmer, Sally and Lawson, Alan, *Portable Australian Authors: Barbara Baynton*, University of Queensland Press, St Lucia, 1980.

Langley, Eve, *The Pea-pickers*, Angus & Robertson, Sydney, 2001.

Lindsay, Norman, *The Magic Pudding*, Angus & Robertson, Sydney, 1987.

McAuley, James, *A Map of Australian Verse: The Twentieth Century*, Oxford University Press, Melbourne, 1975.

McCann, Andrew, *Marcus Clarke's Bohemia: Literature and Modernity in Colonial Melbourne*, Melbourne University Publishing, Melbourne, 2004.

Mailey, Arthur, *10 for 66 and all that*, Phoenix Sports Books, London, 1958.

Malouf, David, *An Imaginary Life*, Chatto & Windus, London, 1978.

Marr, David, *Patrick White: A Life*, Random House Australia, Sydney, 1991.

Moorhouse, Frank, *Grand Days*, Random House Australia, Sydney, 1993.

Morgan, Sally, *My Place*, Fremantle Arts Centre Press, Fremantle, 1987.

Murnane, Gerald, *The Plains*, Norstrilia Press, Melbourne, 1982.

Murray, Les, *Hell and After: Four Early English-language poets of Australia*, Carcanet Press, Manchester, 2005.

Murray, Les, *New Collected Poems*, Carcanet Press, Manchester, 2003.

Neilson, John Shaw, *Selected Poems*, Angus & Robertson, Sydney, 1980.

Prichard, Katharine Susannah, *Coonardoo*, Angus & Robertson, Sydney, 1998.

Richardson, Henry Handel, *The Getting of Wisdom*, Clive Probyn and Bruce Steele (eds), University of Queensland Press, St Lucia, 2001.

Roderick, Colin, *Henry Lawson: A Life*, Angus & Robertson, Sydney, 2001.

Samuels, Selina, *Dictionary of Literary Biography, Volume 289: Australian Writers, 1950–1975*, Gale, Detroit, 2004.

Samuels, Selina, *Dictionary of Literary Biography, Volume 325: Australian Writers, 1975–2000*, Thomson Gale, Detroit, 2006.

Scott, WN, *Judith Wright*, University of Queensland Press, St Lucia, 1967.

Shoemaker, Adam and Hergenhan, Laurie (eds), *Oodgeroo: A Tribute*, University of Queensland Press, St Lucia, 1994.

Sladen, Douglas, *Adam Lindsay Gordon: The Life and Best Poems of the Poet of Australia*, Hutchinson & Co, London, 1934.

Slessor, Kenneth, *Selected Poems*, Angus & Robertson, Sydney, 1993.

Strauss, Jennifer (ed), *The Collected Verse of Mary Gilmore, Volume I: 1887–1929*, University of Queensland Press, St Lucia, 2004.

Stead, Christina, *The Man Who Loved Children*, Angus & Robertson, Sydney, 1994.

Stow, Randolph, *Visitants*, Taplinger Publishing Company, New York, 1981.

Thiele, Colin, *Storm Boy*, New Holland Publishers, Sydney, 2001.

Thiele, Colin, *With Dew on My Boots*, Thomas C Lothian, Melbourne, 2002.

Turner, Ethel, *Seven Little Australians*, Ward, Lock & Co, London, 1912.

Turner, Ethel, *The Diaries of Ethel Turner* (compiled by Philippa Poole), New Holland, Sydney, 2004.

Walker, Kath, *My People: A Kath Walker Collection*, Jacaranda Press, Brisbane, 1970.

White, Patrick, *Voss*, Penguin Books, Harmondsworth, Middlesex, 1987.

Winton, Tim, *Cloudstreet*, Penguin Books, Melbourne, 2004.

Wright, Judith, *A Human Pattern: Selected Poems*, Angus & Robertson, Sydney, 1990.

Wright, Judith, *Preoccupations in Australian Poetry*, Oxford University Press, Melbourne, 1965.

JOURNALS

Astley, Thea, 'The Idiot Question', *Southerly* #1, 1970.

Catalano, Gary, 'The Bread We Eat: On Mary Gilmore', *Quadrant*, April 2001.

Goldsworthy, Kerryn, 'No Comfort in the Stars', *Australian Book Review*, July 2001.

Jose, Nicholas, 'Chords of the Great Dead', *Australian Book Review*, April 2001.

Lawson, Valerie, 'Hazzard Country', *Sydney Morning Herald*, 19 June 2004.

ELECTRONIC

http.blogs.smh.com.au/entertainment/archives/undercover

www.abc.net.au/gnt/Transcripts

www.abc.net.au/rn/bigideas/stories

www.abc.net.au/tv/enoughrope/transcripts

www.australianbiography.gov.au/keneally

Australian Dictionary of Biography, www.adb.online.anu.edu.au.

Allen, Brooke, '"A real inferno": the life of Christina Stead', *The New Criterion* online.

Behrendt, Professor Larissa, 'Law Stories and Life Stories: Aboriginal women, the law and Australian society', Clare Burton Memorial Lecture 2004, http:/lsn.curtin.edu.au.

www.clivejames.com

www.cultureandrecreation.gov.au

www.golvanarts.com.au/clients/murnane.htm

www.harpercollins.com.au

www.lesmurray.org

www.lib.monash.edu.au/exhibitions/sport

www.nla.gov.au/events/doclife/brady.html

www.randomhouse.co.uk

www.peterweircave.com

www.timesonline.co.uk/tol/comment/obituaries

www.uqp.uq.edu.au

www.users.bigpond.com/kgrenville/

Permissions

Thank you to the following for permission to reproduce the poems of Mary Gilmore, Kenneth Slessor, AD Hope, Judith Wright, Oodgeroo Noonuccal and Les Murray:

The poems of Mary Gilmore are reproduced courtesy of Tom Thompson & ETT Imprint.

Extracts from *Five Bells* by Kenneth Slessor from his *Selected Poems* are reproduced by permission of HarperCollins Publishers.

The poems of AD Hope are reproduced by arrangement with the licensor The Estate of AD Hope c/- Curtis Brown (Australia) Pty Ltd.

The poems of Judith Wright are reproduced from *A Human Pattern: Selected Poems* (ETT Imprint, Sydney 1999).

'No More Boomerang' by Oodgeroo of the tribe Noonuccal, from *My People*, 3e, The Jacaranda Press, 1990, reproduced by permission of John Wiley & Sons Australia.

The poems of Les Murray are reproduced by permission of Les Murray c/o Margaret Connolly & Associates.

Acknowledgements

My enormous thanks go to the following people:

To Michael Hill, who made this book possible.

To my publisher Jane Palfreyman, whose boundless passion for books and writing continues to thrill and inspire me, for all her support and guidance.

To my agent Jenny Darling, for her wisdom and expertise.

To publishers Sue Hines and Patrick Gallagher, for their enthusiasm and martinis.

To Clara Finlay, my editor at Allen & Unwin, for her wonderful grace and efficiency, and her astute proofreading.

To Gayna Murphy, for her beautiful cover and page design.

To Nadine Davidoff, freelance editor, for her attentive and thoughtful edit.

To all those writers and others who so generously responded to my invitation to contribute lists of their favourite Australian books to *Australian Classics*.

To Jackson and Scarlet Hill, who continue to make my days.

To Alison Craig, for her organisational talents and countless acts of kindness.

To my family and friends, for abiding with me while I wrote this book.